ENDORSEMENTS

The Power of Surrender drove me to my knees—the only place where true revival begins.

    —John Bisagno, Pastor Emeritus
    Houston's First Baptist Church
    Houston, Texas

The greatest need for the church today is true, genuine, Spirit-sent revival. That is what this book is all about. Read it and weep, pray, repent, and beg God for His mercy. Thank you Michael Catt!

    —Philip Roberts, President
    Midwestern Baptist Theological Seminary

Never in our generation has the moment been more ready for a movement of God. It ALL begins with us. In Michael Catt's newest book, *The Power of Surrender*, we read, "Surrender begins in the heart. Revival begins in the church." That statement convicts me as a Christ-follower and a pastor. Nothing attracts the God of heaven any more than a humble person before God that raises their heart and hands in ultimate surrender to Jesus! May this be the moment God rains His power upon us! I need this book. You need this book. Every Christian in our churches needs this book. Get it. Read it. Share it. Most of all, live it to God's glory.

    —Ronnie Floyd, Senior Pastor
    First Baptist Church of Springdale
    The Church at Pinnacle Hills, Arkansas

This book is filled with food and water for hungry and thirsty hearts, those longing for more than typical twenty-first-century Western Christianity has offered us. But let me warn you, get ready to have your world shaken. Michael Catt doesn't sugar-coat the message. He confronts the critical issues of our day with the time-tested truths of God's Word. He challenges us to seek God to revive our hearts and transform our lives. I encourage you to read and apply the truths in this passionate plea for a mighty revival in our generation.

—**Sammy Tippit, Evangelist and Author**

THE POWER OF SURRENDER

BREAKING THROUGH TO REVIVAL

MICHAEL CATT

B&H
PUBLISHING GROUP

NASHVILLE, TENNESSEE

978-0-8054-4869-6

B&H Publishing Group

Nashville, Tennessee

www.BHPublishingGroup.com

Dewey Decimal Classification: 234.4

Subject Heading: Revivals \ Repentance \ Confession

Unless otherwise noted, all Scriptures are taken from the
New American Standard Bible (NASB) Copyright © 1960,
1962, 1963, 1968, 1971, 1972, 1973, 1975, 1977, 1995 by The
Lockman Foundation. Used by permission. Other translations
used include The Message (MSG) Copyright © 1993, 1994,
1995, 1996, 2000, 2001, 2002. Used by permission of NavPress
Publishing Group. The Holy Bible, New Living Translation
(NLT) Copyright © 1996, 2004. Used by permission of Tyndale
House Publishers, Inc., Wheaton, Illinois. All rights reserved.

Quotations at the beginning of each chapter and other
uncited quotes are taken from John Blanchard's *The Complete
Gathered Gold* (Webster, NY: Evangelical Press, 2006).

Printed in the United States

1 2 3 4 5 6 7   13 12 11 10

Dedicated to my daughters

ERIN AND HAYLEY

whom I pray will see a genuine revival
in our nation in their lifetime

TABLE OF CONTENTS

FOREWORD

Few people know about the private aircraft headed home to Lancaster, Pennsylvania, on the morning of 9-11. The control tower from Harrisburg radioed the pilot with a simple instruction: "Land immediately at Harrisburg." Realizing he was not far from home, the pilot responded, "I want to go a short distance further and land in Lancaster." The tower forcefully responded, "Land immediately at Harrisburg." Again the pilot replied, "No, let me just go a little further to Lancaster." A few minutes later the tower gave one more command: "Look out your right wing." The pilot glanced right and saw two F-16 jets. Without hesitation he blurted, "I will land immediately at Harrisburg!"

Why is it that we don't obey God's commands immediately even though we know He is more powerful than all the world's fighter jets combined? Is it because we are not really a surrendered people? Is it because our surrender is based upon our full agreement with the command—even though we don't see the big picture? If we really knew God for who He is, in all His love, all His wisdom, and all His sovereignty, would we not be quick to trust and obey, surrendered even to the most inconvenient command?

Nothing has propelled me to a place of fresh surrender more than being in Romania shortly after the fall of communism. After a week of speaking, I was invited by a leading pastor to his home following our final service late one December evening. He wanted to fellowship one more time before we left early the next morning. As we were preparing to leave his home, my pastor friend went into the kitchen and soon returned with a cup of tea. He asked if he could share a story.

As we sat down at the table, my friend held up his teacup and shared a story about a pastor and wife who were captured by the communist regime and taken to a labor camp. En route, the wife escaped but her husband, like many before him, ended up losing his life in the cold snows of Siberia. My friend and his family took care of the pastor's wife for several years. Just weeks before this dear widow went home to be with the Lord, they were having tea together when the godly widow stopped my friend and asked, "Do you know whose cup you are drinking from? It was my husband's cup. I took it with me when I escaped. It is a martyr's cup. I want you to have it."

I will forever remember what my pastor friend said next: "Tonight I want to invite you to drink of the martyr's cup, realizing that those most responsible for the fall of communism are not the strategists in Washington, D.C. Those most responsible for the fall of communism are those whose bones lie in the cold snows of Siberia."

When I took hold of that cup, the Lord seemed to say to me, "Byron, those who will be most responsible for the fall of evil and wickedness in America and bring about the next great revival will be those who are willing, if necessary, to drink of the martyr's cup." That moment became a launching pad for daily surrender at a level I had never previously experienced.

I have had the privilege since 1975 of helping thousands of churches prepare for a corporate move of God in revival. With few exceptions I have reminded them that full surrender to the authority of God's Word and the Lordship of Christ is a precursor to revival. I tell congregations that there is a greater chance of God sending revival if there is one person who is 100 percent surrendered than if there are a thousand people who are 99 percent surrendered. It only takes one.

Michael Catt has been tutored by choice men of God who knew what surrender is all about. Both from the pulpit, in his writings, and as executive producer of Sherwood Production's array of movies, Michael has carried a passion for surrender. The theme of surrender is the grand take-away of *Fireproof*, *Facing the Giants*, *Flywheel*, and now *Courageous*. Is it the grand take-away of your life?

My daughter and her husband recently moved to Winona Lake, Indiana. They felt prompted to ask the owner of an old home if he would be willing to sell the house, even though it was not actually for sale. Within a couple of months they had moved in. A few weeks later, they discovered that the songwriter

Judson W. Van DeVenter, author of the hymn "I Surrender All," once resided in the home. A few days later, I discovered that Mr. Van DeVenter wrote the tune to another hymn. Entitled "Sweeping This Way," the author makes the same connection between surrender and revival that Michael Catt does in the pages of this book:

Over the hilltops, down from the skies,
Coming from glory—lift up your eyes!
While we are watching, and while we pray,
A mighty revival is sweeping this way. . . .
Keep on believing, trust and obey;
A mighty revival is sweeping this way.

The connection between surrender and revival is not new. It is as old as the history of revival. The hope of revival today is not lying in some new initiative but an old one. It rests in every heart that fully trusts the Reviver and surrenders every ounce of their being to the control of the Holy Spirit.

Unquestionably we can say there is no hope apart from revival. But the exciting news is that we can say with even greater confidence—there is no hope *like* revival! Throughout history it has proven to be the one thing that produces the most change in the shortest period of time. It is your only hope; it is our only hope as a country. And it is the hope of the nations.

Byron Paulus, President
Life Action Ministries

INTRODUCTION

I am a man who lives with the thought of "What if?" What if God sent revival to my heart? To our church? To our land? What would change? What would we do away with? What would we begin doing? Where would it take us? What if we were willing to lay hold of the altar and not let go until the Lord blessed us and changed our lives? What if we stopped our conniving and started a concentrated emphasis on seeking Him?

We'll never know if we never start.

The late Ron Dunn was pastor of MacArthur Boulevard Baptist Church in Irving, Texas. During Ron's pastorate, God moved in that church, and they lived in revival for nearly five years. Ron and I often talked about those days. He longed to see one more move of God like that before he died. In trying to summarize the experiences of this remarkable season, he wrote that it could "only be described as earthquake power, a power that transformed the countenance and composure of our church," marked by the following results:

> *Shaken with an overwhelming awareness of God's presence.* Without a doubt the greatest thing that's happened is this: Jesus has become real. God is no longer something we pray at, but a Father we pray to. The actuality of the indwelling Spirit has become a reality. Milkshake religion has become an earthquake experience, shaken with unbroken unity and harmony. One heart and one soul. The fiery heart of the Holy Spirit melted differences and welded hearts together in a loving fellowship that grows sweeter each time we meet to worship.
>
> *Shaken with supernatural power for living and witnessing.* God has consistently done "exceeding abundantly above all that we ask or think." We've seen things happen that two years ago we would have never believed. People who never witnessed before (never had the course!) found themselves gossiping about Jesus wherever they went. Sinful habits and attitudes have been conquered through the power of the Holy Spirit. We've come to know that if it isn't supernatural, it's superficial.
>
> *Shaken with an overflowing liberality.* Until revival came, we had never met a budget in our

church's history! Then the Holy Spirit revealed a fixed law of heaven. When a man's lordship is right, his stewardship will be right! The issue isn't "Will you tithe?" but "Is Jesus Lord?" With no budget drives or pledge campaigns of any sort, we have met our budget and finished the year with no unpaid bills—and have tripled our giving to world missions.

Shaken with a knowledge that it is God's doing. What has happened in the past two years, the increased growth in every single area of church life, is not—I repeat, is not—the result of hard work, clever programs, keen administration, intelligent leadership, etc. It is the result of God's Spirit breathing new life into these old bones. And nobody knows it better than this pastor. God forbid that we should ever glory in any of these things.

It is not overstating the issue to say that revival is our key to survival. The Bride of Christ today is unkempt, tangled up in secondary issues, dirty and defiled. We have been unfaithful to our Savior. We are like the people in the days of Hosea, guilty of spiritual adultery. Surely we don't want to meet the Bridegroom in the shape we are in right now. We need to pray for the "something more" that God wants for His Bride. We need a wind from heaven and a housecleaning. We need a purging and a purifying. It may seem that things can't get worse, but they can.

The hour is late; the time is now. We must surrender ourselves to God in total abandonment.

There is power in surrender.

I had a roommate in college who didn't like the word *surrender* when associated with the Christian life. He thought the word was offensive. I find it refreshing. It's an admission that "I can't, but He can." It's the awareness of my desperate need for something or someone to lift me out of the miry clay and set my feet on solid rock.

We need God to rend the heavens. We need the Spirit to blow out the cobwebs of carnality. We must see a return to holiness. We don't need help; we need deliverance.

Much like the days prior to the American Revolution, this nation is immoral. Out of a population of five million in 1776, as many as 300,000 were confirmed drunkards. Profanity was common. The streets were not safe to walk on. At the same time, the churches were dying. The Methodists were losing more than they could add. The Baptists struggled with the same problem. One Congregational church did not have one new member in sixteen years. The Lutherans were so weak in number that they talked about uniting with the Episcopalians, who were in equally bad shape. The chief justice of the United States, John Marshall, wrote to the bishop of Virginia, saying the church was "too far gone ever to be redeemed." Thomas Paine said, "Christianity will be forgotten in thirty years." Universities like Harvard and Princeton, founded for the training of preachers and missionaries, could only count two in their number who claimed to be believers. Only five at Princeton were not a part of the filthy speech movement. There were anti-Christian plays at Dartmouth. It was a dark hour.

But it was dark enough for the remnant to seek the light. Jonathan Edwards was so burdened by the need for revival, he wrote a book with this remarkably long but passionate title: *A Humble Attempt to Promote Explicit Agreement and Visible Union of all God's People in Extraordinary Prayer for the Revival of Religion and the Advancement of Christ's Kingdom on Earth, Pursuant to Scripture Promises and Prophecies*. In due time the first Great Awakening was born as the result of desperate praying and seeking the Lord. The impact on our nation is still felt in part by those who know the true history of America.

The last great revival in Western Civilization was probably the Welsh Revival of 1904. It began in prayer. A Presbyterian preacher named Seth Joshua prayed in a meeting, "O God, bend us." A young coal miner turned ministry student, Evan Roberts, was in the crowd that night. He went to his room and prayed, "O God, bend *me!*" From the depths of God's dealing with his heart, he began leading prayer meetings with young people, putting forth his four keys to revival: 1) You must confess any known sin to God and put any wrong done to others right; 2) You must put away any doubtful habit; 3) You must obey the Spirit promptly; 4) You must confess your faith in Christ publicly.

The resulting impact on Wales was undeniable. The names of those saved were listed in the newspapers. Police officers formed quartets to sing in churches because there was no crime. There were no reported rapes, burglaries, or murders. The mules in the mines had to be retrained because the miners no longer beat them and cursed but sang songs and praised God. Even the mules could tell that revival had come!

That is the purpose of this book—to raise the possibility of another movement of God. There are many excellent books on revival; I have more than a hundred in my library. But unfortunately most of them speak of revivals long since forgotten. We need a twenty-first-century movement of God the next generation will talk about. We need God once again to move in our midst in these last days.

My prayer is that this book will spur your thoughts about revival. It is my hope that you will take some of the principles you learn here and incorporate them in your personal life and in the life of your church. Unless we have revival, we are sunk. Having been marked and influenced by men who have seen revival, longed for revival, and preached the need for revival, I pray that this simple book will have a profound effect on your life. The need of the hour is for a prophet and a people who will not settle for status quo.

The church today is guilty of having her ear to the ground and a finger in the air to see what the trends are and where things are headed. We need a prophet to call us to revival, one who cares little for what people think, one who will get alone with God and say what God says without any fear of man or the consequences.

We do not lack today for preachers who seek the strategic pulpit and the big church. What we lack is someone who will preach repentance and not stutter or blink. God sends prophets just before He sends judgment. If judgment is coming—and I believe it is—then we'd better start praying for a prophet and heeding his words before it's too late. We need an Amos or an Elijah or a John the Baptist who will not settle for business as usual. We need men to match our mountains. We need camel-knee Christians who wear themselves out before the throne of God, pleading for divine intervention.

Our churches do not need another tune-up of old programs or a face lift. We need an overhaul. We need fire in our bones, in our sermons, and in our hearts. It's not too late. God is looking for a remnant, for kindling wood He can use to start the fires of revival.

And it all begins with surrender.

How I pray I'll live long enough to see it. I want it for my church, for myself, and for my children. I don't want them to live their whole lives without seeing a mighty move of God.

Michael Catt
Albany, Georgia

CHAPTER 1

WHAT TIME IS IT?

Hosea 10

It is easier to speak about revival than to set about it.
—Horatio Bonar

Sow with a view to righteousness, reap in accordance with kindness; break up your fallow ground, for it is time to seek the LORD until He comes to rain righteousness on you.
—Hosea 10:12

IN THE 1970S we almost saw a sweeping revival in our land. The revival at Asbury College in Wilmore, Kentucky, impacted not only that school but also hundreds of churches across the country. We stood on the precipice of what could have been another awakening. Bible conferences and revival meetings were extended, sometimes lasting three or four weeks. Prayer meetings lingered long into the night.

Much has been written regarding the movement of God on the Asbury campus. There was no announcement. Nothing extraordinary was planned that morning when God broke loose during a normal chapel service. The scheduled, routine, fifty-minute meeting on February 3, 1970, ended up lasting 185 hours non-stop. It continued for weeks to come.

There was no preaching that morning. Custer Reynolds, Asbury's academic dean and a layman, was in charge. He shared a brief testimony and then asked students if they wanted to talk about their experiences with Christ. Students began to respond. Soon the room was filled with confession, prayer, and weeping. Students got right with one another. People lingered because they were afraid to leave. The atmosphere was thick with the presence of God.

Nothing was orchestrated or organized. There was no order of service, yet the service was ordered by the Holy Spirit. The president of the school, Dr. Dennis Kinlaw, was out of town when the meeting started. He returned to Asbury two days later and went to the chapel in the wee hours of the morning. When a reporter later asked him to explain what was happening, the president replied, "Well, you may not understand this at all, but the only way I know how to account for this is that last Tuesday morning, the Lord Jesus walked into Hughes Auditorium and has been there ever since."

An article describing the meeting said, "The marathon service was uncannily orderly. Worshipers did not become loud, did not speak out of turn, did not fall down on the floor in religious ecstasy. The feelings were subtle, yet, in their own way, overwhelming." Dr. Kinlaw continued, "There was this sense of the divine presence that one doesn't have often in his life. And when you do have it, you never quite get over it. You know. You *know*. You know it in your bone marrow."[1]

From this point the revival spread. People came from all around to be part of what was happening. The media picked up on it, and reporters and television crews showed up. Students from the school even began to travel across the country and show up unannounced at churches to see if they might be given a few moments to share a word of testimony. By summer the impact of this revival had been felt in hundreds of churches and more than 130 college and seminary campuses.

Two students from Asbury came one night to First Baptist Church in Moss Point, Mississippi, where my wife, Terri, grew up. They asked if they could speak and were given permission. God showed up that night. Terri was a teenager then during the early days of the Jesus Movement. She said, "It was the first time I had ever seen anyone on their knees in First Baptist Church."

Two men showed up that same year at First Baptist in Ada, Oklahoma—the first church where I would later pastor—and a very similar thing happened. No one remembers their names. They simply shared and God came down. People went to their knees in prayer and confession. The two left before the service was over on their way to another church.

I've often wondered, What stopped those meetings? How can one see something so real and so powerful and ever want to go back to the way things were? All I know for sure is that we should be pleading with God for another movement of His Spirit in our midst.

Perhaps the bigger question is this: Do we want it?

TOO COMFORTABLE TO CARE

I begin this book by strongly suggesting that the answer to this question is no. We don't want revival. The churches don't want it; the members don't want it. Very few pastors even want a genuine, heaven-sent revival. We like things the way they are. After all, revival means change, and we don't want change. We're too comfortable with the way things are at present.

By *revival*, I mean an across-the-board movement of the Holy Spirit as He touches hearts, changes minds, melts pride, and transforms sinners. Now logically most Christians would like these things to occur. In our heart of hearts, we know this is what's going to be required for God to transform the modern church and make it a missionary organization once again. We know the people of our community are not going to be reached in numbers big enough to have any kind of impact until the Lord's people have a new touch of God in their lives. We say we want revival.

But we don't. Not really.

Everything inside us resists change. Our ego resists anyone else sitting on the throne of our lives. Our spirit rebels at another person calling the shots. Our bodies are afflicted with inertia, preferring to remain at rest.

Oh, I've seen revival, and perhaps you have too. When the Lord's Spirit moves in and begins to touch lives, you can throw away the schedule and the printed order of worship. Everything else goes out the window when the Holy Spirit sets up shop. People are confronted with their sinful ways. Hearts are broken over their wickedness. Husbands confess to their wives, mothers apologize to their children, and children start obeying their parents. Friends reconcile with friends and then turn to their enemies in humility. Bosses ask employees to forgive them. Employees confess wrongdoing and face up to their poor work ethic. Pastors get saved; pastors' wives get saved; deacons and their wives get saved.

Tears are shed by the buckets. Prayer meetings become loud and long and unstructured. Meetings get interrupted by church members walking in with a neighbor or coworker they have just led to Christ. The pastor is no longer the only one hearing from God. Church members testify of what God told them this morning in prayer time. Those who never heeded anything in their lives now find themselves leading Bible studies and witnessing projects. The timid suddenly become outspoken.

The lid is off their faith. They now believe God can do anything and that they can do all things through Him. Nothing is off-limits anymore, nothing out of bounds, nothing unthinkable.

They are free in their giving, loving, serving, and most of all in their thinking.

Invariably spectators and outsiders—those untouched by the Holy Spirit and uncertain that God has had any part in these shenanigans—condemn the excess, resent the disorder, suspect the new people who have begun coming to church, and look for occasions to attack the ringleaders. Revivals drive some people away from the church. On the other hand, revivals attract a lot of new people, often those who have not been brought up in a religious tradition and do not know how to behave in a sanctuary. Revivals disrupt the flow of things, end the tyranny of the calendar and the clock and the Pharisees, and rearrange a church's priorities. Revivals produce an entirely new set of leaders for a church. In fact, it is not an exaggeration to say that revival kills off the old church and leaves an entirely different one in its place.

Now all of this is painful, uncomfortable, disruptive, and even expensive. And being human, we don't like the pain, discomfort, disruption, and expense. We like our comfort. We prefer our complacency. It feels good to see the same faces at church every Sunday, all of them occupying the same pews they've held down for ages. There's a warmth about sitting in Bible study class with the same eight people we've known for years. Newcomers and visitors are an intrusion. The pastor may not be saying anything we haven't heard him say time and again, but even the drone of his voice carries a certain kind of comfort. We're satisfied with the old when God wants to do a new thing in our midst.

So what is the answer if God wants to send revival and we don't want one? Where do we begin to address this stalemate, this breakdown, this crisis of revival?

TIME TO BE WATCHING

Many Christians today have no clue what a critical hour we are living in. The hour is urgent, the Lord is willing, the devil is hard at work, and too many church members are sitting in the grandstands enjoying the view instead of being suited up and on the field. "Woe to those who are at ease in Zion" (Amos 6:1). Someone needs to tell God's children today that the house is on fire. It's time for us to get off the couch and get busy. When we lay hold of God, we can face any crisis. We can overcome any fear and win the day.

It's time, don't you think?

I have an atomic clock in my office. It sits on a table where I can see it when I'm seated at my desk. It's one of the most accurate clocks you can have. I always assume the time on that clock is right because it resets itself. I like clocks. I'm a time-conscious guy. I like to be early for meetings and events. In my mind, "on time" is late. I want to allot for traffic delays or unexpected interruptions. But I wonder, do we know what time it is? Are we able to discern the times and see how dangerously close we are to judgment?

We rush to grab a cup of coffee on our way to work. We rush to the drive-through. We rush to church because we're running late. We hurry and scurry. But when it comes to revival, we seem to have little time to think about it or act on it. Churches no longer allot time on their calendars for revivals. We're too busy rushing to our Pilates class and our comfortable homes to take time for revival.

Since 2003 we've held an annual conference on revival at our church the third week of September. Every year I've invited pastors in our area to come. We promise to feed them three free meals a day. But never have we had more than three or four pastors attend. They're too busy with stuff that doesn't matter, I'd suspect. Some of them give me excuses that sound like a high school student explaining why he didn't do his homework.

TRUE REVIVAL BEGINS WITH CONVICTION AND REPENTANCE BY BELIEVERS IN THE CHURCH.

Pastors can pretend to be busy in ministry when they're really just spinning their wheels and getting dirty doing things that don't matter in eternity.

We have members of our church who have never attended one of these conferences. Even though we've seen hundreds of significant decisions, they still have no curiosity or interest in attending. They're busy. They know what time their kids' games start, but they don't know what time it is on God's calendar.

I'm concerned that even with all the strife, terrorism, economic problems, and social issues of our day, most folks don't know what time it is. They're clueless. Jesus said His coming would be as it was in the days of Noah. What were they doing in the days of Noah? Eating, drinking, marrying, going to events. They didn't hear, see, or understand that the hour was upon them for judgment.

I was speaking at a state evangelism conference, where I heard Richard Blackaby say, "God will send a catalyst for revival. But if you don't respond to the catalyst, He will send a prophet. Failure to respond to the invitation of God will result in the announcement of the judgment of God." We need to know what time it is.

I've asked God to make me a catalyst for revival. The children of Issachar were said to have an understanding of the times and knew what Israel ought to do (1 Chron. 12:32). In a world where we are bombarded by news 24/7, you would think we would have enough information to change the way we are living. But today I see little awareness of the need and less ability than ever to discern the times. Why? We listen to pundits when we should be listening to the prophets. We bend our ear toward the government when we need to bend our knee to God. God's people need to understand the times, and we need to act, react, pray, and stand accordingly.

WHAT'S WRONG WITH US?

Real revival doesn't begin with praise and worship, nor does it begin with evangelism. These should be the outgrowth of a movement of God among His people. True revival begins with *conviction* and *repentance* by believers in the church.

The psalmist said, "It is time for the LORD to act, for they have broken Your law" (Ps. 119:126). If the people of that long-ago day had broken God's law, how much more have we? In an age of postmodern secularist thinking, are we holding up the standards of God? I'm not talking about legalism, rules, and regulations. I'm talking about moral absolutes and holiness. Would the world examine the average church and find her living what we say we believe? Would they see us seeking God with all our heart, soul, mind, and strength? Would they find us making the kinds of adjustments that occur when crisis time arrives, when you do whatever you have to do to get things back where they're supposed to be?

We had a 500-year flood in Albany in 1994. For months our church was a center for feeding volunteers from around the country. We served tens of thousands of meals in our small fellowship hall. We housed workers from more than thirty states for months. We rebuilt homes all across our community. It was time to do something, and we couldn't pretend as if nothing had happened. Yet every week God's people gather and act as if nothing is wrong in this land of ours. We are living in a time of anarchy. Gangs are a major problem in our towns and cities. We have serious gang issues in the town where I live. Three girls with suspected ties to gangs recently tried to firebomb our preschool area. They were caught on tape seeking to destroy the part of our building where we minister to babies. Evil is rampant. It knows no boundaries or shame.

America has become heathenistic and animalistic in its behavior. We show off half-naked bodies, not just on magazine covers but at the shopping mall. Suggestiveness has given way to blatant flaunting. Things that used to be limited to porn sites are now in prime time.

Our culture shows a disrespect for authority and absolutes. If you have any doubt about that, read the paper or turn on the news. Reporters treat presidents and authority figures with little or no decorum. There is little respect for the law of the land because there is little respect for the law of God. Instead of the spirit of revival, we have the spirit of pandemonium.

But the greatest problem is that the church seems to be apathetic. At a time when the world needs the church at her best, we are not doing what God has left us on the planet to do. *We are in a spiritual crisis!* We are entertaining ourselves toward judgment. We are sin-sick, but we are not sick of sin. Someone needs to sound the alarm, to say that the church in America today is a long way from revival. It's time we woke up to the fact that judgment begins at the church house, not the White House. And if it doesn't begin soon at the church house, we're going to be in the outhouse.

When a disaster hits, it's too late to prepare for it. When the storm is just off shore, it's too late to evacuate. When we see signs of a coming judgment, we must not wait long to act. For what grace does not accomplish, judgment will. God will send us through a season where He sacrifices our comfort to conform our character. He's not interested in our performance; He wants our heart. Our *surrendered* heart. The times demand nothing less.

Now is the time to act! The situation is desperate. The only way we can overcome the anarchy, apathy, and fleshly attitudes of our culture and our churches is to begin seeking the Lord. So what time do you have? Is your watch synchronized with God's timepiece? He says it's time to seek the Lord. If that's not the time you have, you need to make an adjustment.

GROUNDBREAKING

Surrender begins in the heart. Revival begins in the church. We cannot point fingers at the devil's crowd because Jesus has given us everything necessary to overcome the world, the flesh, and the devil. We cannot blame the secularists and humanists because they are just acting like themselves. If they had heard all the Bible preaching and teaching we've heard, they would likely have repented by now. We cannot blame all the forces arrayed against us. We can't blame the secular media and Hollywood. We've been told we are more than conquerors. Why then do we act as if defeat is our only option? Look at the times—it's no time to make excuses. The problem is apathy and self-justification, settling for a form of religion without power. We are a Body with dry eyes and lukewarm hearts.

What do we do about it?

Speaking to this sort of condition, the prophet Hosea had this to say: "Sow with a view to righteousness, reap in accordance with kindness; break up your fallow ground, for it is time to seek the LORD until He comes to rain righteousness on you" (Hosea 10:12).

In studying Hosea you discover that the root of evil was (and has always been) a divided heart. The people were guilty of spiritual adultery. They had been unfaithful to God by loving other gods, having been accused of whoredom sixteen times in the book of Hosea. In reality all sin is spiritual adultery—unfaithfulness to the lover of our soul. It is a thumbing of our nose at grace. It is a rejection of God's love. When I choose to sin, I choose to grieve the One who loves me most.

Understand that the "fallow ground" in Hosea's prophecy—the ground in need of being broken up—was not a reference to the lost world but to God's own people. I've never farmed a day in my life. I have relatives who have worked a farm, but I've never been behind a plow myself. I do, however, think I understand what a plow is for. You use a plow to break up the ground and prepare for a harvest. If the ground is not plowed, the seed will not get deep in the soil.

My first full-time church out of seminary was in Yukon, Oklahoma. We bought a brand new house and immediately set about turning our red clay yard—which didn't have one blade of grass growing in it—into an honest-to-goodness lawn. We borrowed a tiller and cranked it to the deepest setting, but we could barely break up two inches of soil. In fact we broke the tiller in the process! I learned something that day: plowing won't produce productive soil. We have to keep plowing until the hard areas are soft, until every rock is removed and every obstacle to the seed of the Word bearing fruit is gone.

Charles Finney said, "To break up the fallow ground is to break up your hearts, to prepare your minds to bring forth fruit unto God . . . to bring the mind into such a state that it is fitted to receive the Word of God."[2] As Warren Wiersbe writes in his commentary on Hosea, "The plow of conviction must first break up hard hearts before the seed of the Word can be planted and the gracious rain be sent from heaven."[3]

In Finney's lecture on fallow ground, he made note of what he called "sins of omission"—ingratitude, lack of love for God, neglect of the Bible, unbelief, neglect of prayer, neglect of the means of grace (making excuses regarding the things of God), lack of love for souls, lack of care for the lost, neglect of family duties, neglect of watchfulness over your own life, neglect to watch over your brethren, and neglect of self-denial. He followed these with "sins of commission"—worldly mindedness, pride, envy, a bitter spirit or harboring a grudge, slander and gossip, levity before God, lying, cheating, hypocrisy, robbing God, temper, and hindering others from being useful. He exhorted people to go over the ground of their hearts and minds carefully, making sure any area that could hinder the Word from bearing fruit in a believer's life was clear and clean. Then he gave this warning, "It will be of no benefit to examine yourself unless you determine to change in every particular area that which you find wrong in heart, temper, or conduct."[4]

Fallow ground has two primary characteristics. First, it is *unproductive*. It yields no harvest. All it contains are weeds and rocks. It may have once produced a harvest, but that day is long past. Second, it is *undisturbed*. It is currently being ignored or has been forgotten. It can be filled with weeds, thorns, or scrub brush, but whatever its condition, it is not fulfilling its purpose. Yet that's not all that can be said of fallow ground.

Fallow ground can be hard. Like the seed in Matthew 13, the Word falls on us but rarely gets into us. The devil snatches away the seed. This can happen in a multitude of ways. We can second-guess the preacher or actually place ourselves as a judge over Scripture. Fallow ground is the heart that says, "I'll believe what I want to believe." It's a denial that every part of the Word is inspired and profitable.

Fallow ground can be cluttered. We have more time-saving devices than any generation in history and yet less time than ever. We're busy, but rarely busy about things that matter for eternity. We've put family, football, fun, fellowship, food, and foolishness above the Word and our relationship with Christ. You can't break up the fallow ground and bear spiritual fruit if you are only feeding on the Word with one sermon a week.

SOME PEOPLE REFUSE TO LET THE BIBLE SAY WHAT IT SAYS.

Fallow ground can be shallow. We know just enough about the things of God to be dangerous to ourselves and to others. We own a Bible, but we don't read it. We carry it, but we never allow it to confront us. While we may have once been open to the Word and receptive to it, now we let it go in one ear and out the other.

Fallow ground can be critical and analytical. While we are commanded to study to show ourselves approved (2 Tim. 2:15), it doesn't mean we are to pick the Word apart. Some people refuse to let it say what it says. Our carnal flesh doesn't *want* to know what it says. But "I think" or "I feel" doesn't matter when it comes to Scripture. It is wholly and fully inspired. Leviticus is just as inspired as Romans. It is the infallible, indestructible, inexhaustible, incorruptible Word of God. Don't pick at it. Rather, dig deep in it and let the Holy Spirit speak to you. Mark Twain said, "It's not the parts of the Bible I don't understand that bother me: it's the parts I do understand." A. W. Tozer, in his book *Paths to Power*, wrote these words:

The fallow field is smug, contented, protected from the shock of the plow and the agitation of the harrow. Such a field, as it lies year after year, becomes a familiar landmark to the crow and the blue jay. . . . Safe and undisturbed, it sprawls lazily in the sunshine, the picture of sleepy contentment. . . . Fruit it can never know because it is afraid of the plow and the harrow.

In direct opposition to this, the cultivated field has yielded itself to the adventure of living. The protecting fence has opened to admit the plow, and the plow has come as plows always come—practical, cruel, business-like, and in a hurry. Peace has been shattered by the shouting farmer and the rattle of machinery. The field . . . has been upset, turned over, bruised, and broken, but its rewards come hard upon its labor. The seed shoots up into the daylight its miracle of life, curious, exploring the new world above it. Nature's wonders follow the plow.

There are two kinds of lives also: the fallow and the plowed. The man of fallow life is contented with himself and the fruit he once bore. He does not want to be disturbed. He smiles in silent superiority at revivals, fastings, self-searchings, and all the travail of fruit bearing and the anguish of advance. The spirit of adventure is dead within him. . . . He has fenced himself in, and by the same act he has fenced out God and the miracle.

The plowed life is the life that has . . . thrown down the protecting fences and sent the plow of confession into the soul. . . . Such a life has put away defense and has forsaken the safety of death for the peril of life. Discontent, yearning, contrition, courageous obedience to the will of God: these have bruised and broken the soil until it is ready again for the seed. And as always, fruit follows the plow.[5]

We live in a tough world. If the Lord is going to send revival, it must begin in the hearts of His people. It's time to seek the Lord. We can no longer be like the man "who hears the word, and the worry of the world and the deceitfulness of wealth choke the word, and it becomes unfruitful" (Matt. 13:22). How much time at church is wasted on talking about the worries of the world and the deceitfulness of riches? Hallway conversations orbit around football games, ballet practices, picnics, 401k statements, and the economic situations of our day. Rarely do you find people gathering at church with one thing on their mind—the Lord Jesus Christ.

Many a good sermon has been wasted on a preoccupied crowd. Many a worship experience has been wasted in stewing over preferences rather than focusing on worship. Any church that has become inward focused is unproductive ground, not wanting to be disturbed. Their hearts are cluttered, corrupted, and carnal, and the Word of God can't break through because of the resistance.

When is the last time God disturbed you? When's the last time you allowed Him to do something that wasn't in the bulletin, something that didn't accommodate your planned-out, prearranged schedule? The Word of God will either harden or soften you, depending on whether you allow the plow of conviction to break your heart.

I'm writing this on a Monday, and just yesterday at church it seemed right to call people to the altar after the special music, before the sermon. The altar was flooded. I gave people permission to come, and they rushed down the aisle. Many bowed as low as they could and wept. Tears were flowing. God was moving. It caused me to change my message. I had to ask God in the moment to show me what to say. It was one of those services where He softened our hearts.

At the same time, there were people in attendance who just sat and stared. The presence of the Holy Spirit was obviously in force, but they just looked straight ahead and scratched their heads. They didn't get it. They may *never* get it. Don't assume revival means everyone will get with the program. If you're waiting on the majority, you'll never see it. Some will be clueless. Two people can sit in the same service: one will be moved while the other will think it was a waste of time. It's a matter of the heart. The condition of our soil determines if we can see a great work of God in our lives.

THE TIME IS NOW

The coming of revival in our time will demand *personal preparation* among God's people. Jeremiah said, "Thus says the LORD to the men of Judah and to Jerusalem, 'Break up your fallow ground and do not sow among thorns'" (Jer. 4:3). We must sow our seed in anticipation of a harvest. We must sow with prayerful expectation. As we prepare our hearts, souls, and minds for God to work, we position ourselves to expect Him, to hear Him, to see Him.

Let it start with you. You can have revival even if no one else does. The choice is yours. Do you want to live with all God has for you, or are you willing to settle for less than God's best? Surrender is a personal issue before it ever becomes a corporate issue. Revival always begins with the remnant. It never begins with back-row Baptists who can take it or leave it. It will rarely, if ever, happen with the Sunday morning crowd. We must sow into fertile ground.

How are we to sow? Hosea tells us how: "with a view to righteousness." Israel had plowed iniquity; the only cure now was to sow righteousness. As Alexander MacLaren once noted, "Sowing is not all; thorns must be grubbed up. We must not only turn over a new leaf, but tear out the old one. The old man must be slain if the new man is to live. The call to amend finds its warrant in the assurance that there is still time to seek the Lord, and that, for all His threatenings, He is ready to rain blessings upon the seekers."[6]

True, sowing is not enough. There must also be reaping. Hosea told the people, "You have plowed wickedness, you have reaped injustice, you have eaten the fruit of lies" (Hosea 10:13). Therefore the nation was broken. Relationships were shallow, barren, and tumultuous, in need of change and restoration. Sounds like a lot of churches I know of today.

You can always discern the vertical by the horizontal. How do I know someone is seeking the Lord? I see them dealing with others in kindness. John said you can't love God and hate your brother. Jesus told us to love the Lord with all our heart, soul, mind, and strength, and to love our neighbor as we love ourselves. We're good at loving ourselves, but do we have the same kind of love for our neighbor? I've met people who would rather die than get right with someone else. But sowing should result in the reaping of new, holy desires.

Not only will revival demand personal preparation but also *persistent supplication.* How long do we have to pray for revival? Until we have surrendered to His will alone and until He comes. How long? Until God shows up. Until God is enthroned in His rightful place. Until He rains down righteousness on us.

I've seen mercy drops of revival, but I'm asking God for showers. Are you pleading for showers, or are you content with a few mercy drops? To see the showers of blessings, we must surrender. We must break up our fallow ground and sow seeds of righteousness. We must be tender toward God. Nothing is settled until it is settled right, and nothing is settled right until it is settled with God. People who can hold on to sin and selfishness and say they have a "peace about it" are lying. When revival starts to come to the surface, all the things that stand in the way are removed. Seeking revival doesn't mean we're asking for a new manifestation of God. We're not begging for an event, a method, or a feeling. To pray for revival means to surrender, to get our minds on the same page with God's sovereignty.

And perhaps most of all, it means we are to seek nothing else. Israel's heart was divided. They worshipped for a while, then walked back to their idols—faithful for a season, then back to business as usual. They would go to Jerusalem to check the box and take the offering, then head back to their idols and altars. Their faithfulness was fickle. There was no surrender, just stroking their conscience. James said that a double-minded man is "unstable in all his ways" (James 1:8). The saints today are unstable because they have not bowed the knee in surrender. They stand on shaky ground and shifting sand.

Are you surrendered to nothing less than the God of revival? Do you want anything more than you want Jesus? Is your one goal and passion to see God arrive on the scene in a fresh wind of revival? I'm not talking about the thrill of the fill. If all you want is a thrill, put your finger in a light socket. You'll get a feeling you won't forget! If you want a simple test for surrender, ask yourself, "Am I willing to settle for anything less? Is seeking the Lord the one thing that dominates me, drives me, motivates me, and sustains me?" Don't settle for something almost as good as Jesus—*get Jesus!* There's more to Jesus than you know right now, for His well has no bottom and His sky has no limits.

Have you ever lost something and gone on a mad search for it? I'm an only child. My dad always said, "You won't have to worry about arguing over the will with relatives when I die." He was right. I didn't have to argue with relatives. But I did have to argue with the government . . . because my dad hid his will. It was nowhere to be found after his death.

I looked everywhere. I found his fireproof safe, but it wasn't in there. I looked through all his files, but it wasn't in there. I searched high and low. Meanwhile, I was paying tens of thousands of dollars in taxes because I couldn't produce a valid will. I was unable to prove I was the sole heir, and it was costing me major money in lawyer's fees and other red tape, not to mention untold amounts of time and frustration.

I finally found my dad's will—not in a place I would have ever thought to look—hidden behind his college diploma. Locating his will was a relief, though unfortunately it was long after the time had passed to refile taxes on his estate. I spent a lot of time thinking, What if? But one of the greatest thoughts that came to mind was why for most of my life I haven't sought the Lord with that kind of diligence. I haven't spent the time I should in desperate pursuit of Him. It's my loss. Not in money but in blessings beyond measure.

One revivalist author addressed this issue:

> For decades sincere believers have asked, "Why don't we have revival?" And for decades the answer has always been the same: We don't have revival because we're willing to live without it! . . . Sure we want revival. But we don't *need* revival. That's the difference. God will meet us at the point of our need, not our point of preference. Revival is God's radical measure

to get the church in a given area or at a given time back to normal before it falls into spiritual oblivion and cultural irrelevance. Revival comes when we realize that it's either revival or death, revival or continued backsliding, revival or the world around us goes to hell.[7]

We're at the point where we need to pray for God's will to be done on earth as it is in heaven. That's the simplest definition of revival you'll ever find: God putting His will into place for vast numbers of His people. So the prayer we pray for revival may come down to being the simplest prayer one can ever lift heavenward: "Lord, we want Your will to be done in us." In so saying, you are handing Him the keys, moving out of the driver's seat, and yielding your will to His. It's a lordship issue.

But if the pleasures of this world have you in a death grip and will not let go—as in, you could not possibly imagine leaving home on a Tuesday night to perform a deliberate act of Christian ministry because you'd miss your favorite television show—and you cannot honestly pray for God's will to be done in your life, then there's another prayer for you. This prayer is the key to the first one. "Father, I cannot say that I want Your will to be done in my life, but I wish I could. Therefore I pray I will have the 'want to' to desire Your will to be done. I ask you to change my heart and give me a desire for You alone."

It is time to seek the Lord. It's past time.

The time is now.

CHAPTER 2

IT'S LATER THAN YOU THINK

Revelation 2–3

No repentance is true repentance which does not recognize Jesus as Lord over every area of life.
—John C. Chapman

Therefore repent and return, so that your sins may be wiped away, in order that times of refreshing may come from the presence of the Lord.
—Acts 3:19

SOME TIME in the sixteenth century, a Scottish gentleman named John Maxwell built a watchtower near his Hoddam Castle home, one of a chain of defensive posts in the area. According to some historians, Maxwell was bribed to change sides just before a great battle in exchange for the hand of Agnes Herries—a decision that cost the lives of twelve of his kinsmen who had been at Carlisle Castle as hostages. One of the dead was Maxwell's twelve-year-old nephew. In a sign of his great remorse, he placed an inscription above the door to the tower, naming it "Repentance Tower." It stands to this day.

Could I be so bold as to ask, When was the last time you went to Repentance Tower? When was the last time you responded to a sermon on repentance? The Scriptures are full of the message of repentance, but we don't hear much about repentance anymore. The three hardest words to say in the English language could be "I have sinned" or "I was wrong." We've confused repentance with weakness, but in reality the lack of repentance weakens the believer and the church.

Thomas Manton said, "Holy tears are the sponge of sin." When was the last time you found yourself brought to tears over your sins or the sins of others? We have many cleansing products today for our faces, but what we really need are tears of repentance that cleanse our hearts, tears that come as the result of comprehending how far we've fallen, tears that are the outward manifestation of an inner awareness that we have sinned against a holy God. As Chuck Colson writes, "When we truly comprehend our own nature, repentance is no dry doctrine, no frightening message, no morbid form of self-flagellation. It is, as the early church fathers said, a gift God grants which leads to life."[1]

The psalmist made a connection between sowing in tears and reaping in joy. The lack of revival should bring the church to tears. Today it seems we can never stop sending text messages, yet we can't start the tears. We've lived so long without revival, we think we can get by without it. It's been so long since this world, especially America, has seen a sweeping movement of God, most folks have no clue what we're talking about. We have never seen the former glory, so we think smoke and mirrors are signs of glory. But they are merely a cover-up for departed glory. You can name the great denominations that once experienced revival, but where are the denominations experiencing revival today? Where's the force rising out of the ashes and reclaiming what the enemy has stolen? Where are the tears of repentance at our denominational offices? Where are the altar calls by pastors crying out to Jesus? We are lacking because we fail to understand the necessity of repentance.

On July 8, 1741, Jonathan Edwards preached his famous sermon, "Sinners in the Hands of an Angry God." The response to his call to personal salvation and revival in the land was amazing. Before he could even finish his message, people were shouting, "What must I do to be saved?" In calling the listeners to repentance, Edwards closed the sermon with one final appeal, "Therefore let everyone that is out of Christ, now awake and fly from the wrath to come." His words on the wrath of God, hell, and repentance still serve as the leading example of a Great Awakening sermon.

Real repentance produces confession and forsaking of sin, reconciliation and restitution, separation from the world, submission to the lordship of Christ, and the filling of the Holy Spirit. Real repentance doesn't just strike at the *fruit* of sin; it cuts to the *root* of sin. Someone has said that faith and repentance are the hinges to the door of revival.

The prophet Isaiah recorded these words, "Alas, sinful nation, people weighed down with iniquity, offspring of evildoers, sons who act corruptly! They have abandoned the Lord, they have despised the Holy One of Israel, they have turned away from Him" (Isa. 1:4). The word "alas" is not so much a sigh of regret as it is an "aha!" It's laced with God's indignation over His rebellious children. Can we admit that in many ways the church is "weighed down with iniquity," that we've "abandoned the Lord" for other things? God's people in Isaiah's day abandoned God because they despised Him. Thus they were alienated from Him. Only repentance could bring restoration. God's church of our day needs to hear the same message. We need to clean up. We need to repent.

Beth Moore tells the story in one of her Bible studies of being in an airport, needing to get some work done with her down time. She noticed an old man in a wheelchair nearby, unkempt, with tangled hair, and wearing his pajamas. She started arguing with the Lord for fear that He might tell her to go witness to him. The Lord spoke to her heart and said, "I want you to brush his hair." She thought, "Lord, how about if I just witnessed to him?" But she obeyed the Spirit's prompting and asked the man if she could brush his hair. She had to repeat herself loudly a few times because the man was hard of hearing. It didn't take long before he started thanking her. He was on his way to see his wife whom he hadn't seen in a long time, and he was embarrassed by the way he looked. Moore said God spoke to her heart, saying, "That's My church—unkempt, dirty, not ready to meet the bridegroom."

TIME FOR A CHANGE

What does repentance mean? The word is used forty times in the Old Testament, meaning to change your mind, heart, or disposition. The message of John the Baptist in the New Testament was "Repent!" Jesus, of course, preached repentance. When others were pointing fingers and trying to figure out what deserves the judgment of God, Jesus said, "Unless you repent, you will all likewise perish" (Luke 13:3). Peter and Paul called on both the Jews and Gentiles to "repent and return" to God (Acts 3:19). The last book of the New Testament, Revelation, gives a stern call to the churches to repent. There can be no doubt that repentance is a strong and much-needed word for our time.

The revivalist Leonard Ravenhill wrote, "When the Church gets a divorce from the world and worldliness . . . when we cease from the strivings of the flesh and recognize that the Bible written yesterday is also for today and for tomorrow, and that it and it alone has the formula for revival, we shall at least have started on the road to the reformation of the Church, which must precede the true spiritual awakening which alone can save our generation."[2]

We need to repent as long as we have religion without the Holy Spirit, Christianity without Christ, forgiveness without repentance, salvation without regeneration, and heaven without hell. And that's where we are! We've settled for Christianity Lite in America today. We have crowds, but where is the congregation? We have Starbucks in our Sunday school classes, but where is the Spirit? We are politically correct and socially active but spiritually dead. We live in a day of smooth talkers, stage lighting, and flattering tongues. And we don't know how to blush. Preachers are actually using vulgarity in the pulpit. They call it relevant; I call it repulsive. Props have replaced prayer. Preachers and churches are playing fast and loose with the Scriptures.

Some of the key movements of our age are leading us down the broad road toward the cliff of certain destruction. Whether it's the late Norman Vincent Peale's positive thinking or Robert Schuller's emphasis on self-esteem, today's self-help theology is foreign to the Scriptures and to repentance. Similarly, the Word of Faith movement and the prosperity gospel run counter to the New Testament. While the message is spreading like wildfire, there is no fire on the altar. Try selling the health-and-wealth gospel to anyone in a third-world country!

In his book *Christless Christianity*, author Michael Horton comments on those who continue to peddle such "theology" today. He writes, "To the extent that it reflects any theology at all, [it] represents a convergence of Pelagian self-help and Gnostic self-deification."[3] Basically, it's a therapeutic deism that says, "God is here for you and your happiness." There is little emphasis on holiness and generally no emphasis on repentance, either for salvation or for sanctification. The success of some of today's best-selling books that water down the gospel could have just as easily been written by Oprah.

Continuing to describe and challenge this message, Horton says, "There is no condemnation . . . for failing to fulfill God's righteous law. On the other hand, there is no justification. Instead of either message, there is an upbeat moralism that is somewhere in the middle: do your best, follow the instructions I give you, and God will make your life successful."[4]

It is time for us to make adjustments in our thinking. While I am all for reaching the world, we can only reach them after we have repented. A carnal church cares nothing for the lost or the least. Revival is a fresh moving of the Holy Spirit among the saints. We cannot stay the same. Repentance must come in the pews before we can expect to see it in the people of this world. Vance Havner wisely said, "Many a so-called revival is only a drive for more church members, which adds more unsaved sinners, starched and ironed but not washed, to a fellowship where even the true believers have not been aroused for years." The church needs to return to the mourner's bench because the mourner's bench is for the members first.

TRY SELLING THE HEALTH-AND-WEALTH GOSPEL TO ANYONE IN A THIRD-WORLD COUNTRY!

Notice the obvious order of Psalm 51:12–13: "Restore to me the joy of Your salvation and sustain me with a willing spirit.

Then I will teach transgressors Your ways, and sinners will be converted to You" (italics mine). This is God's plan and pattern: repentance and restoration first, followed by evangelism. Repentance removes any thought that "easy believism" is acceptable. There is no room for La-Z-Boy believers. Convenience store or cafeteria Christianity—where you run in, get what you want, and leave the rest—is not New Testament faith, nor is it adequate for the hour.

If you are listening to a preacher or reading a Christian author who never uses the word "repentance," change churches or start reading someone else. They aren't helping you. They have adjusted the gospel to be more acceptable. They have cut out the bold, prophetic voices of the Scripture. If it's good enough for Isaiah, Jeremiah, John the Baptist, and the Lord Jesus, it should be good enough for us, no matter how weird the world thinks we are.

Any dedication that does not include separation is ultimately superficial. "Do not be conformed to this world, but be transformed by the renewing of your mind" (Rom. 12:2). Phillips translates the verse, "Don't let the world squeeze you into its mold." *The Message* paraphrases it this way: "Don't become so well-adjusted to your culture that you fit into it without even thinking." As John added, "If anyone loves the world, the love of the Father is not in him" (1 John 2:15). James spoke to the same sentiment when he wrote, "Whoever wishes to be a friend of the world makes himself an enemy of God" (James 4:4). I love what Billy Sunday said, "To talk about a worldly Christian is like talking about a heavenly devil."

Vance Havner once surmised, "When I see a bird that looks like a duck, quacks like a duck, has webbed feet like a duck, paddles in the water like a duck, and prefers the company of ducks, it is hard for me to resist the conclusion that it must be a duck! . . . When I see a Christian who looks like the world, talks like the world, walks like the world, goes places where the world goes, and prefers the company of the world, it is hard for me to resist the conclusion that they are of the world."

TRUE TO HIS WORD

G. Campbell Morgan, in his commentary on 1 Corinthians, divides Paul's letter into two sections. The first section deals with carnality, and the second with spirituality. Paul had to deal with their flesh before he could lead them deeper into faith. Our problem is that we are Corinthian in our thinking. God cannot speak to us as spiritual people because we aren't. Our churches are filled with people who do not have a biblical worldview. They are gray in areas where the Word is black and white. They stutter and shrink when they should be standing tall.

We've bought the lie that the power of positive thinking can change lives. I remember being with the late Lehman Strauss one day, and he was telling me about preaching at the old Winona Lake Conference with Vance Havner. Havner began his sermon by saying, "I got up this morning and read a little from the Apostle Paul. Then I read a little of Norman Vincent Peale. Personally, I find Paul appealing and Peale appalling." Lehman said the crowd broke out into applause and started shouting. Today he would be rebuked for being negative.

You'll find little in common with the success, health, and wealth of the prosperity gospel and the Word of God. Paul didn't live in a mansion and cross the Mediterranean in a luxury liner. He spent most of his life running from town to town, being beaten up, attacked, chased around by the Gnostics and Judaizers, and chained to Roman soldiers. Not the glamorous life we see in preachers today. Paul would never say "I don't know" when asked if other religions were misguided or if he was comfortable using the word "sinners"—the way some modern preachers have answered interviewers' questions about their beliefs and practices. Paul clearly said in Romans 7, "I know that nothing good dwells in me, that is, in my flesh" (v. 18). That's an admission of sin from a sinner. You can't read Romans and miss the fact that we are sinners. Any trivialization of sin reveals a total lack of understanding or a denial of the authority of God's Word.

In addition to this, Paul knew what the calling of God meant and what it cost. He said, "I know how to get along with humble means, and I also know how to live in prosperity; in any and every circumstance I have learned the secret of being filled and going hungry, both of having abundance and suffering need" (Phil. 4:12). He knew what he believed and knew where he was headed. We need more men like Paul and fewer like the above-mentioned smooth talkers.

One last word on why this concerns me. Horton quotes one particular pastor as saying that talk of God's judgment "was for a time," perhaps a generation ago. "But I don't have it in my heart to condemn people. I'm there to encourage them. I see myself more as a coach, as a motivator to help them experience the life God has for us."[5] Sounds good, but not if you have a biblical worldview and understand what God says about sin, hell, and judgment. Why not have the integrity to stop calling himself a preacher, resign his church, and hit the road as a motivational speaker? At least he wouldn't be leading the sheep astray with his errant view of God and man.

I don't say this to pick on one person but to warn the Body of Christ about false teaching that soothes people's hearts and smooths over their sin, belittling the glories of life with God. If I read my Bible correctly, I don't get to pick the message; I'm just the messenger. God wrote it, and I'm to deliver it as written. It's not up to me to redefine biblical words to appease the crowd or my seared conscience. There is a need for us to understand why repentance is necessary. If we don't repent, we'll be dull of hearing, and the warnings of Jesus will go unheeded.

> Beware of the false prophets, who come to you in sheep's clothing, but inwardly are ravenous wolves. You will know them by their fruits. Grapes are not gathered from thorn bushes nor figs from thistles, are they? So every good tree bears good fruit, but the bad tree bears bad fruit. A good tree cannot produce bad fruit, nor can a bad tree produce good fruit. Every tree that does not bear good fruit is cut down and thrown into the fire. So then, you will know them by their fruits.

Not everyone who says to Me, "Lord, Lord," will enter the kingdom of heaven, but he who does the will of My Father who is in heaven will enter. Many will say to Me on that day, "Lord, Lord, did we not prophesy in Your name, and in Your name cast out demons, and in Your name perform many miracles?" And then I will declare to them, "I never knew you; depart from Me, you who practice lawlessness." (Matt. 7:15–23)

The church must repent of wanting to have her ears tickled. The preachers must repent of trying to please *people* rather than God. The laity must repent of wanting a message that makes them comfortable but does not transform them into the image of Christ.

Truthfully, you have to be negative to get to the positive. You can't talk about sin, indifference, idolatry, materialism, carnality, and apathy in a positive light. The only answer is: Repent! We are sick, and we need the Doctor of our souls to diagnose our specific illness. Then we need to take the prescription, as bitter as it may taste, to cure what ails us.

The New Testament teaches we are to live not only *ready* for His return but also *expectant* of His return. That being the case, I wouldn't want to meet my Lord in a backslidden condition. A revived church is up-to-date on repentance, prepared for Jesus to return. There's no putting off till tomorrow. Revival is a time of *expectation*. We prepare for it, pray for it, and then expect God to honor His Word. We must repent if we are going to survive. We must wake up to the reality of our desperate situation. We must surrender our lives to Jesus. Repentance is an admission that this is no time for business as usual.

Vance Havner said, "I have observed in the past few years that a strange stupor has fallen over the church of God. They come to church with their fingers crossed, ready to take what they hear with a grain of salt, and the preacher has two strikes against him before he utters a word. Besides that, the devil has cocained and chloroformed this present age, until a strange coma has settled over the saints. . . . Our eyelids are heavy and our brains are clouded, and unless we stir up the gift of God within us and get down to the business of watching and praying, our Lord shall come suddenly and find us sound asleep."

I've preached hundreds of revival meetings. I've preached nearly two thousand sermons and Bible studies at the church where I pastor. There are times when I grow weary of this message. After all, it would be easier and my sermons would be less offensive if I watered them down and went with the flow. We'd probably have more members, and I would be more popular among my peers. But I would be miserable and a traitor to the Scriptures and my Savior.

There are a few things I know for certain: 1) I cannot bring revival, preach it down, or work it up. It has to begin within the remnant. 2) If we don't have revival, every statistic will continue on a downhill slide. Giving, baptisms, and missions will all cave and ultimately collapse. 3) The choice is in the body, especially among the remnant.

Do you want to live the rest of your life in a typical church? Do you want services that start on time and end with little or nothing happening? The world expects some preachers to stand on this, but what the world needs (including the Sunday morning church crowd) is to see the laity standing on this truth.

CALLED TO REPENTANCE, TO REVIVAL

The book of Revelation reveals the glorified Christ walking among the candlesticks—the churches—just sixty years after His ascension. And what He saw didn't please Him for the most part. To five of the seven churches in Revelation, Jesus said, "Repent or else." This could be the message to five out of seven churches today, maybe more than that. Not one of those churches from the book of Revelation exists today. In fact, because they didn't heed the warnings, most were insignificant by the time the next generation passed away.

Over this land you will find once great churches now dying or empty. Some have been converted, like the cathedrals of Europe, into museums and coffee shops—because God is not obligated to bless us. We are obligated instead to align ourselves with Him. Do you want to leave a legacy? Do you want to make a difference? It begins with repentance that removes every obstacle from the road to revival.

There will never be a spiritual awakening and moral renewal in the nation until we have dealt with the root problem facing this generation. Boomers have largely rejected the Word of God as the basis of their authority and become gods unto themselves, bowing down to five gods who have "self" as their first name: self-will, self-righteousness, self-confidence, self-pleasing, and self-exaltation. We must tear down the altars of self and return to the God of our forefathers if we are to undergo a national revival. Sammy Tippit wrote, "We will never have spiritual awakening in the nation until we first see corporate revival within the church. The church needs to take a long hard look at itself. We must ask God to search our hearts and see where we have worshiped at the altar of self. The time has come for Christians to fall on our faces in repentance."[6]

The straying churches in Revelation were much the same:

1) *Ephesus* lacked love. They were busy and energetic with a full church calendar and sound doctrine. They could debate the meaning of Scripture, but they didn't have any love—the one thing Jesus said would characterize His disciples. You can be as straight as a gun barrel doctrinally yet still be empty. When our love for Christ dies, so does our love for others, the Word, and the lost.

Our churches today fuss and fight. We aren't committed to the things God is committed to. That's the only explanation for how we can justify gossip, meddling, envy, strife, slander, hatred, and unforgiveness. We act like the devil because we have no desire to repent and be right with God and man. When iniquity abounds, as Jesus said, the love of many will wax cold. Lawlessness doesn't just *exist* in our churches—it's abounding! There is no fear of God in the average church gathering. People can live in sin and feel very comfortable in many congregations. Ephesus was told to remember and repent or God would remove the candlestick, and the church would be put on the shelf.

2) *Pergamum* was told to repent because of their laxity. They loved the broad road and being open-minded, but they lacked discernment and discipline. The Lord also addressed their acts of immorality. The one with the sharp, two-edged sword in His mouth confronted them for allowing immorality into the church. We are to hate evil, not tolerate it. Churches today accept members who are living together in sin, hoping they will eventually work it out if they hang around church people long enough. We're so scared of offending someone, but we have no fear of offending God, who said, "Avoid sexual immorality."

3) *Thyatira* looked like the "Church of the Year" at first glance, but they too needed to repent. "You tolerate the woman Jezebel, who calls herself a prophetess, and she teaches and leads My bond-servants astray so that they commit acts of immorality and eat things sacrificed to idols. I gave her time to repent, and she does not want to repent of her immorality" (Rev. 2:20–21). This prophetess was guilty of teaching false doctrine. Any philosophy that makes it easier to sin is of the devil.

A LOT OF EXCITING CHURCHES ARE IN DESPERATE NEED OF REVIVAL.

Manley Beasley used to say that when revival came, it would cross denominational lines. But he didn't believe that God would honor people or denominations that dishonored certain truths. Tolerance usually ends up in compromise. Vance Havner wrote, "Beware of people who think they have seen visions when they have only had nightmares. Do not be hoodwinked and taken for a ride and sold down the river by new 'trends' and 'approaches,' popular deluxe brands of Christianity streamlined to suit a generation that cannot endure sound doctrine."[7]

4) *Sardis* was lifeless. So the Lord acted as the coroner. He saw the body and looked for vital signs but found none. Some churches think they're alive because they're busy, because they have the doors open with activities and programming for all age groups. God might not think so. There is not one word of praise for Sardis as a whole. On the surface they were alive, but in the eyes of God they were dead.

I've been to churches that made me think of Disney World, but I've been to others that made me think of the New Jerusalem. A lot of exciting churches are in desperate need of revival. Sardis had a form of godliness but lacked power. The salt was there, but it had no flavor. They needed unction in their functions. Jesus warned, "Repent or I'm coming like a thief." They weren't ready for His return. If we thought He was coming back tomorrow, I bet we would get right today!

5) *Laodicea* was lukewarm—a little too hot to be cold, and a little too cold to be hot. Jesus said, "I know your deeds, that you are neither cold nor hot; I wish that you were cold or hot. So because you are lukewarm, and neither hot nor cold, I will spit you out of My mouth." They said to themselves, "I am rich, and have become wealthy, and have need of nothing" not realizing they were actually "wretched and miserable and poor and blind and naked" (Rev. 3:15–17). They were clueless and so out of touch with God that they flunked His examination and didn't even know they were being tested. God's evaluation

would seem undignified if it weren't straight from the lips of our Lord. They were pitiful and pathetic. They made God nauseated. G. Campbell Morgan said, "Lukewarmness is the worst form of blasphemy."

So he that has ears, let him hear what the Spirit says to the churches. Are you listening? The Laodiceans were strutting around—naked! How many churches invite us to come and see how they do it—how they grow their ministries and organize their programs—when in fact, in the eyes of God, they are naked. If we could only see our churches the way God sees them!

Every year I get this package that must cost at least $100 from a very well-known church. It's an invitation to attend their conference where I'm supposed to learn how to really do church. The package is usually full of silly stuff I pass on to children because it has nothing to do with building a church based on what God says about building a church. There is a world of difference between a crowd and a congregation. If that church started preaching repentance, the crowd would leave and the gimmicks would be taken to the toy store where they belong.

J. Edwin Orr wrote, "The rebuke given Laodicea may be fairly applied to believers. Lukewarmness, self-satisfaction, halfheartedness, backsliding, formalism, indifference, self-righteousness, greed for gold, worldliness, pride, self-deception, spiritual destitution, blindness and lack of vision, easily seen through—these are the characteristics of Laodicea, and these are the characteristics abounding today. . . . If a majority of your church members share a majority of these indications of spiritual poverty, then your church is a Laodicean church. And if the majority of churches in your district are thus backslidden, then everything said to Laodicea applies to your neighborhood."[8]

But there is hope. There is the possibility of God once again moving among His people. "Those whom I love, I reprove and discipline; therefore be zealous and repent. Behold, I stand at the door and knock; if anyone hears My voice and opens the door, I will come in to him and will dine with him, and he with Me" (Rev. 3:19–20). We've mistakenly used these verses as an invitation to the lost. Jesus, however, is standing outside the door of His church, asking if He can come in.

He stands at the door of the self-sufficient, self-satisfied, self-righteous, self-justifying church today and knocks. Will you let Him in? Or will you be too busy to notice? Paul reminded the Corinthians, "Therefore, having these promises, beloved, let us cleanse ourselves from all defilement of flesh and spirit, perfecting holiness in the fear of God" (2 Cor. 7:1). Cleansing is essential in revival. It means to purify or prune the evil out of our lives. We are to make a clean break with sin. Obviously we can't be sinless, but we can cooperate with the Spirit by perfecting holiness in the fear of God and rooting out the weeds that choke the Word in our lives.

LET IT START WITH US

When asked what role the church might play if God sends revival, Manley Beasley said, "As a local assembly, some will sit by and the church next door will be aflame and they won't even know it. During the days of Wesley and Whitefield, the glory of God could be in a block, and the next block over they didn't know it was happening. They had ears but could not hear and eyes but could not see."[9]

Ron Dunn talked about how two people could sit in the same service and hear the same sermon. One could walk out changed, and the other could just walk out. How can that happen? Sensitivity to the Spirit. One is listening and the other isn't. One is receptive and the other is resistant. One repents and the other argues with God. You can be close and miss it. Sin is deceptive.

Repentance is the prelude to revival, a biblical principle that cannot be avoided. We must not let the attitudes of the indifferent or insensitive stop us. We must not let the carnal block the door. Jesus didn't say, "If you can get the majority to vote for revival, I will come in." Repentance and response to the Spirit are individual matters both in salvation and sanctification.

It only took four young men to get hold of God and pray down revival in Ulster in 1859. Evan Roberts and a handful of others prayed down revival in Wales in 1904. If we want revival, we cant wait for the corporate body to repent while there is repenting for us to do ourselves. Nor can we wait for the church to decide there's a need for revival. If we know it, then we need to act.

You may be God's "anyone"—the person He will use to open the door and let Him in. He's more than ready. He's willing to come and meet with you. Don't wait on the other person. You open the door. You take the first step. It just takes one to start a revival. Jesus isn't waiting on the results of a poll or committee meeting. He's waiting on a person. And He'll keep on waiting as long as we . . .

- lack any real discernment in the preaching and teaching we listen to
- delay acting on what God has clearly said
- deny a coming judgment
- think the sermon is for someone else
- think the church exists to make us feel better instead of pointing us to holiness
- maintain an apathetic attitude

Vance Havner warned, "The hour is too late and the need is too great for business as usual. Start with yourself, get right with God, and then seek others of like mind and heart. It is time for holy desperation because it is too late for everything else."

One of the most convicting messages Ron Dunn ever preached was entitled "One More Year." His text was Luke 13:

> Now on the same occasion there were some present who reported to Him about the Galileans whose blood Pilate had mixed with their sacrifices. And Jesus said to them, "Do you suppose that these Galileans were greater sinners than all other Galileans because they suffered this fate? I tell you, no, but unless you repent, you will all likewise perish. Or do you suppose that those eighteen on whom the tower in Siloam

fell and killed them were worse culprits than all the men who live in Jerusalem? I tell you, no, but unless you repent, you will all likewise perish."

And He began telling this parable: "A man had a fig tree which had been planted in his vineyard; and he came looking for fruit on it and did not find any. And he said to the vineyard keeper, 'Behold, for three years I have come looking for fruit on this fig tree without finding any. Cut it down! Why does it even use up the ground?' And he answered and said to him, 'Let it alone, sir, for this year too, until I dig around it and put in fertilizer; and if it bears fruit next year, fine; but if not, cut it down.'" (vv. 1–9)

Twice Jesus said, "Unless you repent." Stop pointing fingers at others. God is examining us on an individual basis. The question is, What if God said He would give you one more year? If God came looking at your life, looking for the fruit of repentance, the fruit of souls, and the fruit of the Spirit, what would He find? Ron's preaching outline forms a fitting conclusion to this chapter:

1) *God has a right to expect fruit from us* because of our privileged position as His personal property with a primary purpose. There were plenty of fig trees growing wild,

but this one was planted in a vineyard to receive special care and nourishment. Fig trees were created to bear figs. Apart from that, they are useless and worthless.

2) *God has a right to examine us for fruit.* He came seeking fruit and scrutinizing every tree. Since it's His vineyard and His trees, He will examine our fruitfulness.

3) *God has a right to expel us for fruitlessness.* "Cut it down!" I'm convinced that more believers than we know have been set aside from great service and others planted in their place. Uselessness invites disaster and promotes further uselessness.

4) *God has a right to extend mercy.* "Wait one more year." In the Old Testament, the expression was "break up your fallow ground." We must repent with a broken and contrite heart, and then fertilize, feed, and nourish our lives with prayer and the Word of God.[10]

If we fail to repent today, we have one more day to repent of, and one less day to repent in. Thomas Fuller wrote, "You cannot repent too soon, because you do not know how soon it may be too late."[11]

CHAPTER 3

CLEANING OUT THE CLUTTER

Ezra and Nehemiah

The characteristic of revival is that a profound consciousness of sin is produced in many persons at the same time by an awareness of God.
—Iain H. Murray

But now we have been given a brief moment of grace, for the LORD our God has allowed a few of us to survive as a remnant. He has given us security in this holy place. Our God has brightened our eyes and granted us some relief from our slavery.
—Ezra 9:8 NLT

WHEN MY PARENTS DIED, my wife and I had the responsibility of cleaning out the house where they had lived for nearly fifty years. The attic was packed with old toys, magazines, Christmas decorations, and all the prescription files from my dad's drugstore. To say that my parents never threw anything away would be an understatement. I once told them they would not die of old age but of the attic falling in from the weight of all that junk!

So there we were, working through our grief and filling up trash bags. One day I put thirty-six full-sized plastic yard bags at the curb. It was exhausting work. We had to decide what to keep while preparing the rest of the house for an estate sale. Terri organized the sale because she knew it would be hard for me to watch people, many whom I would know, go through my old house, bargaining and bickering over prices. I still owe her for that!

Clutter is a problem. It bogs down not just homes and families but also churches. If you walk through the average church, you'll find old Sunday school quarterlies that were never used the first time, old hymnals stacked on the pianos, and used coffee cups under the chairs because people were too lazy to throw them away. Every church could use a good spring cleaning.

I hate clutter. I hate it in my office and in my study. Having piles of stuff around drives me crazy. I want things clean, neat, and organized. My rule is: when in doubt, throw it out. But what about the clutter we often overlook? The clutter of busyness, for example. Lacking any real sense of priority and purpose, we clog our schedules with so much stuff, we have little time for God.

How about the clutter in our minds? We are bombarded with constant information from e-mail, cell phones, television, talk radio, and a host of other media outlets used to "save time." There are so many voices shouting for our attention, it's hard to hear God speaking.

God longs for us to clear out the clutter, to throw away the junk and eliminate the nonessentials so we might see clearer and know Him better. The fact that our lives are cluttered is an indication that we do not believe God is sufficient. We have additives (which are really subtractions) because we can't fix our hearts on Jesus really being the answer.

God revealed Himself as the great I Am. This apparently means that everything else in life could be called "They Are Nots." Because what God can do, others can't do. Fame can't satisfy us. Stuff can fill us like cotton candy, but it melts before we can even swallow. Yet wherever there is a legitimate need, we'll find God there. In this chapter we'll meet two men who trusted God to use them as instruments of revival—two men who made God the primary focus of their lives—Ezra, a scribe, and Nehemiah, a layman.

APPALLED AT SIN

Many years before the people of Judah had been carried off into Babylonian exile, God had inspired Isaiah to mention the very name of the ruler who would initiate their return: Cyrus, king of Persia. He was the key to the beginning breezes of what is known as the post-captivity revival, the longest revival recorded in the Scripture. A casual observer will miss this: God called Cyrus "His anointed" (Isa. 45:1). It may be hard for us to get our head around this, but God used a pagan king for His purposes "so that you may know that it is I, the LORD, the God of Israel" (v. 3). Like always, God showed up in the darkest times.

In the first year of his reign, Cyrus announced he would allow some of the Jews to return to the land. He said he had been appointed by God "to build Him a house in Jerusalem" (Ezra 1:2), and he called for an offering to be collected. Talk about God being in control! But while many Jews across the land rejoiced, some chose to stay behind rather than return.

It's easy to talk about Promised Land living, but it's another thing to go fight for it. A church can experience a few movements of God and think it's revival. But we must be careful to "calculate the cost" (Luke 14:28) if we say we want to see the glory of God restored to our life and our church. Most of us, if we knew the cost of revival, would stop praying for it. We like a little stirring, but that's not enough for a genuine move of God to transform the landscape.

Later under the leadership of the scribe Ezra, another group returned to Jerusalem. By now the temple had finally been rebuilt, but it was nothing like the first temple. Ezra arrived to find the city walls still in shambles and the gates wide open, offering no protection from enemy nations. But his was a heart uncluttered when it came to wanting God's desire for His people. "The good hand of his God was upon him. For Ezra had set his heart to study the law of the LORD and to practice it, and to teach His statutes and ordinances in Israel" (Ezra 7:9–10).

When God's hand is on someone, you know it. You see God guiding and protecting him. God comes alongside and burns within that person a holy confidence that the Lord is on his side. It takes a man with unwavering conviction to face the adversity and opposition to revival. This is why Ezra was a key to revival.

For while he found upon his return that the people had rebuilt the temple, he also recognized they had embraced pagan practices. "The people of Israel and the priests and the Levites have not separated themselves from the peoples of the lands, according to their abominations" (Ezra 9:1). When he saw this, Ezra tore his garments, pulled hair from his head and beard, and sat down "appalled" (v. 3). The word means to be shocked, horrified, astonished, or desolate. The things Ezra did in response to hearing of these sins was the same thing one would have done to grieve over the dead. "Then everyone who trembled at the words of the God of Israel on account of the unfaithfulness of the exiles gathered to me, and I sat appalled until the evening offering" (v. 4).

Why doesn't sin in the camp or in the church affect us that way anymore? We generally turn a blind eye to sin in the church for fear of offending someone in the membership. Have we forgotten that it's God's church? He is offended that we are not offended by sin! But the sin of the people drove Ezra to prayer.

> At the evening offering I arose from my humiliation, even with my garment and my robe torn, and I fell on my knees and stretched out

my hands to the LORD my God; and I said, "O
my God, I am ashamed and embarrassed to lift
up my face to You, my God, for our iniquities
have risen above our heads and our guilt has
grown even to the heavens. Since the days of
our fathers to this day we have been in great
guilt, and on account of our iniquities we, our
kings and our priests have been given into the
hand of the kings of the lands, to the sword, to
captivity and to plunder and to open shame,
as it is this day. But now for a brief moment
grace has been shown from the LORD our God,
to leave us an escaped remnant and to give
us a peg in His holy place, that our God may
enlighten our eyes and grant us a little reviving
in our bondage." (Ezra 9:5–8)

Oh, how quickly we forget promises made at the altar. How
quickly we forget the blessings of God and go back to our clutter and baggage that should have long since been kicked to the
curb, especially the spiritual clutter of ongoing sin.

As one preacher has said, "We've forgotten how to blush."
We are no longer shocked by sin. We need an Ezra to remind us
that we can build all the temples we want, but if we don't deal
with sin, those temples will just be houses for sinning. Until we
see sin the way God sees it, we're just having religious meetings
without experiencing revival. Where is the preacher who will
preach against sin? Not just the sins of the homosexuals and

adulterers, but the other works of the flesh like gossip and slander. The one who walks in pride in the church is an offense to God. Who will confront him? What about the ungodly attitudes in the church—unforgiveness, bitterness, anger? I've seen the same sorry attitudes on church softball teams as from a bunch of beer-drinking, foul-mouthed pagans.

Do we see the need for the leadership to grieve and confess like Ezra? Until change comes, there will be no revival. Walter Kaiser wrote, "Generally there is some single pressing issue that presents itself as one of the key reasons for the need for revival. But the factor that decides whether a reformation or a revival has occurred is the effect it has on the whole inner disposition and hearts of the people."[1]

A BURDEN FOR SEEKING GOD

Nehemiah arrived on the scene because of a burden for his people. One day men came from Jerusalem, and Nehemiah asked how things were going. They replied, "The remnant there in the province who survived the captivity are in great distress and reproach, and the wall of Jerusalem is broken down and its gates are burned with fire" (Neh. 1:3). The news from Jerusalem broke Nehemiah's heart, and he spent days weeping, mourning, fasting, and praying.

In our ReFRESH™ Conferences, I try to encourage pastors to bring a few key laymen with them. They need someone who catches the vision and shares the burden to return with them to their churches and communities and seek the Lord for revival and renewal. If it's just the pastor, it often ends up being written off as "preacher talk." But if a layman gets on fire for God, the other laity will stand up and take notice.

Here was a godly layman—a cupbearer with power, access, and influence—who was grief stricken over the condition of the people, just as Ezra was. Where can we find laity who are burdened over decreasing baptisms, increasing divorces, fallen preachers, carnal church members, and a discredited gospel because of sinfulness in the body? God's people have compromised, and the walls have been breached. We are no longer storming the gates of hell. We're merely holding on against the onslaught of the enemy who has broken down everything sacred in our society.

Can we pray the prayer of Nehemiah?

> I beseech You, O Lord God of heaven, the great and awesome God, who preserves the covenant and lovingkindness for those who love Him and keep His commandments, let Your ear now be attentive and Your eyes open to hear the prayer of Your servant which I am praying before You now, day and night, on behalf of the sons of Israel Your servants, confessing the sins of the sons of Israel which we have sinned against You; I and my father's house have sinned. We have acted very corruptly against You and have not kept the commandments, nor the statutes, nor the ordinances which You commanded Your servant Moses.

Remember the word which You commanded Your servant Moses, saying, "If you are
unfaithful I will scatter you among the peoples;
but if you return to Me and keep My commandments and do them, though those of you who
have been scattered were in the most remote
part of the heavens, I will gather them from
there and will bring them to the place where
I have chosen to cause My name to dwell."
They are Your servants and Your people whom
You redeemed by Your great power and by Your
strong hand.

O Lord, I beseech You, may Your ear be
attentive to the prayer of Your servant and the
prayer of Your servants who delight to revere
Your name, and make Your servant successful
today and grant him compassion before this
man. (Neh. 1:5–11)

Nehemiah knew the Scriptures. He knew God's character
and promises, and he knew the nation's hopes were bound up in
their uncluttered devotion to Him. Our hope is not so much in
God's promises as in the character of the One who *makes* those
promises. The God who does not change and does not lie is
the God who invites us to boldly approach the throne of grace.
Nehemiah didn't just pray one time; he prayed for months,
looking for an opportunity and an open door. He put himself in
position to be used of God by making himself usable.

Throughout my ministry I've had to listen to the "someday" crowd. These are the ones who say, "I'm in high school and I want to enjoy it, but when I get out of school, I'm going to serve God." Then they go to college and say, "I'm preparing for my career. It's hard, but when I get out, I'm going to settle down and serve God." Then they get married and make excuses about getting adjusted as a couple and then getting adjusted with the kids. One thing leads to another, and they've spent their whole lives saying "someday." But someday never comes.

Life is not a dress rehearsal. You don't get a second chance. You get one shot at serving God, so whatever you are going to do for His name—do it now! The Israelites delayed and doubted God, and it cost them forty years in the wilderness. The three men who met Jesus in Luke 9:57–62, saying they would become His followers when they could get around to it, all made excuses. They said they wanted to follow God, but they had something else they needed to do "first." Jesus never comes next. Delay is denial. He is either Lord *of* all or not Lord *at* all. Whatever you plan to do for God, do it now. Nehemiah was ready and available. He just needed the signal from heaven that it was time.

One day he took the wine to the king, and the king asked him, "Why is your face sad though you are not sick? This is nothing but sadness of heart" (Neh. 2:2). Trembling, Nehemiah replied, "Why should my face not be sad when the city, the place of my fathers' tombs, lies desolate and its gates have been consumed by fire?" (v. 3). When the king asked, "What would you request?" Nehemiah's first response was to pray to the God of heaven (v. 4). Is this not an instance of a man who already knew the principle of praying without ceasing? In the midst of every obstacle and opportunity, Nehemiah first turned to God in prayer.

After a season of fervent prayer, Nehemiah made his request. "If it please the king, and if your servant has found favor before you, send me to Judah, to the city of my fathers' tombs, that I may rebuild it" (v. 5). And in Nehemiah's own words, "the king granted them to me because the good hand of my God was on me" (v. 8). Here was a man who was available to God. He was willing to pay the price to be the answer to his own prayers. When the opportunity presented itself, he was prayed up and prepared. Nehemiah knew what needed to be done, and he knew God had called him to do it.

> **YOU GET ONE SHOT AT SERVING GOD, SO WHATEVER YOU ARE GOING TO DO FOR HIS NAME—DO IT NOW!**

How burdened are you? How willing are you to be the answer to your prayers? How long are you willing to pray for an open door? Prayer is warfare. Our praying must be persistent, pointed, and purposeful. Nehemiah started winning the battles he would face in Jerusalem before he ever arrived on the scene.

In Ephesians 6, after Paul described the details of the armor of the saint, he reminded us that a prayerless saint is a defeated one. He said we are to "pray at all times in the Spirit, and with this in view, be on the alert with all perseverance and petition for all the saints" (v. 18). Every piece of the armor is put on in prayer, and then we are commanded to keep persevering in prayer.

Ray Stedman writes, "Immediately after listing for us our spiritual armor, Paul instructs us in the final complement to the full armor of God: prayer. Notice the order in which Paul discusses these issues. He does not reverse the order and say, 'First pray, then put on the armor of God.' No, we put on the armor first, then pray. We tend to reverse this order, and that is why our prayer life is frequently so feeble and impotent. Our prayer life would be stronger and more effective if we would carefully observe the designated order of Scripture."[2]

Long before Paul wrote Ephesians, Nehemiah embodied these characteristics of prayer. He was a man totally devoted to seeking his God—a man with uncluttered passion for the will and strength of the Lord—a man God could use to bring forth revival.

FEARLESS TOWARD OPPOSITION

When a person starts moving out to reclaim ground that has been stolen by the enemy, he will face battles. Sin had led to the captivity of Israel. Nehemiah's return to Jerusalem would not be a cake walk either. The devil and the harsh critics did everything they could to thwart his work. Remember, the enemy will connive every conceivable way to get you to stop short of what God has called you to do.

Nehemiah set out with the blessings of the king and of God. And when he arrived in the land, he began inspecting the walls. Finally he called the city leaders together and said,

"You see the bad situation we are in, that Jerusalem is desolate and its gates burned by fire. Come, let us rebuild the wall of Jerusalem so that we will no longer be a reproach" (Neh. 2:17). The walls had to be rebuilt for security purposes. Once the walls were built, watchmen could stand on the walls and keep an eye on any approaching threats. Immediately Nehemiah found favor with the leaders. They said, "Let us arise and build," and they "put their hands to the good work" (v. 18).

But like any work of God, Nehemiah and the people faced their share of critics.

Do not underestimate how much Satan hates the thought of a revived people and a restored church. "When Sanballat the Horonite and Tobiah the Ammonite official heard about it, it was very displeasing to them that someone had come to seek the welfare of the sons of Israel" (Neh. 2:10). Don't miss this. Not everyone is going to be excited about what God is doing in your life. Not only will you battle with the world, the flesh, and the devil, but you'll also have to battle with the carnal members of your church. Revival is a threat to those who live in the flesh, those who want power, and those who hate change, even if it's change for the good.

Any great work of God will be opposed. Some will lack faith. Others will lack vision. A few will feel threatened because they've lost control. Keep your eyes on Jesus. Expect opposition. It will come from one of three crowds: the "It can't be done" crowd, the "It won't be done" crowd, or the "It shouldn't be done" crowd. The enemy is quick to rear his ugly head to oppose what God initiates.

Don't expect these naysayers to go quietly into the night. Notice their persistence against Nehemiah's rebuilding project. First it was "displeasing" to them (Neh. 2:10), then their displeasure turned to mocking and despising (v. 19), and finally they became so enraged that they conspired to "fight" (4:7–8). They resorted to deception and slander, accusing Nehemiah of establishing his own kingdom for his own glory. When they saw his plan succeeding, they appealed to him to reason with them, further trying to distract the forward momentum. The people were moving forward while these men were left in the dust.

The devil is ticked off by any demonstration of the power of God. He will meet a demonstration with a *demon*-stration, hoping to strike fear into our hearts. The devil will attack anyone God is using in revival. His attacks can be frontal or subtle. He can entice us to compromise, or he can question our motives. The opposition may be outward and vocal, or it may be subtle attacks and murmuring in the hallways. Either way, it's a strategy to get you off task and off target.

He will even use people who want to imply they are speaking for God. That's what happened with the so-called prophet who tried to persuade Nehemiah to run into the temple and hide. I can't tell you how often people have tried to redirect me, telling me to lighten up and relax. But if I'm on a mission, I can't go AWOL or take a break for rest and relaxation. That would mean forsaking my post. Compromised thinking will always cloud our vision.

The devil will also use *good things* to divert our energy and attention. I've been asked to serve on boards and organizations that were good and noble, but they weren't what God had called me to do at the time. If I had agreed, I would have been worn out in doing *good* things but not the *best* things. I attend very few denominational meetings. It's not because I'm not interested. I just don't have time to sit around drinking coffee, singing, "Nobody knows the trouble I've seen." There's work to be done, and the sun is setting. We can get sidetracked by the good, which is the enemy of the best. This can be as much a work of Satan as an outright frontal attack.

Revival will not occur amid that kind of clutter.

We need to address one more diversion. "Also in those days many letters went from the nobles of Judah to Tobiah, and Tobiah's letters came to them. For many in Judah were bound by oath to him" (Neh. 6:17–18). No one speaks to the verse better than Warren Wiersbe:

> If you can't see Satan working, it's probably because he has gone underground. Actually, we are safer when we can see him at work than when his agents are concealed. Open opposition is good for God's work and God's workers because it keeps us alert and trusting the Lord. . . . It seems incredible that any Jew would secretly cooperate with the enemy, let alone Jews who were nobles from the royal tribe of Judah! If any tribe had a stake in the future of "the city of David," it was the tribe of Judah. . . . When these nobles cooperated with Tobiah,

they were resisting the Lord, disobeying the Word, and jeopardizing their own future. Why would they do such a treacherous thing? For one thing, Tobiah wrote them letters and influenced their thinking. Instead of seeking the truth, the nobles believed the enemy's lies and became traitors to their own people.[3]

I've walked through this very thing in my ministry. I've been burned more than once by a disloyal staff member. Private conversations were used against me. Confidences were betrayed. You can tell the character of a man by how he leaves a church; he'll either walk out like a man or crawl out like a worm. It is a sad commentary that many ministers and staff members leave blood on the walls, shooting over their shoulders when they leave a church. This neither glorifies God nor advances His kingdom.

This can also happen with disgruntled church members. In the 1960s Sherwood had a chance to buy several houses across the street from the church. The vote passed, but one lady started a telephone campaign because she didn't want it to happen. In the interest of unity, the church rescinded the motion the following month, and the deal was dead. When I first came to Sherwood in the 1990s, we were landlocked. We needed to buy the houses across the street. The delay of thirty years cost us nearly a half million dollars. Delay in doing the will of God is costly. You can't let the few who will not go forward with God run the church of God. They aren't qualified.

CLEANING OUT THE CLUTTER

We've survived letters to the editor. We've been attacked by caustic comments in the Squawk Box, a section in the local paper where you can anonymously write a one or two-sentence beef about anything or anyone. I believe columns like these do more to divide a city than to build it up. Proverbs 29:8 warns, "Scorners set a city aflame," and they will also destroy a church.

Attacks will surely come, and you must meet them with courage and boldness. Notice how Nehemiah responded to his critics and cynics. He was too smart to be duped by them. He was too discerning to fall into their trap. He was too in tune with God to listen to them. His heart was uncluttered enough to keep his focus clear.

You have to meet their persistence with holy boldness. Nehemiah dealt with them head-on. He wasn't the coward of the county; he was the man appointed by God, and he acted like it.

Everyone has a thorn in the flesh. They are in every church. They love friction. They instigate dissension. They are "enemies of the cross of Christ . . . whose god is their appetite, and whose glory is in their shame" (Phil. 3:18–19). They should be dealt with accordingly. Don't ask God to use you if you can't stand up to your critics and detractors.

Look back at Nehemiah's words to the critics in chapter 2: "So I answered them and said to them, 'The God of heaven will give us success; therefore we His servants will arise and build, but you have no portion, right or memorial in Jerusalem'" (v. 20). In other words, when all was said and done, those opponents would be cut out of the will. This was no casual statement. One of the men was the governor of Samaria, one was the governor of Ammon, and the other was a leader overseeing the Arabs. Nehemiah was surrounded by powerful men, but he wouldn't surrender. They had the "We were here before you came, and we'll be here after you're gone" attitude, but Nehemiah stood firm in the Lord.

Eight times in this book, Nehemiah declared his allegiance and dependence on God. He and He alone can grant success as we trust in Him and stand on His Word. No matter what, those on the Lord's side win in the end.

When God is at work, there is no time for appointments with the carnal. "I am doing a great work and I cannot come down," Nehemiah said to them. "Why should the work stop while I leave it and come down to you?" (Neh. 6:3). You don't have to entertain the thoughts of every critic. If you do, they will wear you out with their words and their so-called concerns. They aren't concerned about you; they are concerned about how the situation will affect them. They will make up things to put fear in your heart, but the fear of man is a snare. "Such things as you are saying have not been done, but you are inventing them in your own mind" (v. 8).

When given the opportunity to run, Nehemiah stood his ground. "Should a man like me flee? And could one such as I go into the temple to save his life? I will not go in" (v. 11). Too often we quit just before the victory is ours. If you are a pastor and don't plan to stay at your current church, don't make a lot of changes. Just preach the Word, love the people, and leave.

But if you are intent on revival, you'll have to weather some dangers, toils, and snares. People will tempt you to take a short-cut or settle for something less than God's best. You have to be careful who you allow to speak into your life.

A man who fears God fears no man. Fear is the beginning of defeat. The only fear you should have is a fear of losing the touch of God on your life. If you want to direct the choir, you must turn your back to the audience. You'll hear statements like, "Folks are concerned," "People are worried," "I've had some of the members come to me about this," and all kinds of similar statements. Can I give you some advice? If people won't name the details of the situation, ignore it. The proverbial "they" is usually two or three. Most pastors leave a church because a handful of people sound like an army. Change the channel on your spiritual radio, and tune in to the voice of God.

With the popularity of blogs, we are all just one nut case away from a battle. Don't be sucked in by the dissenting minority. If you are a person God wants to lead in revival, then you are speaking on His behalf, the Lord God Almighty. So don't let the crowd shout you down or drive you out. "Greater is He who is in you than He who is in the world" (1 John 4:4). "Submit therefore to God. Resist the devil and he will flee from you" (James 4:7). Stay uncluttered in your devotion.

A. W. Tozer said it well:

> Fear broods over the church like some ancient
> curse. Fear for our living, fear of our jobs, fear
> of losing popularity, fear of each other: these

are the ghosts that haunt the men who stand today in places of church leadership. Many of them, however, win a reputation for courage by repeating safe and expected things with comical daring. Yet self-conscious courage is not the cure. . . . The ideal seems to be a quiet courage that is not aware of its own presence. It draws its strength each moment from the indwelling Spirit and is hardly aware of self at all. Such a courage will be patient also and well-balanced and safe from extremes. May God send a baptism of such courage upon us.[4]

CLEANUP DAY

We don't have time in this chapter to go into all Nehemiah did, but he cleared out the rubble and rubbish in two areas: first, he dealt with those who were blocking his way; then he dealt with the rubble that was keeping them from rebuilding the wall. He got the people to see the possibilities, and they did what was needed and expected. Revival may begin with one man, but it never ends there. "Me" has to become "we." It's *our* work, *our* calling, *our* task. We find out what God has in mind for us, and we partner with Him in the work. His work, our hands.

In the days following the rebuilding of the walls, worship was restored. Ezra read from the book of the law. The people stood in honor of the Word of God. The famine of hearing the Word of God was finally over. The people were now hungry for the Scriptures.

Ezra would read first. Then the people would break up into smaller groups, and the Levites would explain what they had heard. This is apostolic, exegetical, expository preaching at its best. The reading came first, followed by observation, interpretation, and application.

Our churches have a hunger for everything but the Word these days. Too many sermons today are too full of illustrations, much like a house made of glass. Impressive, but not where you want to be in a storm. Revival preaching has to be a return to Scripture—line by line, precept upon precept, text in context. Our opinions do not matter; what God says matters!

When we built our new facility, I marked off a six-by-eight-foot section around where the pulpit would be, and I wrote on the exposed concrete with a permanent marker. I wrote Scriptures about the authority and power of the Word, quotes from my favorite preachers, and more. Immediately behind the pulpit I wrote in large letters, "Let him who stands here and preach not Jesus be accursed."

REVIVAL PREACHING HAS TO BE A RETURN TO SCRIPTURE—LINE BY LINE, PRECEPT UPON PRECEPT.

I tell visiting preachers about what's written beneath their feet when they stand in our pulpit. Charles Spurgeon said, "A sermon without Christ as its beginning, middle and end is a mistake in conception and a crime in execution. . . . If any man can preach one sermon without mentioning Christ's name in it, it ought to be his last, certainly the last that any Christian ought to go to hear him preach. . . . When we preach Christ crucified, we have no reason to stammer, or stutter, or hesitate, or apologize; there is nothing in the gospel of which we have any cause to be ashamed." God will empower the pulpit that has one object—the exaltation of Christ through the preaching of His Word.

In Nehemiah's day, the people revered the Word. They didn't question it; they obeyed it and responded to it. The reading and explanation of Scripture led to conviction and worship among the people. God became their central focus. Fifteen times in Nehemiah 8 you find the phrase "the people." God longs to do a great work among His people, but they must be receptive. Is there an air of expectancy in your church? God often meets us at the level of our expectations. Will this Sunday be just another Sunday, or will it be the day that a weeping preacher brings the Word and the people begin to weep as well? How sad that on most pews this Sunday, the Word that set these people and the early church on fire will put many to sleep. How can one sleep when the Word of God is being proclaimed? Faith without works is dead. Revival is not a static thing; it's active.

This work of God in Nehemiah and Ezra's day was far-reaching and long-lasting. There is no record of idolatry after this revival. It brought an end to much of the previous acceptance of compromise. The revival fires burned the dross and left the gold. The emotions of revival may end, but its effects can last for generations.

If we would have the courage to stand up to the critics and cynics . . . if we would clear out the secondary things that clutter our lives and water down our priorities . . . if we would learn how to get hold of God and then let God get hold of us through His Word, we might have a move of God that could last for generations.

It begins with people who cannot accept the status quo any longer. It starts in the heart of one or a few who are weary of their cluttered, meaningless lives. It brings us to a place of determination and desperation. It continues with a desire to hear the Word and obey it.

With that in mind, what is it right now that you need to stop doing? What causes you to stumble? What is cluttering your mind and heart? Are you willing to let some things go that don't need to be there? Let the Lord purge and purify.

There is much rubble to be removed, but the labor is worth it. Like a ship at sea in a storm, there comes a point when you must throw overboard everything that is not necessary for survival. You can't get sentimental and expect to survive. You can't reach land when you're weighed down by things that will easily beset you. Why would anyone want to live with rubble when you can have revival? Why look at ruined walls and live in fear when God has more in store for us? Removing the rubble is preparation for revival. It's preparing the ground for God to work, paving the way for God to move in. It's setting our sails to catch the wind of the Spirit. When we remove the rubble, we get rid of anything and everything that keeps us from the "this one thing I do" mind-set.

We need churches full of people who have a mind to do the great work of preparing the way for the Lord. We need to pray to the Lord of the harvest to send forth laborers into the fields.

We don't need any more people who just sit, soak, and sour. We need those who allow God to squeeze them out in His service.

I can't think of one thing we threw away or sold when cleaning out my parents' house that I miss or wish I could get back. Perhaps this is the day you need to do some housecleaning of your own. For when Jesus fills your heart with nothing other than Himself, you'll be too full to miss what you threw out in the process. If revival is to come, the clutter must go.

CHAPTER 4

THE WORD OF GOD

2 Timothy 3

The foundation of every reformation of the Holy Spirit is the Word of God made plain to the people.
— Frank Cooke

The law of the Lord is perfect, restoring the soul; the testimony of the Lord is sure, making wise the simple.
— Psalm 19:7

ONE OF THE GREAT FEARS I have is the growing biblical illiteracy among God's people. We are no longer a nation of readers, thanks in large part to our developing technologies. Yet I am firmly convinced that if we want to see revival, we need to be students of the Scripture and students of the history of revival. If we don't know what God has said, we will not know how to act and respond . . . to anything.

These are perilous times. We are witnessing a great cultural shift, yet many believers are unaware of it. We do not understand the hour in which we live. Most of us own multiple copies of the Scriptures, but how often do we sit down to read, meditate, study, or memorize them?

The Word is a lamp, but we seem to continually walk in darkness. The Word is bread, but we live off the crumbs of secular philosophies. The Word is honey, but we have no appetite for it. Our eyes have been trained to see the news ticker scrolling across the bottom of the screen, but we lack the ability to focus on what God says. Ron Dunn wrote,

> I'm afraid many Christians look at the promises of God as I looked at the Sears catalog as a boy. When I was about ten, I spotted a .22 rifle in the catalog, and I had to have it! It cost $25.00, but it might as well have been a thousand. Knowing it was beyond my reach, I would get out the catalog, turn to the page that displayed the picture of "my rifle," and dream. No wonder the catalog was called "the

wish book." I wished and wished, but I knew
I couldn't have it. And to many Christians the
Bible is just that—a wish book. They read the
promises with enthusiasm and shout "Amen"
when they are preached from the pulpit, but
never really expect to see them fulfilled in their
own lives. But the Bible is not a wish book; it
is a faith book. And for those who, by faith,
cross over into victory, all the promises of God
become real.[1]

The prophet Amos recorded words that should shake us to
the core: "'Behold, days are coming,' declares the Lord God,
'when I will send a famine on the land, not a famine for bread
or a thirst for water, but rather for hearing the words of the
Lord'" (Amos 8:11). This saying came true. After the prophecy
of Malachi, God went silent throughout the next four hundred
years. During those days generation after generation heard no
prophet. God had spoken, but the people had ignored what He
said.

Are we paying attention to His Word today? Are we declaring it with clarity and boldness, as the Scripture compels us?

We have gained much attention at Sherwood because of
the success of our movies through Sherwood Pictures—movies
that are being used by God around the world to impact lives.
We've heard from thousands of people who have given their
lives to Christ as a result of the messages in these films. But my
greatest fear is that we would only be known as "the church that

makes movies." We are so much more than that. I see among many of our people a hunger for prayer and revival, a desire for pure and undefiled worship, a true servant spirit.

As I've been thinking about the impact of all this attention garnered from our movie-making, I've asked God to protect us from resting on our laurels. I've also prayed we would not allow the movies to do our missions for us. It would be easy for us to pat each other on the back about all the e-mails and stories we get and therefore never get our hands dirty. We must be hands-on with missions. We can't let our movies do that for us.

I would say we're on the cutting edge as a congregation. Certainly the number of churches that have made movies is a short list. Yet I can say with God-fearing confidence that we have never compromised the Word in our scripts. We are clear on the gospel. Why? Because whatever you *reach* people with, that's what you *keep* people with. If you reach them with gim-micks, you'll lose them when you start talking about the price of discipleship.

True revival can only spring from the Word of God.

That's because revival is costly. It sifts out the insincere. It is a confrontation with the carnal and fleshly. It demands a response of repentance. There is no other way to get to the heart of people's issues than through the uncompromising truth and power of God's Word. Yet many churches have substituted good things for the best thing. They've settled for programs, methods, and events in place of sound biblical preaching. The exaltation of God through the exposition of Scripture has been replaced by stuff. These churches do a lot, but do their people hear the Word proclaimed on a weekly basis? Are they respond-ing to the call of God to seek Him with all their hearts?

This is no time for dabbling. We need a focused faith on what God has said and what He demands. Revival will not come through a sports program, a building program, or better Sunday school classes or home groups. All these are good, but nothing can take the place of the Word of God. "An indispens-able sign of true revival," Errol Hulse said, "is that the Word of God grows mightily and prevails—it spreads widely and grows in power."[2]

OUT OF THIS WORD

We owe our existence today in large part to Martin Luther. He saw the excesses, indulgences, and corruption of the Catholic church in his day, began to study the Scriptures, and was cap-tivated with "justification by faith" as it was revealed to him through the Bible. The Reformation was birthed in a study of the Word.

Luther stood before the Holy Roman Emperor in 1521 to answer charges of heresy regarding his views.

MANY CHURCHES HAVE SUBSTITUTED GOOD THINGS FOR THE BEST THING.

He was asked, "How can you assume that you are the only one to understand Scripture? Would you put your judgment above that of so many famous men and claim that you know more than they all?" Luther responded, "Unless I am convinced by Scripture and plain reason—I do not accept the authority of popes and councils, for they have contradicted each other—my conscience is captive to the Word of God. I cannot and will not recant anything, for to go against conscience is neither safe nor right. God help me, here I stand."[3]

I agree with John Wesley, who said, "O give me that book! At any price, give me the book of God! I have it: Here is knowledge enough for me. . . . I sit down alone. Only God is here. In his presence I open, I read his book; for this end, to find the way to heaven."[4]

We live in an age where we want our ears tickled and our backs scratched. We don't want a prophet; we want political correctness. We don't want exhortation; we want entertainment. Paul warned of those "whose god is their appetite, and whose glory is in their shame" (Phil. 3:19). From heaven's perspective this might define the problem with American Christianity today. Lacking knowledge of the Word has led to increased secularism and humanistic thinking in our pulpits and pews. Far too many church members lack a biblical worldview. They don't know what the Bible says about life.

I go to conferences and listen to pastors talk about how they no longer carry their Bibles to the pulpit. They just put their sermon and text on their Blackberry or iPod and scroll down. Are they ashamed to be seen with a Bible? Like a politician without a teleprompter, they might be sunk if the battery ever died on their gizmo.

I hear others talk about how teams write their sermons and pool their ideas for the message. Where is the man of God with the Word of God for the people of God? We are so impressed with our shovels, we've forgotten the diamond we're digging for.

Today anyone who speaks of biblical holiness, purity, righteous-ness, and the need to cry out to God in repentance is considered a fanatic. A person on fire for Jesus has to backslide if he wants to fellowship with the average Sunday morning saint. John said of Jesus, "As He is, so also are we in this world" (1 John 4:17). I don't see much of that today. I see little evidence of the Spirit-filled life and the presence of the Spirit in most churches. I know this, however—there can be no revival without a return to the Scripture as the final authority for life.

F. B. Meyer, one of the most profound devotional writers in Christian history, became lifelong friends with D. L. Moody during the great evangelist's tour in England. For many years Meyer went at Moody's invitation to preach at his Bible confer-ence in Northfield, Massachusetts, the place of Moody's birth. After attending several of these events and listening to the pas-tors there, Meyer wrote the following observations in 1897:

> For many years the pulpit in America has been too much given over to sensational preach-ing. Instead of what we should call textual, expository preaching, the great preachers have sought rather to develop topics, and they have therefore given themselves up to the treatment of subjects of burning interest, either in the political or social world.
>
> Then there has been a growing worldliness on the part of the churches . . . the introduc-tion into the house of God of elements which

we should taboo as being altogether unworthy have been in vogue.

Not only has there been a tendency in the direction of sensationalism and worldliness, but also of a spurious revivalism; that is to say, when the numerical increase has been unsatisfactory, and when the life of God in the churches has been diminishing, instead of going back to God Himself and to His Word and prayer to revive the churches, there has been too large a disposition to call in revivalistic preachers and to use every method in newspapers by advertising, and in every way to get up a revival, the reaction from which has been disastrous.[5]

After reading Meyer's words from so long ago, I thought, "There is nothing new under the sun." We are still dealing with the same issues more than a hundred years later. Preachers are more concerned about hot topics than delving into the holy text. The Scriptures, however, are not geared to being frivolous. There is no such thing as a biblical revival that starts with laughter or barking like dogs, as in the so-called "Laughing Revival." Hell laughs at that thought, while heaven weeps!

Why are we so obsessed with fads, gimmicks, technology, drama, and a thousand other things? Because at our core we don't really believe the Word of God is powerful enough to change people's lives. We think the gospel needs some additives to help it sputter along. So it's vogue to be vague. We have countless sermon series on how to be a better husband, better wife, better family member, or better employee. But we fail to remember that we'll never be better in our earthly relationships if we aren't right with our heavenly relationship. We may as well be delivering messages that Charles Finney called, in an aptly titled sermon, "Preaching So As to Convert Nobody." As Vance Havner observed in commenting on an earlier era, while also speaking prophetically speaking of our own times,

> The art of almost saying something is quite in vogue these days. The speaker gets off to a good start and you feel that he will hit the nail on the head. But no; just before he gets to the point he deftly swerves to one side and makes a neat detour. He almost says it but not quite. He never really goes through to name things. He sounds as though he might do it any minute, and shallow listeners sometimes think he does, but when you have checked over the performance, there are slim pickings.
>
> The art of almost saying something is very clever. It sounds smart and will not offend anybody. It will help the speaker get ahead in this world, but this world is not the right world to get ahead in. At the end of the road stands God, and God always says something. His book does not almost state the case. We need to be saying something these days. Let us hear from men

with a double resolve: "I will hear what God the Lord will speak" (Ps. 85:8); "what the Lord says to me, that will I speak" (1 Kings 22:14).[6]

The Word of God was never given to make our flesh feel good; it was given to confront us with our worldly and fleshly thinking. The Word takes us to the cross.

BACK TO THE BOOK

In Paul's second letter to Timothy, we see the importance of the Word of God in the context of revival. If we don't grasp this basic truth, we are sunk.

> Indeed, all who desire to live godly in Christ Jesus will be persecuted. But evil men and impostors will proceed from bad to worse, deceiving and being deceived. You, however, continue in the things you have learned and become convinced of, knowing from whom you have learned them, and that from childhood you have known the sacred writings which are able to give you the wisdom that leads to salvation through faith which is in Christ Jesus. All Scripture is inspired by God and profitable for teaching, for reproof, for correction, for training in righteousness; so that the man of God may be adequate, equipped for every good work. (2 Tim. 3:12–17)

Under the inspiration of the Holy Spirit, Paul told Timothy that all the issues and sideshows and problems could only be addressed by going back to the Word and giving people the truth of God. This is exactly what happened in Nehemiah's time, as recalled in the previous chapter. The leaders assembled the people to hear the reading of the Scriptures. And when they heard the Word, they listened and repented.

The Word of God is able both to convict and comfort, to tear apart and build up, to cut and to heal. How? Because it is God-breathed. God speaks to man through His inspired Word. The words were given by God to men, and they wrote them down under the inspiration of the Spirit of God. If you don't believe the Word is inspired, inerrant, and infallible, you won't see revival. Because if the Word is wrong on one subject, it's wrong on all subjects. If there is error regarding the flood, it could be assumed there is error regarding saving faith. If it's not true regarding repentance, it's not true regarding the depravity of man. You can't cherry-pick the Scriptures. If you really stand on the authority of the Bible, it will lead to persecution. Such a stand is not popular, which is all the more reason for making sure people hear the truth when they hear from us. The Word of God goes against the grain of culture and unbiblical world-views. It goes against the desires of our flesh—my flesh too. But we cannot shirk our duty to declare it.

Yes, we know this world is headed for destruction, with everything proceeding "from bad to worse" (2 Tim. 3:13). Even if God does bring a season of revival, it's not going to change the end of the story. Judgment is coming. But will the church be judged for her lack of hunger for God? Or will we hear "Well done" for standing strong in this day of apathy, carnality, and laziness? We should be heeding what God said to Joshua:

> Be strong and very courageous; be careful to do according to all the law which Moses My servant commanded you; do not turn from it to the right or to the left, so that you may have success wherever you go. This book of the law shall not depart from your mouth, but you shall meditate on it day and night, so that you may be careful to do according to all that is written in it; for then you will make your way prosperous, and then you will have success. (Josh. 1:7–8)

Most preachers I hear talking about success don't tie it to obeying the Word of God. The westernization of Jesus must be nauseating to the Almighty. While we've allowed culture to define success, I would like to define success as the victorious Christian life. Revival results in victory. God's army marches on with a quickening in their step, a song in their heart, and the gospel on their lips. But lack of attention to the Scriptures will result in a lack of passion for the things of God. We will fall short of the divine intention. As Ron Dunn used to say, "While the Bible admits defeat, it never assumes it." We've accepted defeat as normal. We've accepted the onslaught of evil as unstoppable.

I believe the preceding verses from the book of Joshua give us God's program for success. It's also a key to true revival. The Word gives us direction. It is God's GPS to lead us to our destination. Old-fashioned Bible preachers may be irritating to the "joy boy" prophets of the new school. But like those who came to Jesus with a question about marriage in heaven, Jesus might say to them today, "You are mistaken, not understanding the Scriptures nor the power of God" (Matt. 22:29).

Some preaching and teaching today is nothing more than putting our ignorance on display. It is "mistaken" preaching, leading others off course, causing them to stray from the truth. If we are going to see people at the altar, we must believe the Word. If we are going to see lives surrendered completely to Christ, we must stand strong on a call to repentance. If we are going to see revival as in days of old, we've got to get back to the Book.

GOING ALL IN

I don't know about you, but I like a dogmatic preacher. My dad was a pharmacist. When he filled a prescription that required the mixing of ingredients, I'm sure his customers appreciated the fact that he was dogmatic in his portions. When I get on an airplane, I want the pilot to be dogmatic. I want the air traffic controller to be dogmatic. I don't want them trying to figure it out on the fly.

I know dogmatism is not politically correct today. But without it we'll halt between two opinions. We'll run to preachers and teachers who tickle our ears and tell us what we want to hear. We'll read books that neither challenge nor stretch us to be holy. I don't need any more fiction; I need facts. Tell me what I need to do to see God move and work.

Listen, we are headed toward the edge of the cliff, and we must turn back. As Americans, we pride ourselves in being able to fight back from adversity. Whether through wars or depressions, we are a nation that faces adversity head-on. But my fear is that since it's been so long since we've seen a sweeping move of God in our land, we might not survive the current crisis we are facing. We're in trouble, and we need to admit it. Only truth can get us out of the mess we're in.

There is a sinister, threatening breeze blowing today—deceptive and demonic. It is a wind whispering that we can have the favor of God without repentance, revival, and surrender. We are being lulled to sleep by it. It will take wisdom from on high to discern and distinguish between the sheep and the wolves. This is no time for us to bury our heads in the sand. We must face it without fear, with a full knowledge of what God's Word says about our times, our future, and our lives. It's time to sound the charge and not retreat. This is the day for a call to arms, and you and I are the buglers. As I heard Vance Havner say one day, "This is a day for voices, not echoes."

Four months after Pearl Harbor, Colonel Jimmy Doolittle led a group of volunteers on a secret mission to bomb Tokyo. The goal was to bring the war to the enemy. Doolittle's raid was our first strong response to the Japanese attack.

One of the members of Doolittle's Raiders was a bombardier named Jacob DeShazer. After the raid he was captured along with seven others. Three of them were executed. Another died of starvation. But Jacob and three of his fellow airmen came home after being tortured for forty months.

While he was in prison, however, someone had given Jacob a Bible, where he read Romans 10:9—"that if you confess with your mouth Jesus as Lord, and believe in your heart that God raised Him from the dead, you will be saved." A man once filled with bitter hatred for his captors asked Christ to deliver him from his sin. Later, in fact, he went back to Japan as a missionary. First he responded to the call of his nation, then he responded to the call of the Captain of the Lord of hosts. He took the real battle to the real enemy.

This is no time for the church to wallow in self-pity or decry what is going on in the culture. The level of our obedience will determine the level to which God can work. Ezekiel's audience heard what he said but didn't do anything about it. James said if we hear and don't act, we deceive ourselves. Jesus told us not just to hear His commandments but to keep them. Revival is the result of obeying God without hesitation or reservation. There is no such thing as partial surrender. We're all in, or we're all out.

There's a scene in *Fireproof* after Caleb Holt's salvation experience when he's talking to one of his firehouse buddies, Michael Simmons. When Caleb tells Michael that he's "in," Michael questions him to make sure of his commitment, reminding Caleb that you can't be halfway in. It's either all or nothing. When it comes to your sanctification and the necessity of revival, are you all in? Are you sold out? Is the song of your heart, "I have decided to follow Jesus, no turning back; though none go with me, I still will follow"?

But be prepared: this world is no friend to revival—it will resist it. The flesh is no friend to revival either—it will fight it. What, then, will be said of our generation? Will we be known as the generation that sought God for revival? Or will we be the generation that passed on a legacy of lethargy? If our heart's cry is to see revival in our nation, we—like young Timothy—must give attention to the Word. We must stand on God's promises. We must believe He wants to send fresh wind and fresh fire across this land. We must believe He wants revival even more than we do. We must heed His Word and cooperate with Him. Not everyone will. Will you?

In *The Message* we read:

> The Spirit makes it clear that as time goes on, some are going to give up on the faith and chase after demonic illusions put forth by professional liars. These liars have lied so well and for so long that they've lost their capacity for truth. . . .
>
> You've been raised on the Message of the faith and have followed sound teaching. Now pass on this counsel to the followers of Jesus there, and you'll be a good servant of Jesus. Stay clear of silly stories that get dressed up as religion. Exercise daily in God—no spiritual flabbiness, please! . . .

Get the word out. Teach all these things. And don't let anyone put you down because you're young. Teach believers with your life: by word, by demeanor, by love, by faith, by integrity. Stay at your post reading Scripture, giving counsel, teaching. And that special gift of ministry you were given when the leaders of the church laid hands on you and prayed—keep that dusted off and in use.

(1 Tim. 4:1–2, 6–7, 11–14)

Those who desire revival must stay with the stuff. We must stick with what's true. The Scripture is sufficient, and Christ is all-sufficient. God has given us "sacred writings," not opinions and speculations written according to the whim of the times. We need to have enough discernment to know when the Word is being compromised. God expects the man of God to have the mind of God and always to be filled with the Word of God.

THE BIBLE AND REVIVAL

If we are going to see God move, we must have the right view of Scripture. Our attitude toward the *Word* will determine our actions in the *world*. We have no right to hold a different view of the Bible than the one held by Jesus and the disciples. We cannot accept what the Bible says about Christ and then reject what Christ said about the Bible. We'll never discover all God has for us without first embracing the truth and authority of Scripture.

If Scripture is true and profitable, we must let it work itself out in our lives. After all, it is "the wisdom that leads to salvation" (2 Tim. 3:15). It is not "the word of men" but rather "the word of God, which also performs its work in you who believe" (1 Thess. 2:13). God's Word is powerful and able to change lives. Just as we hear it and believe it for salvation, we hear it and believe it for sanctification. There can be no revival apart from a hunger for and obedience to the Word.

The Bible is a mirror that shows us our desperate need for God. Jesus said, "He who does not love Me does not keep My words; and the word which you hear is not Mine, but the Father's who sent Me" (John 14:24). In this world of postmodern, relativistic thinking, we need a clear word. We're investing tons of our time, money, and energy into being current and trendy, but the problem of man is as old as the Garden of Eden. The answer is where it's always been—in the pages of God's Word.

> **THE BIBLE IS A MIRROR THAT SHOWS US OUR DESPERATE NEED FOR GOD.**

Why am I harping on this? It's because we cannot compete with the world on their terms. Their shows are better. They throw more money into one beer commercial than most denominations will spend on missions in a year. We weren't called to beat them at their game—not when what we have to offer is so much better! As the writer of Hebrews talked about Jesus being better than the angels and the old covenant, what we are able to proclaim is better than anything the world has to say.

Since the Garden of Eden, Satan's question remains the same: "Has God said . . . ?" The reason we're in the position we're in today is because Adam and Eve didn't take God at His Word. We are to be guardians of the truth and defenders of the faith. We need to study the Scriptures and accurately handle them. There's power in the Word of God.

I have been privileged to learn from some of the best Bible teachers in the last hundred years. Men like Ron Dunn, Warren Wiersbe, Lehman Strauss, and others have challenged me to be a student of the Word. They have forced me to think so I could grow. If you are not sitting under the teaching of a man of God who preaches the Word of God unapologetically, get out now. Find a church where Christ is Lord and the Scriptures are taught.

You can't sit under the Word without it bringing reproof to your life. It will refute you, rebuke you, and correct you. It will reprove sin in your behavior and error in your doctrine. The writer of Hebrews reminds us, "The word of God is living and active and sharper than any two-edged sword, and piercing as far as the division of the soul and spirit, of both joints and marrow, and able to judge the thought and intentions of the heart" (Heb. 4:12). God's Word is like a great surgeon. It cuts and misses nothing. It goes to the core and cuts to the chase.

People who live in sin don't want to be in church because it's too convicting. If a carnal man is comfortable in church, something's wrong with either the message or the messenger—or both. The book we call the Bible is not just a collection of random thoughts. It is life-changing. In the Word we find demands that require us to make a decision. God is ready to breathe life into any person or any church that will take Him at His Word. Only the Word can cut through our façades. Augustine said, "If you believe what you like in the Bible, and reject what you do not like, it is not the Bible you believe but yourself." We must surrender ourselves to the Spirit and the Scriptures when the sword cuts through our phony exteriors.

Let's say you went to the dentist and he found you needed a root canal. You would be foolish to say, "But the rest of my teeth are fine." If you went to the doctor and he said, "You've got a spot on your lungs we need to run some tests on," you would be foolish to say, "But the rest of my vital organs are fine." Why is it, then, that people reject and resist preachers who deal with sin, who deliver the Word in all its might and truth? There were many good, godly church members in Corinth, but Paul didn't ignore those who were corrupting the congregation. Nor did he ignore the two gossips in Philippi. The preacher who doesn't reprove and rebuke is not worth the paper his ordination is printed on.

The writer of Hebrews goes on to point out that "all things are open and laid bare to the eyes of Him with whom we have to do" (Heb. 4:13). The word translated "open" in this verse pictures the Roman soldiers who would march a criminal down the street, sticking a small dagger under his chin to make him look up and not drop his head, fully exposing the face of the criminal for all to see. We can't hide from what God says and what He expects. If we want to see revival, we need to confess according to the revelation of the Word.

THE WORD OF GOD

Revival is a straightening up. That's what the Word does. It is profitable for "correction" (2 Tim. 3:16)—the only time this particular Greek word is used in the Bible. It communicates the idea of thoroughly restoring something to an upright position. While the Word can tear you up, it can also put you back together. While it exposes error, it also imparts truth. While it leads you to repentance, it also restores you. As Warren Wiersbe summarizes this verse, the Scriptures "are profitable for doctrine (what is right), for reproof (what is not right), for correction (how to get right), and for instruction in righteousness (how to stay right)."

The Word is simply imperative to revival.

During the years we've held our annual ReFRESH™ Conference, we've seen God work. Singing is kept to a minimum, and we have two preachers every night. So during the four days we'll hear somewhere between eighteen and twenty sermons. There always seems to be a point when the Word breaks through our fallow ground, a moment when the seed and the soil are in sync.

Do these meetings accomplish everything I would like to see? Not at all. There is always more work to be done. But every year we see more and more people catching and understanding the message of revival. Pentecost did not lead to the conversion of all Jerusalem, but it did impact the city, and the subsequent preaching of the early church led to the conversion of thousands upon thousands. Pentecost did what God intended it to do. And when we keep the Word central in our preaching, our churches, our ministries, and our lives, we will find ourselves doing what God intends us to do. In the book *Will Revival Come?* Ernest M. Wadsworth writes:

> Modern preaching seems to have lost much of its power over people. This is not because people have changed nor because times have changed, nor because the gospel is outworn; but apparently it is because ministers have changed and preaching has changed. . . . The imperative need of the hour is for revival sermons. Revived ministers need to be preaching revival messages. Church members need to be awakened. . . .
>
> The great Reformation under Luther and the reforms under Calvin and Knox were effected by God-honored declarations of faith. The mighty revivals of Church history, born in prayer, were ushered in by the preaching of Biblical revival sermons. . . . The same kind of men today, preaching the same kind of messages, would witness the same effects. . . .
>
> When God's truth is as fire in our bones, thoughts and utterances will be painful because the speaker feels the burden of the Word of the Lord. It is one thing to know the truth, another to understand it, but still a rarer thing to feel its power.[7]

In revival I'm just asking God to fulfill His purpose in my life, in the church, and in this world. Not all will change. Not all the lost will be saved, but I can position myself to hear a mighty rushing wind. Revival will call us out to further His purposes as we keep ourselves in His Word.

CHAPTER 5

OH, THAT HE WOULD REND THE HEAVENS

Isaiah 64, Psalm 63

Revival is not some emotion or worked-up excitement; it is an invasion from heaven that brings a conscious awareness of God.
—Stephen Olford

Oh, that You would rend the heavens and come down, that the mountains might quake at Your presence.
—Isaiah 64:1

MY MOM was not in good health the last few years of her life. She would spend hours sitting in a recliner, wasting away and watching television. She loved game shows. I can remember hearing "The Price Is Right" in the background many days when I would phone her. Having watched it myself a few times, I can still see Bob Barker standing on stage, directing the announcer to call a random contestant out of the audience to "Come on down!" The crowd would applaud, and the person would bound up the aisle with anxious anticipation of what new appliance they might win.

"Come on down!"

Isaiah was a prophet of God in a nation headed down the tubes. Sin was abounding. God had been abandoned. False prophets filled the land, much like the prosperity preachers of today, promising peace. Isaiah was a man of high caliber, conviction, and character. He saw God, and it changed Him for the rest of his life.

In Isaiah 64 we find the prophet sizing up the situation. His mind went back to the days when God thundered from Sinai, when the nation walked in power and blessings from heaven. Comparing those past years with the distressing present, he pleaded for God to "rend the heavens and come down" (v. 1).

"Come on down!"

What about us? What about now? It doesn't take much looking around at the day in which we live to know that we need God more than ever—not just to "come down" but to bound out of heaven and take center stage. Our only hope is in a return to righteousness. If we were to bounce back from our economic downturns and repel every terrorist threat, yet not have the blessings of God, we would still be done for.

We need a divine intervention. Our problems can't be fixed by money, machines, politics, or philosophy. Looking around should make us look up to God. Revival is not worked up; it is prayed down. It is when God breaks through into the life of a person, a church, or a land and puts things back in order. God has answered this prayer throughout church history. In church revivals, national awakenings, and great movements across all boundaries, God has come down on His people. We need Him to do it again.

A PLEA FOR HOLINESS

The days were dark during Isaiah's time. The people were in captivity, the temple had been destroyed, and Jerusalem was desolate. God had judged the land. It was a low watermark for His people. They were living in a spiritual drought, much like the one we are experiencing today, where we accept moral decay and political corruption as a way of life. Read carefully this plea for revival from the lips of Isaiah:

Oh, that You would rend the heavens and come down, that the mountains might quake at Your presence—as fire kindles the brushwood, as fire causes water to boil—to make Your name known to Your adversaries, that the nations may tremble at Your presence! When You did awesome things which we did not expect, You came down, the mountains quaked at Your presence. For from days of old they have not heard or perceived by ear, nor has the eye seen a God besides You, Who acts in behalf of the one who waits for Him. You meet him who rejoices in doing righteousness, who remembers You in Your ways. Behold, You were angry, for we sinned, we continued in them a long time; and shall we be saved? For all of us have become like one who is unclean, and all our righteous deeds are like a filthy garment; and all of us wither like a leaf, and our iniquities, like the wind, take us away. There is no one who calls on Your name, who arouses himself to take hold of You; for You have hidden Your face from us and have delivered us into the power of our iniquities. (Isa. 64:1–7)

> **FAILURE TO SEEK THE LORD WILL BRING CONSEQUENCES WE DON'T EVEN WANT TO THINK ABOUT.**

One ministry God is using today to stir the fires of revival is Life Action Ministries. These men and women go to churches and "camp out," if you will, until God breaks through the façades that hinder revival. Del Fehsenfeld Jr. envisioned this ministry in a youth prayer meeting during the Jesus Movement. From this vision came a passion for revival and awakening. Today I consider Life Action to be one of the strongest voices for revival in America, if not the world.

In his book *Ablaze with His Glory*, Del wrote, "Even the most optimistic observer must admit that the escalation of social and moral ills in our society is alarming: pornography, adultery, divorce, abortion, alcoholism, and homosexuality have all become accepted elements of our social landscape. Ours is a shattered society, strewn with the wreckage of broken hearts, lives and relationships. Our political, civic and religious leaders have exhausted their resources seeking human solutions to the great social evils of our time."[1]

As a nation we are committing moral and ethical suicide. Relativistic thinking has replaced revelation. God made us a great nation, but we are ignoring Him. For this reason alone we should expect judgment. Like the people of God in biblical times, we may wake up one day to a spiritual wilderness and desolation—guilty as charged. Our failure to seek the Lord will bring consequences we don't even want to think about. In fact, some of these consequences are already evident. Hosea warned, "My people are destroyed for lack of knowledge. . . . Since you have forgotten the law of your God, I also will forget your children" (Hosea 4:6). Is this what we want for our children and grandchildren? Are we willing to sacrifice their future on the altar of our flesh?

We must pray and plead for God to come down. We can no longer call acceptable what God calls sin. We can no longer ignore the need of church discipline just because we live in a lawsuit society. We cannot resist or ignore the clear teachings of the Word of God, and we cannot tell God how to do His work. We can no longer continue to show disrespect for the man of God.

We work at play, and play at work. This has to stop. The punishment for sin is sin. Romans tells us that "God gave them over" (Rom. 1:24). Why? Because they rejected the revelation they had been given. Spirituality is not measured by the church calendar but by our conscious commitment to holiness, without which no one can see God. He is looking for clean hands and a pure heart. I see a lot of raised hands in worship these days, but I wonder if they are holy hands.

Isaiah asked God to step into history in a powerful, earth-shattering way. Likewise, the church today—the called-out ones—need to start calling out to God. Just because the lights are on at church doesn't mean the light and life of Christ are being manifested there. There was a day when the church lived in revival fire. Now it just sifts through the ashes. The meeting house is quickly becoming a mausoleum. Pews sit empty. Prayer meetings are nonexistent. The median age of the church is old and older. The glory has departed, and we are trying to figure out better ways to light the stage.

We need an invasion from heaven. We must ask God to stir Himself to act. We must be stirred to intercede. In Isaiah 62 we read, "On your walls, O Jerusalem, I have appointed watchmen; all day and all night they will never keep silent. You who remind the LORD, take no rest for yourselves; and give Him no rest until He establishes and makes Jerusalem a praise in the earth" (vv. 6–7). Who is on the walls pleading day and night until He makes His church a praise in the earth?

People drive by our churches and never even think about us. We have better church signs today but few signs of His power—and we aren't looking for signs of His coming. We often ask, "What's wrong with the church?" The same thing that's always been wrong with her: we are lazy after God. As long as we are content with attenders and members and not disciples, we will not see God rend the heavens. Until there is great praying, there will not be great power. It's not enough for God to look down upon us; we need Him to "come down." We need a church like the one in Acts that starts in a prayer meeting and waits for power from on high.

PRAYER AND REPENTANCE

Isaiah's prayer is one of the greatest revival prayers found in Scripture. Just as God came down in fire at Sinai, Isaiah was imploring Him to come down again and reveal His awesome power to the nations. Yet God was not working because of sin among His people. He wanted to bless them, but their sins built a barrier to His blessings. They were fulfilling what had been spoken of them long before, despite their arrogant promises that they would never do the same thing.

> This people will arise and play the harlot with the strange gods of the land, into the midst of which they are going, and will forsake Me and break My covenant which I have made with them. Then My anger will be kindled against them in that day, and I will forsake them and hide My face from them, and they will be consumed, and many evils and troubles will come

> upon them; so that they will say in that day,
> "Is it not because our God is not among us
> that these evils have come upon us?" But I will
> surely hide My face in that day because of all
> the evil which they will do, for they will turn
> to other gods. (Deut. 31:16–18)

It seems we can't get away from this need to repent. Prayer and repentance go hand in hand. When we confess our inability, desperation, and hopelessness before God—if not for His divine intervention—then we have a chance to see revival. We must not limit the term "repent" to what lost people are supposed to do. God has not given us that option. Is the church in such a pathetic state and spiritual stupor that we cannot recognize how far we've drifted from God's design? If the Lord did rend the heavens, He would find most believers sound asleep.

It's been well over a hundred years since our Western culture has seen revival. While God is moving in South America, Africa, and the Far East, we are dying in the West. The sun is setting. The cloud of blessing is moving away. Today, for instance, there are more lost people in the state of California than in all but seventeen countries where Southern Baptists send missionaries.

Where is God? He used to be here. In the days of the Great Awakenings He was here. It's a question we seemingly can't answer, which plays right into the hands of our enemies and detractors. "My adversaries revile me, while they say to me all day long, 'Where is your God?'" (Ps. 42:10). But "why should the nations say, 'Where is their God?'" (Ps. 79:10). We need a revival of God's power in the land. We need God in the center, not on the periphery. It's not enough to compliment God with an occasional nod in His direction. We must confess Him without apology. Those who are on the Lord's side need to show up, stand up, and speak up. We cannot be casual and careless about what God calls sin. The only fire I see in most churches is in the kitchen.

Isaiah saw people acting like pagans. There was little difference between the children of the world and the children of God. Does that ring a bell? What's the difference between the average church member today and a lost man? Not much. We must pray until something happens, until this changes, until God comes down and wakes us from our sleep. James A. Stewart said, "True intercession is the costliest of all Christian service. It is no mere lip service. It is the heart-agony of the Father expressed through us by the Holy Spirit. . . . We never really pray until our hearts and minds become the praying-ground of the Spirit."[2]

Revival will come when we cleanse ourselves of that which is an abomination to God, when we cry out to Him in prayer for the restoration of our churches, our people, and our land. When we return to our first love and rend our hearts of our double mindedness, God might just rend the heavens and come down.

We must also pray for a revival and reorganizing of our priorities. Today's technology allows instant communication with everyone but God. We text, e-mail, and talk on our cell phones incessantly, yet we can't spend two minutes with God. We spend more time watching television in one day than we spend in prayer and Bible study all week.

Look back at Isaiah 64: "There is no one who calls on Your name, who arouses himself to take hold of You; for You have hidden Your face from us and have delivered us into the power of our iniquities" (v. 7). Note that their worship was insincere and halfhearted. The Hebrew word for "arouse" refers to the effort required to stir oneself when he is sleepy or groggy. We must admit that our churches are in a spiritual stupor. No man seeks God without making some effort. Revival doesn't come to the lazy and disinterested.

Why should we be aroused? To "take hold" of God. It means to bind and gird tight, then to make firm and strong—to bind ourselves to the strength of God who makes mountains quake. If God is withholding His favor, we need to plead for Him to open the doors of heaven. If we are headed for judgment, we need to wake up. Our only hope is for God to come down now! We need a divine visitation that changes the spiritual landscape. The favor of God is our only hope. The presence of God is our greatest need. The power of God is what we lack most.

Will you ask God to act in a way that exceeds your expectations? Will you ask Him to do in you and in your church what you've never seen done before? I'm not talking about wildfire. I'm talking about the fact that most of us have no fire. As Vance Havner said, "It's easier to calm down a fanatic than to breathe life into a corpse."

Do we really believe that God is able to do exceedingly, abundantly beyond what we hope or imagine? Too much of our praying is not worthy of the God of glory. We *have* not because we *ask* not, or because we want God to operate in ways that won't upset our apple cart. The Lord of Hosts doesn't come to take sides; He comes to take over. We must want what happens whenever God comes down.

KEYS TO REVIVAL

Richard Owen Roberts, a longtime champion of spiritual awakening, gives three characteristics of revival:

1) *It is extraordinary.* "Without organization, advertising, or even sometimes, human leadership, revivals have altered the hearts of men, the social attitudes of millions, and the destinies of nations. True revival cannot be confined by state lines, national boundaries, economic class systems, facial characteristics, skin coloring, educational distinctions, social status, or denominational preferences."

2) *It is a work of God.* "No amount of human effort can produce true revival. Everything God has told us to do we ought to do, but having done it all, we must still wait upon Him to do what He alone can do."

3) *It produces extraordinary results.* "Conduct that has always seemed acceptable will appear unbelievably wicked. Prejudices that have characterized professing Christians for decades will be revealed for the grievous sins they really are. Private indulgences upon which a person has looked with favor for years will suddenly seem to merit all the wrath of God poured out forever. Prayerlessness,

ignorance of Scripture, sins of omission, and failure in good works will no longer be defended by a myriad of excuses, but will be laid open."[3]

What kind of person can God use as an instrument of revival like this? The answer is found in Isaiah 64: "him who rejoices in doing righteousness, who remembers You in Your ways" (v. 5). Observe the three key words that point to the keys to revival: rejoice, righteousness, and remember.

The person God uses will be one who *rejoices* in righteousness. Today's church tries to manufacture joy, but there's really no secret to its origins. We should rejoice in God first and foremost. He inhabits the praise of His people. We are to rejoice in the Lord always. Is your life a life of praise? When revival comes, praise is evident. We stop worrying about how our singing sounds—we just sing! I'll tell you how much we need revival. When's the last time you heard a good, loud "amen" in church? I can't think of a time when anyone has shouted me down in holy agreement with the Word. We clap at the end of our songs and when someone shares a testimony, but when's the last time you heard someone clap after the reading of the Scripture or during the offering?

Then there is *righteousness*. We are called to work out what God has worked in us. If you are in Christ and Christ is in you, then the world should see nothing else. If I want to be like Christ, I've got to be in Christ. Andrew Murray said, "Conformity to the world can be overcome by nothing but conformity to Jesus." But there is no real righteousness without repentance. Our righteousness must exceed that of the Pharisees if we expect revival. "For all of us have become like one who is unclean, and all our righteous deeds are like a filthy garment; and all of us wither like a leaf, and our iniquities, like the wind, take us away" (Isa. 64:6).

Vance Havner wrote, "Our iniquities have separated us from our God. Our self-righteousness, like rags, does not cover us, but like filthy rags, defiles us. We therefore need nothing less than a mourners-bench revival in the church of God that will bring His people down on their knees confessing and forsaking their sins, for we cannot expect God to take away sin by forgiving it if we do not put it away by forsaking it; we need a revival that will empty theaters and fill churches and shut the mouths of critics and show this unbelieving world that what God has done He can do again."[4]

We must also *remember* who we are dealing with. God is holy. We hear much today about how God is love . . . and He is. But that doesn't negate His holiness. His character is holy. His Word is holy. His Spirit is holy. His acts are holy. God's resources are not limited. There is no limit to what God can do in us, for us, and through us if we position ourselves in surrender.

George Fox, founder of the Quaker movement, was mightily used of God during his lifetime. "The Lord said to me," Fox wrote, "if but one man or woman were raised up by His power to stand in the same spirit that the apostles and prophets were in, that man or woman would shake all the country for miles around." When British revivalist Henry Varley said, "The word has yet to see what God will do with and for and in and by the man who is fully consecrated to him," D. L. Moody resolved to be that man.

Then there was Jonathan Edwards. He said, "If it were revealed to me that in any stage of history there could be but one man who were in all to fulfill the will of God, I would strive with all my might to be that man." God used Jonathan Edwards as the catalyst for the rending of the heavens in the First Great Awakening.

At the turn of the twentieth century, God found a man in Wales that He could trust with the message of revival. Evan Roberts prayed that God would rend the heavens, and He did. The Welsh Revival is one of the most chronicled in church history. In every century it seems God has found such a man. Who will be the man or woman of the twenty-first century?

OF MOUNTAINS AND DESERTS

When God rends the heavens, the church will be revived and the lost will then be saved. Isaiah prayed "that the mountains might quake at Your presence . . . to make Your name known to Your adversaries, that the nations may tremble at Your presence!" (Isa. 64:1–2).

Mountains are immovable objects, but God has a way of dealing with mountains. There are people you've given up on, but God can still move in their lives. Recently during a Mother's Day sermon, I asked moms and dads to stand if they had a prodigal child or grandchild. Several hundred people stood up. My encouragement to them was this: Don't give up! Bombard heaven on their behalf. Ask God to deal with that which is destroying them or delaying them from coming to Christ. For when God steps in, no Pharaoh, Goliath, or Babylon can stop Him. If God rends the heavens, the hearts of many who are now hard-hearted and cold will melt like an iceberg at the equator.

We need God to kindle the fire and cause the water to boil. This is no time for lukewarm commitment, dry bones, or dead churches. We must live with a holy anticipation that one day—maybe today—God will show up.

THERE IS NO ONE ALIVE WHO HAS EVER EXPERIENCED A NATIONAL REVIVAL.

Vance Havner urged, "When men get hold of God and God gets hold of men, He can do more for them in five minutes than they can do for themselves in a million years. When God's people get right and sinners are saved, it means better people, better homes, better churches, better communities, better everything."[5]

Today we find ourselves in a desert experience. It seems the days have turned into weeks, weeks into months, and months into years. It's been so long since we've seen God move upon this land, there is no one alive who has ever experienced a sweeping, national revival—not since the 1800s. Countries where we now send missionaries are sending them to us and praying that America will have revival. What must we do in light of this? *Pray!*

"There is no one who calls on Your name," Isaiah cried—no one "who arouses himself to take hold of You" (Isa. 64:7). No one! We get stirred up listening to talk radio. We get stirred up at a ball game. We get stirred up when someone pulls out in front of us in traffic. We get stirred up by a thousand things, but who is getting stirred up to lay hold of God? God's not going to stir us. He expects us to stir ourselves. He will not do for us what we are supposed to do.

I believe the hardest group to stir up today is believers. We are lukewarm and disinterested if we can't see a personal benefit in it. We have the truth in our heads, but it's not in our hearts. There is no fire burning within the heart of the average church member today. There will never be a rending of the heavens until we are stirred to do more seeking than this. R. A. Torrey said:

> I can give you a prescription that will bring revival to any church or community or any city on earth. First, let a few Christians (they need not be many) get thoroughly right with God themselves. This is the prime essential. If this is not done, the rest I am sorry to say will come to nothing! Second, let them bind themselves together to pray for revival until God opens the heavens and comes down. Third, let them put themselves at the disposal of God to use all of them as He sees fit in winning others to Christ. That is all. This is sure to bring a revival to any church or community. I have given this prescription around the world. It has been taken by many churches and many communities and in no instance has it ever failed. It cannot fail.[6]

If we were only to focus on our circumstances, we would despair. The obstacles seem insurmountable. The days are difficult but not impossible. There is hope in the Lord. When David wrote Psalm 63, he was going through a difficult time. (The background for this psalm is found in 1 Samuel 15–19.) David and his followers had fled from Jerusalem, most likely during Absalom's rebellion. Maybe they were traveling down the old Jericho road (which still exists), headed into the northern part of the Judean wilderness. David's heart was heavy and he was exhausted. The king, once surrounded by all the glory of Jerusalem, had become a fugitive.

And yet David was not without hope. Nor are we. As long as God is enthroned in heaven, there is hope. His Word is true. I love what Spurgeon said about this psalm: "David didn't leave off singing because he was in the wilderness, neither did he in slovenly idleness go on repeating psalms intended for other occasions; but he carefully made his worship suitable to his circumstances and presented to God his wilderness hymn when he was in a wilderness. There was no desert in his heart, although there was a desert around him." He may have been at a low ebb, but the guy could still hit the high notes.

Psalm 63 is a good reminder of how to pray when we wonder if God is really interested in rending the heavens. It's a psalm that gives perspective in desperate places. The landscape in many ways is a picture of David's heart. He was restless. He remembered the days when everything was on track; now he was being tracked down. But what David lost in leaving his capital city, he found in the Lord. In the desert God came down and blessed him in a new and refreshing way. David was, as the old preachers used to say, "shut up to faith." He was right where God wanted him, right where God could bless him.

"O God, You are my God; I shall seek You earnestly; my soul thirsts for You, my flesh yearns for You, in a dry and weary land where there is no water. Thus I have seen You in the sanctuary, to see Your power and Your glory" (Ps. 63:1–2). This is a revelation of godly priorities from a man after God's own heart. I believe David reached the point where he was willing to say, "Absalom can have the kingdom and Jerusalem—just give me God." What an incredible affirmation and declaration of faith! David reminds us that what God teaches us in the sanctuary should encourage us in the wilderness, and what God teaches us in the wilderness should lead us to praise Him in the sanctuary.

Can God turn your sorrow into songs? Can you sing songs in the night, in the dark night of the soul? Times when you see your need for God are times when you can learn great things about God. The wilderness doesn't have to be wasted time. It can give you a hunger for the Promised Land. It can teach you that there is no hope or abundant life apart from abiding and obeying.

- Hagar saw God in the wilderness. (Gen. 16)
- Moses saw God in the wilderness. (Exod. 3)
- Israel was led by God in the wilderness. (Deut. 8)
- Elijah saw God in the wilderness. (1 Kings 19)

In Psalm 63, David called God "Elohim"—the name for God that emphasizes His strength and power over all other so-called gods. Notice how personal and focused his prayer is. *You are right here, right now, my God. I know You, and You know me. My desperate situation is not beyond Your knowledge. You are the only one who can deliver me.* Although his son was rebellious and his friends had betrayed him, David didn't let circumstances sour him. Instead they caused him to seek the Lord. The phrase "I shall seek you earnestly" encompasses the Hebrew for "dawn." It suggests more of an eagerness of heart than an early hour.

David said his soul was thirsty for God. Literally it reads, "My soul thirsts for you like a parched land. I have an unquench-able thirst." Moffatt translates it, "I yearn for Thee, I thirst for Thee, I long for Thee." *The Message* reads, "I can't get enough of you! I've worked up such hunger and thirst for God, traveling across dry and weary deserts." David was exiled from the throne and the place of worship but not from God. His was not a thirst for revenge or something that would temporarily satisfy. David didn't thirst for water or the blood of his enemies. He thirsted for God. "Blessed are those who hunger and thirst for righteous-ness" (Matt. 5:6). "As the deer pants for the water brooks, so my soul pants for You, O God. My soul thirsts for God, for the living God" (Ps. 42:1–2). "My soul longed and even yearned for the courts of the LORD" (Ps. 84:2). "I stretch out my hands to You; my soul longs for You, as a parched land" (Ps. 143:6).

What fed and drove David? The Lord did. David longed for God as if nothing else mattered. Vance Havner used to say, "It's one thing to say Jesus is all you want until you find He's all you've got. And then you realize He's all you ever needed." Bobby Richardson, the Hall of Fame infielder for the New York Yankees in the 1950s and '60s, once prayed, "God, your will. Nothing more. Nothing else. Nothing less."

David was in a "dry and weary land" (Ps. 63:1). He saw it with his eyes. He felt it in his throat. But make note of the next thing he said: "Because Your lovingkindness is better than life, my lips will praise You. So I will bless You as long as I live; I will lift up my hands in Your name. My soul is satisfied as with marrow and fatness, and my mouth offers praises with joyful lips" (vv. 3–5). What a change! From weary to worship, from dryness to a mouth filled with praise.

PRAYER AND PRAISE

Could it be that one sign of the revived life is praise and worship? Fill in the blank for yourself: God's lovingkindness is better than—what? Can you say the only thing you want more than your next breath is the steadfast love of God? David would have rather had the love of God in the wilderness than the absence of God's presence in the palace. Is the same thing true of us? Can we walk through a dark valley and still sing, "It is well with my soul"? Only the one who is in tune with God can sing in a key that resonates in heaven.

It could be that God designs and orchestrates our dry times to take us to the place of desperation. David was determined to praise God until his final breath. God had placed an eternal perspective in his heart, and David turned his sighing into singing: "I will bless You as long as I live" (Ps. 63:4).

In the early days of the church, believers overflowed with the spirit in power and praise, even in the midst of growing persecution. James A. Stewart says, "Their whole life was flooded with praise. The assembly gatherings were characterized by praise. They praised God for His glorious salvation. They praised Him that they were counted worthy to be ambassadors of the Lord Jesus. They praised Him that they could suffer shame and reproach for His glory. They praised Him that they had something to sacrifice for the spread of the gospel. Deep spirituality and worship go hand in hand. Read the hymns of the past centuries. . . . The saints bursting forth spontaneously into songs of adoration and worship is one of the glories of revival."[7]

An article by Paxton Hood in *Heartcry*, a publication of Life Action Ministries, refers to the revival fires of the eighteenth century:

> One of the great aids to the revival was the music generated through the course of the revival. Until Isaac Watts and Phillip Doddridge appeared, England had no popular sacred melodies. . . . The hymns of Watts as a whole were well suited for expression of the kind of passionate spiritual experience produced in a great revival.
>
> When the revival came, the general public were accustomed to songs that were thoughtless, foolish, and often licentious. New songs of praise were needed. In order to begin meeting

this need, John and Charles Wesley took Count Zinzendorf's hymns from the Moravian community, translated them into English, and immensely improved them. Some of the finest hymns in the Wesleyan collection are these translations.

Probably without knowing it, the Wesleys and their coadjutors did exactly what the Reformers had done. They gave emotional expression to the revival through the ordinance of song, and they preached the Gospel in sweet refrains. The songs written during the revival were remarkably free from rigidity and ritual. As in all great religious movements that have shaken men's souls, they were spiritual, authentic expressions of God's work in the soul. Loud "amens" resounded as the preacher spoke or prayed, and then hearty gushes of song united all hearts.

These songs were boldly evangelical, devoted not to church forms but rather praises to Christ, earnest meditation upon the state of man without His work, and the blessedness of the soul that had been saved by Him. It has seemed to some that the most perfect hymn in the English language is "Jesus! Lover of My Soul." Sentiments may differ, but this hymn undoubtedly captures the essence of all the hymns that were sung in the days of the revival.[8]

When you visit most churches, you find the membership mumbling instead of singing, for fear of someone hearing them. There's a lot of worship and energy on the platform but little in the pews. Instead of participating, the congregation watches the musicians perform. But in revival God directs, orchestrates, and gives birth to our praise. It doesn't have to be worked up; it's the working out of what God has worked in us.

I've never been anywhere with more genuine worship than the Brooklyn Tabernacle, under the leadership of Pastor Jim Cymbala. The membership of the church is made up of the outcasts of society whom God has saved. They are former pimps, prostitutes, transvestites, homosexuals, gang members, and crack addicts mixed in with folks raised in the church. When you visit, the congregational singing is so loud that you can't hear yourself. Your voice blends in with a sea of souls who have been overwhelmed by the grace of God. They've never gotten over being saved.

If there is no song in our hearts, we'll have no song on our lips, only on our iPods. But if David could sing in the wilderness, what's our problem? David was on the run, but he had a song in his heart. Revival awaits when our hearts are fully His.

PRAY HIM DOWN

If you trace the history of revival and awakening in America, the one common theme and thread is prayer. In the

1700s Jonathan Edwards sent out his appeal for Christians to unite together in prayer for a worldwide awakening. William Carey, the father of modern missions, was greatly influenced by this appeal and republished it. Later Charles Finney based all his revival writings on this document. His *Lectures on Revival* are still in print today. D. L. Moody and R. A. Torrey were influenced by Finney's lectures. This proves that what we need today is not something new, but something as old as the cry of the prophet, "Lord, rend the heavens and come down!"

A man named Daniel Nash was Finney's intercessor. Nash pastored for six years and saw two great revivals in his church, then left the pastorate to travel with Finney and bathe the meetings in prayer. Most would agree the power behind Finney was Nash. Read the record of his influence below:

> When God would direct where a meeting was to be held, Father Nash would slip quietly into town and seek to get two or three people to enter into a covenant of prayer with him. Sometimes he had with him a man of similar prayer ministry, Abel Clary. Together they would begin to pray fervently for God to move in the community. One record of such is told by Leonard Ravenhill: "I met an old lady who told me a story about Charles Finney that has challenged me over the years. Finney went to Bolton to minister, but before he began, two men knocked on the door of her humble

cottage, wanting lodging. The poor woman looked amazed, for she had no extra accommodations. Finally, for about twenty-five cents a week, the two men, none other than Fathers Nash and Clary, rented a dark and damp cellar for the period of the Finney meetings (at least two weeks), and there in that self-chosen cell, those prayer partners battled the forces of darkness."

Another record tells: "On one occasion when I got to town to start a revival, a lady contacted me who ran a boarding house. She said, 'Brother Finney, do you know a Father Nash? He and two other men have been at my boarding house for the last three days, but they haven't eaten a bite of food. I opened the door and peeped in at them because I could hear them groaning, and I saw them down on their faces. They have been this way for three days, lying prostrate on the floor and groaning. I thought something awful must have happened to them. I was afraid to go in and I didn't know what to do. Would you please come see about them?' 'No, it isn't necessary,' Finney replied. 'They just have a spirit of travail in prayer.'"

Another states: "Charles Finney so realized the need of God's working in all his service that he was wont to send godly Father Nash on in advance to pray down the power of God into the meetings which he was about to hold."

Not only did Nash prepare the communities for preaching, but he also continued in prayer during the meetings. "Often Nash would not attend meetings, and while Finney was preaching Nash was praying for the Spirit's outpouring upon him. Finney stated, 'I did the preaching altogether, and brother Nash gave himself up almost continually to prayer.' Often while the evangelist preached to the multitudes, Nash in some adjoining house would be upon his face in an agony of prayer, and God answered in the marvels of His grace. With all due credit to Mr. Finney for what was done, it was the praying men who held the ropes. The tears they shed, the groans they uttered are written in the book of the chronicles of the things of God."[9]

James A. Stewart is one of my favorite authors on revival. God used him in a remarkable way. He began his ministry when he was only fourteen years old, and he traveled the world preaching the gospel for forty-five years. Stewart was a student of revival. In his book *Revival and You*, Stewart suggests that every congregation form a prayer circle—without worrying about numbers—to begin to lay hold of God. He considered it "essential that only prepared people, who are willing to pay the price for revival, join the prayer circle." Read carefully these

closing thoughts from the pen of one who knew how to wait on
God and pray down heaven.

One must settle down in the Lord's presence
before he can touch the Throne. It is when we
are quiet that the Holy Spirit prays through
us. . . . Kindly do not pray publicly until the
Lord has given you the spirit of faith to believe
that He is going to fulfill His Word. . . . Prayer
to be vital, must be definite. . . . How few
Christians will keep to the one theme of the
meeting—revival.

Every pastor, the moment he accepts the
pastorate of a church, should seek at the ear-
liest possible moment to establish a circle of
prayer during the twenty-four hours of each
day, when at all times some saint will be on the
"watch tower" (Hab. 2:1). . . . It is good also
for every church to set aside one or two definite rooms for intercession which may not be
used for any other purpose. The setting apart of
these rooms for the definite ministry of intercession somehow has a sobering effect upon
the congregation. . . . Each Lord's Day, gather
for early morning prayer before the services of
the day begin. . . . Have a prayer meeting prior
to every Sunday evening Gospel service.[10]

Having tasted some of the mercy drops of heaven, I thought through what we have done at Sherwood to position ourselves for God to work. I am amazed (but not shocked) that all writers on revival emphasize the same essentials. Praying for revival is not an option—it's essential.

Since 1990 we've had a 24/7 intercessory prayer ministry at Sherwood. We have two rooms set aside—the Prayer Tower as well as Spurgeon's Prayer Closet—for the sole purpose of prayer and intercession. We have a prayer chapel on our high school campus. We have a prayer meeting prior to our Sunday night services. It is in this prayer environment that we have seen God work. The more we pray, the more God seems to work.

There is nothing so sweet and refreshing as seeing God actively moving in our midst. As one author noted, the Old Testament prophets and New Testament writers believed in an "any time revival," but they didn't know when, for how long, or how often. Our attitude must be like Micah who said, "But as for me, I will watch expectantly for the LORD; I will wait for the God of my salvation. My God will hear me" (Mic. 7:7).

There is nothing we need more than for God to rend the heavens and come down. Remember, we're not looking for an event; we're looking for the Lord to show up. Would you pray for one more rending of heaven so that we might see a refreshing work of God in our time? He will step out of heaven when we get serious about prayer.

Lord, do it again!

CHAPTER 6

WHAT KEEPS US FROM HAVING REVIVAL?

Psalm 44

One of the miracles of the grace of God is what He is able to do with the torn nets of lives surrendered to Him.

—G. B. Duncan

For our soul has sunk down into the dust; our body cleaves to the earth. Rise up, be our help, and redeem us for the sake of Your lovingkindness.

—Psalm 44:25–26

IF YOU GO to your average Christian bookstore, you'll find dozens of books on church growth and programs, books on establishing an effective evangelism ministry, and far too many books on earthly relationships. As you walk up and down the aisles, you'll discover a variety of bulletin designs, Bible translations, and church resources. And it won't take you long to discover the Christian fiction section. I enjoy a good fiction book, but it bothers me that so many believers can be biblically illiterate while being so hungry for the newest release by a Christian novelist.

I'm a bookstore addict. But in all my life, I've never found a store with a section dedicated to books on revival. The one thing we need the most is the one topic you can't find.

> **IT DOESN'T TAKE ME LONG IN A CHURCH OR MEETING BEFORE I KNOW IF THERE IS A HUNGER FOR GOD IN THAT PLACE.**

I doubt if the average church member has been part of a heaven-sent revival. I would imagine for most readers, the subject of revival is the smallest section in their personal library. Some call revival an old term. Some say it's worn out and antiquated. Mostly, though, I believe it's misunderstood. We've held "revivals" that were, in essence, evangelistic campaigns. The biblical order is revival first (where the church gets right) followed by evangelism (where the lost are saved). We've often tried reviving people who were lost church members. We've tried to convince the carnal to care about the lost. We've gone outside the biblical order to reverse the patterns of decline in our churches.

We've missed it. And we're missing it still.

I preach every year in Bible and revival conferences. I find most of the crowds have no idea what revival means or looks like. They've never been in a service where a divine visitation rearranged the schedule and cleared out the cobwebs. Churches and denominations are dying. Denominational leaders bemoan a decrease in giving as wealth passes from one generation to another. We try to justify decreases in baptisms while lost people are pouring across our borders and into our communities. We seek to prop up dying churches when the gospel message should be setting the church on fire.

What's wrong with the church in our day, and why are we struggling so to make inroads of impact on our culture? It depends on who you ask. Some blame a lack of leadership. Others point to the growing cultural divide. A few blame the devil. Most don't know and don't care. But we can discover a lot about our churches by what we don't have. It doesn't take me long in a church or meeting before I know if there is a hunger for God in that place. I can almost sense it when I walk on the campus. I can tell it by listening to the hallway conversations. In most churches the men can name the starting lineup of their favorite pro or college team, but they can't name half of the twelve disciples, much less the Ten Commandments.

What's absent is what needs to be present. The church was birthed in power, but it's strangely missing today. Our services are as dry and flat as a three-month-old bottle of open soda. Gimmicks won't mend it. Programs won't solve it. Methods won't change it. Sensationalism is not the solution. What we need is revival! We need a big dose of Spirit-filled Christianity that shows the difference between a farce and a force.

But what is keeping it from coming? What is the missing message of revival? What is hindering our surrender?

CHOKING ON LEGALISM

When I was in college, a group of us went to Louisiana to do a youth revival. We set up the sound and were getting ready for the service. Then totally unexpected, the pastor sent a messenger over to our room to tell us we would have to cut our hair or we couldn't lead the service that night. My hair was long— well, down on my shirt collar, at least (it was the mid-'70s). Either way, it was cut it or leave.

The weather was terrible. The roads and bridges were starting to ice. But we left. And didn't get back to campus till around 3:00 a.m. It was my first real experience with the meanness of religion. I determined in my heart that I would never bend or bow to those who wanted to lay heavy burdens on me or anyone else. I have not and will not let a legalist run or ruin my life.

It seems God has never grown tired of putting me in situations like these. Being a prophet, I can be confrontational. (Can you tell?) I was privileged to be president of the Southern Baptist Convention Pastors' Conference in Indianapolis in June 2008. I told the twelve speakers to wear what they were comfortable preaching in. Whatever was normal for them, go with it. I made this decision because I deliberately wanted to reach across generational lines. Much of what we fight over is rooted in generational preferences, not Scriptural truths.

So the men took me up on my offer. Some preached in a golf shirt and a pair of dress pants. Two preached in suits. Kerry Shook, who pastors one of the great churches in America, preached in jeans and an untucked shirt. That day he lifted up Jesus and showed a video where Fellowship of the Woodlands in Houston, Texas, baptized over eight hundred people. People even got saved watching the baptisms. It was incredible!

The next day I was doing a book signing, when a man walked up to me and asked, "Are you the guy who was in charge of the pastors' conference?" I told him I was. He then poked me and said, "I've got a problem with men preaching without ties." I tried to explain to him why I made that decision, but it was a waste of time and breath. He continued on, "You even had one guy preaching in blue jeans with his shirttail out!" I tried to tell him about Kerry and what God was doing in his church. Kerry is a young guy with a rich heritage. His dad was a preacher. He preaches the Word without apology. I've heard him preach on the judgment seat of Christ and on hell. There's no watering down of the gospel in his preaching. But the man quickly reiterated, "I have a problem with guys who don't wear ties." I noted this as he walked off in his jeans and tennis shoes and golf shirt, and I thought to myself, "That's the first Pharisee I've ever seen in Levi's and sneakers!"

In 2009 I was preaching at the Mississippi Baptist Evangelism Conference, and I shared this story while preaching in a sports coat over a mock turtleneck shirt. After the service an elderly minister came up to me and started talking about preaching and the majesty of Jesus. I couldn't help noting that he kept staring at my neck. Then he poked me in the chest. (What is it with Pharisees and poking people in the chest?) He said, "You can't preach on the majesty of Jesus without wearing a tie."

I let it go. But I thought to myself, as my friend Charles Lowery said, "Yeah, that's what ticks them off about Jesus too. He didn't wear a tie either."

One way we can limit God and hinder revival is by our spirit of preference. Pharisees will always judge by the outside, but a work of God occurs in the heart. I'm not saying we should seek to intentionally offend. I preach most of the time in a suit, but I'm not going to make clothing a matter of fellowship. If I did, I would exclude most of the people groups around the world who are seeing more of a movement of God than we are in America.

When I first came to Sherwood, we were a legalistic church. The church had a great reputation in the community, but there was arrogance among a few. Women were never allowed to wear pants, for example. Even if a woman was bringing her tithe to the church on a Tuesday, she couldn't bring it in while wearing pants. Excuse my sarcasm, but if someone is tithing, they can bring it to the church in a bathing suit, as far as I'm concerned. (Just kidding for the legalists who'll want to write me a "holier than thou" letter.)

There was also an unspoken "no clapping" rule at our church. I had only been at Sherwood a short time when someone sang a solo and I started clapping. Then others in the congregation started clapping. On Monday morning one of the hierarchy of the "let's kill the dreamer and see what becomes of his dream" crowd showed up in my office. He said, "Preacher, I've got a problem with what happened yesterday." I asked what the problem was, and he said, "You started clapping, and clapping is a sin." I had been to college and seminary, and that was news to me! I asked him, "Doesn't the Bible say 'clap your hands, all ye people'?" He said with all the self-righteousness one man can muster, "That's in the Old Testament!" I responded, "What about the fact that Jesus honored the Old Testament and quoted the Old Testament?" Then as only an ignorant Pharisee could do, he angrily responded, "Preacher, I didn't come here to argue the Bible with you. I know what I believe!"

ONE WAY WE CAN LIMIT GOD AND HINDER REVIVAL IS BY OUR SPIRIT OF PREFERENCE.

You can't fix stupid.

Anyway, when I realized how imbedded we were in legalism, I immediately started preaching through Galatians. And yes, we lost some folks. I also started preaching out of the New American Standard, not the King James. We lost some more. People who wouldn't know a Greek participle from Greek pasta left the church because I didn't preach from the KJV. It would have been a waste of time to ask them which King James Version they wanted me to use since, after all, the KJV has been revised more than thirty times. And who authorized it? A wicked king, not the King of kings! (I'm afraid I just lost someone in this chapter.)

What I discovered was that legalism served to cover up a lot of sin. And when the façades were broken down, the fakes were revealed in all their hypocritical glory. The Pharisees fought me, longed for the former pastor, and talked about the good old days. They talked about me when my wife was sitting right in front of them. But I did the only thing I knew to do: I preached the Word in context and let the Spirit do His work. As I preached through Galatians, those who were listening began to discern between rules and true righteousness. The chains of legalism were replaced by the love of God.

I'm not saying rules hinder revival. God has rules, but the rules teach us that we are sinners who can't keep even the ten basic rules. We blow it every time, every day, in every way. We don't need boxes; we only need boundaries—the boundaries of the Word of God and the Spirit of God, the boundaries of the peace of God and the God of peace. With those biblical boundaries in place, you can fling the door open and let the Lord blow out the cobwebs, the grinches, and the grumblers.

If you want revival, there are times you'll have to identify with Jeremiah. When God sent Jeremiah to call His people to repentance, He told the prophet to expect a "fight" (Jer. 15:20). Pharisees don't go down without a fight. Like the church at Sardis in the book of Revelation, many boast of their membership, methods, buildings, and budgets, but there is something missing. It's the presence of God. They have the appearance of life, but they are dead. They are not channels through which the Spirit of God can flow.

Vance Havner once said of this, "Sardis Christians have a name to be alive but are dead. They are in a whirl of religious activity and attend a lot of meetings—but spiritually they are animated corpses. Finney said, 'They are often employed about the machinery of religion and pass for good Christians but they are of no use in a revival.' They may be elders, deacons, choir-singers, Sunday school teachers, with a reputation for church faithfulness, with awards and banners and prizes for religious achievement—but it is all dead works. They are often the last people to wake up in a revival because they mistake performance for experience. They need to repent, confess their dead works, start right in full surrender and be filled with the Spirit."[1]

Have you taken your beliefs and laid them at the cross? Have you run your theology through the grid of God, or is it just a theology of preference? You may be busy, but is God bless-ing the busyness, or are you just stirring up dust like Pig Pen in the "Peanuts" cartoons? Everywhere Pig Pen went, he carried a dust cloud. People choke in a dust storm. Some of our churches are dusty and need a good housecleaning.

PLENTY SATISFIED

There are others in the church who are more like Linus, carrying around their security blankets. They can't imagine life without them. They need something to hold on to because they think Jesus is not enough. They want Jesus plus something else. But Jesus plus anything is nothing.

When our oldest daughter Erin was a child, we worked to get her to give up her pacifier. She called it her "nuk nuk." When she was about two years old, we finally got her to throw it in the trash can, and we praised her for being a big girl. About a week later, as we were getting out of the car at the mall park-ing lot, she noticed a big dumpster by one of the entrances. She asked me what it was, and I told her. She quickly asked me if her "nuk nuk" was in there. It's hard to give up our pacifiers and security blankets, but revival demands that we grow up.

Revival demands a desire to move from milk to meat. Many who hold to rules and regulations still want to be pacified with warm milk. They don't want to chew on the Word. They don't want to wrestle with the mysteries of God. They want salvation, but they think sanctification is in following the rules, not in hungering and thirsting after righteousness.

God wants to send revival to our churches. We talk about it, but few have experienced it. We read of great movements of God in days gone by, but we wonder why it's not happening here. Could I suggest that we are satisfied to live without it? We hinder and limit the Holy One because we don't believe there is any more to the Christian life than what we've experienced or what we want to experience. We are afraid if we let go and let God, we'll lose control. And we will! That's the beauty of it. It is sad to see that some churches would rather have rot than revival. F. Carlton Booth said, "Revival is the exchange of the form of godliness for its living power." We need power in our churches today.

Vance Havner said, "Sunday morning Christianity is the greatest hindrance to true revival. There has never been a real work of God that did not result in heartburn alongside the hallelujahs." Dr. Havner was the boldest preacher I've ever known. Although small and frail, he feared no man. The night he preached in my home church on the lordship of Christ, he walked the aisles and called people out one by one, row by row to confess Jesus as Lord. He had gone several rows when he turned around and shuffled back toward the front where the pastor and his wife were sitting. He walked right up to them, put his hands on his side, looked them both square in the eyes, and asked, "Pastor, are you going to lead your people or follow them? Are you going to confess Jesus as Lord tonight?" Then he did the same thing with the pastor's wife. Havner knew the leader needed to lead, not follow. As I look back on those meetings and their impact, I don't think the pastor and his wife ever "got it." The revival died down after a season. You can't take people where you've never been.

When revival comes, some leaders will no longer be qualified. When revival comes, the bottom falls out and the top blows off. The church changes because it has to. There is a breath of the Spirit that comes on the dead, and a new level of hunger that comes to the living. If you want revival, get in line with what God is doing and go with Him.

I've listened to those who have walked in seasons of revival. I've probably preached a hundred sermons in my life on the subject. I'm a product of a revival movement. If I had waited on someone else, I probably would have never seen it. If I'd waited until my peers or my church "got it," I likely would have missed it. But revival is available to all who long for a fresh work of God in their lives. Don't let others stop you. Don't set a limit on what God can do in you, even if your church never sees it. Revival is not a mystery. God wants to revive His people. He wants to see freedom in the fellowship.

NO STORY TO TELL

The psalmist wrote, "O God, we have heard with our ears, our fathers have told us the work that You did in their days, in the days of old" (Ps. 44:1). Notice that the only reference is to what they had heard, not what they had seen. Isn't that the truth? Most of us today have never seen a great work of God in revival. The twentieth century was the first century when we as Americans did not see an awakening like those who lived in the eighteenth and nineteenth centuries.

On the whole, the church is irrelevant today. About the only time the world thinks of us is when they talk about fanatics or scandals within the church. There are no human solutions to our problems. We need to go backward so we can go forward. We need to go back and say as one great revival leader said, "Holy Spirit, revival comes from Thee; send a great revival, start the work in me."

Three times in Psalm 44 we read the phrase, "We have heard with our ears." I wonder what it was like when Abraham told Isaac of how God called him out of Ur, or when Noah recounted to a new generation how God instructed him to build the ark, or when those who crossed over into the Promised Land told their children about the wilderness wanderings, the manna from heaven, and the pillar of cloud and fire. The psalmist has given us a song about stories he heard from his father. These stories were passed on so that the next generation would remember the faithfulness of God, stand on the trustworthiness of God's Word, and walk in faith with God. The Sunday school of the Jewish home was the home itself. Around the table, over meals, and at the gates, they would tell and retell the great stories of their faith.

One reason we miss revival is because we aren't taking time to tell our kids the stories of God's faithfulness. We talk about the good old days, but we have no revival to refer to. If we do, it's a distant memory, not a current reality. Israel's history was a track record of God's faithfulness. In the mundane routines of life, God showed up. They talked about divine interventions, deliverance, and God's mercy. Today most of our talk is superficial.

We hear what God is doing overseas, but we don't see it here. We've substituted technology for truth, playing for praying, sports for sanctification, and hobbies for holiness. Meanwhile, our families and churches are dying. The majority of churches in my denomination are plateaued or declining. Thousands never baptize a soul. Yet America is one of the largest mission fields in the world. Who is praying for God to raise up a man, a church—someone, somewhere—to be a catalyst for revival in our time?

> For by their own sword they did not possess
> the land, and their own arm did not save them,
> but Your right hand and Your arm and the light
> of Your presence, for You favored them. You are
> my King, O God; command victories for Jacob.
> Through You we will push back our adversar-
> ies; through Your name we will trample down
> those who rise up against us. For I will not trust

in my bow, nor will my sword save me. But You have saved us from our adversaries, and You have put to shame those who hate us. In God we have boasted all day long, and we will give thanks to Your name forever. (Ps. 44:3–8)

Do we expect God to do great things today, or is it all just ancient history? Our faith might grow stronger if we would read our Bibles and take God at His Word. We think that if we don't expect great things from God, we won't be disappointed. I know this: if God is not working today, it's our fault, not His. God hasn't failed us; we've failed Him.

Parents aren't teaching their kids great truths. The church can't go any further than the members and families are willing to go. If you aren't teaching your children to believe great things and seek great things from God, they will grow up not even hearing about revival, much less seeing it.

Are you praying for your pastor and Sunday school teacher to speak with passion and power? Spurgeon said, "I would that I could speak with the fire of some of those men. Pray for me, that the Spirit of God may rest upon me, that I may plead with you for a little time with all my might, seeking to exhort and stir you up, that you may get a like revival in your midst." I would quit the ministry today if I didn't believe that God wants to do a mighty work in my lifetime. I'm not interested in just preaching sermons and filling the pulpit. I want to see God at work in ways that only He can be glorified. I pray with the psalmist, "Rise up, be our help, and redeem us for the sake of your lovingkindness"

(Ps. 44:26). We don't deserve revival, but we desperately need it. We are helpless and hopeless without a divine intervention. We will never have revival until we believe it is God and God alone who is at the center of all we need.

There is little difference today between church members and the lost world. We have the same divorce rate. We have the same issues, baggage, and hang-ups as the lost, but we hide behind our religion and pretend we are better than most. We are much like the rest of the world—"lovers of self, lovers of money, boastful, arrogant, revilers, disobedient to parents, ungrateful, unholy, unloving, irreconcilable, malicious gossips, without self-control, brutal, haters of good, treacherous, reckless, conceited, lovers of pleasure rather than lovers of God, holding to a form of godliness, although they have denied its power" (2 Tim. 3:2–5).

We may keep the rules, but we lack the power. We check the box, but our hearts are not burning within us. We complain about our cities, but we neglect to pray for those in authority. We have raised a generation like those in the days of the Judges, a generation "who did not know the LORD, nor yet the work which He had done for Israel" (Judg. 2:10). We have no great works of God to show them. They don't come because we don't care. We'd rather keep the status quo. We'd rather point fingers at this godless youth culture than let God break our hearts about the false gods they chase after.

Something must change. Someone must break out of the pack. Someone must sound the clarion trumpet. Someone, somewhere must lay hold of God and cry out for a work of God in a land headed toward judgment. If God doesn't send revival soon, He will send judgment, and we can be sure it will begin at the house of God.

If you hunger for revival, I would encourage you to read the great workings of God recorded in Scripture. Read of how God delivered His people from their many years of bondage in Egypt. Read of the revivals under several of the kings. Read of the revival under Nehemiah's leadership.

Read, too, the great accounts of revivals since the time of the Reformation. Someone has pointed out that leaders are readers. If you are going to be a leader and a catalyst in revival, you'd better know what you are talking about and asking for. Don't be a part of the ignorant brethren. Be informed. Pray intelligently. Believe that God can do it again. Read about the Great Awakenings in this land. Read about Charles Finney, the Welsh Revival, the revival in Scotland, and the revival under Duncan Campbell. As you read, ask God to birth in you a hunger for more and much more—not just for yourself but for the generations that follow.

KEEPING IT TO OURSELVES

The prophet Malachi wrote to people who were wondering if the glory days would ever return. He was the last prophet of the Old Testament who wrote the last book and issued the last warning. The people of his time were keeping up the rituals, but the glory of God wasn't there. They were going through the motions, but their heart wasn't really in it. They assumed God was the problem, but God said, "You're the problem."

The people of Malachi's day defiled the altar by their attitudes and pathetic offerings. They weren't giving God their
best. "'You bring what was taken by robbery and what is lame or
sick; so you bring the offering! Should I receive that from your
hand?' says the LORD" (Mal. 1:13). They were thumbing their
noses at God while bringing insufficient, unacceptable offerings
to Him. They had no desire to surrender.

While driving along the back roads of the South, I often
come across road kill. Strewn along the highway will be dead
possums, skunks, raccoons, and deer that have run out in front
of a car and been hit. What God is saying, in effect, is that these
people had so little consideration for the table of the Lord, they
were offering Him road kill. They were bringing offerings not fit
for humans, yet they expected God to accept it. "'Cursed be the
swindler who has a male in his flock and vows it, but sacrifices
a blemished animal to the Lord, for I am a great King,' says the
LORD of hosts" (v. 14).

Our actions reveal our attitudes. Our sacrifices reveal our
surrender. A wrong response reveals a wrong heart. God would
rather His people not worship at all than to offer this kind of
worship. It's like leaving a tip. If you have a bad waitress and
don't leave anything, they may assume you forgot it. But if you
leave them a lousy tip, they know you just didn't like the service. When we fail to sacrifice and surrender, we are saying to
God, "I don't think much of You or what You have to offer." It's
a greater insult to give a lousy gift than no gift at all.

"'For from the rising of the sun even to its setting, My name
will be great among the nations, and in every place incense

is going to be offered to My name, and a grain offering that is pure; for My name will be great among the nations,' says the LORD of hosts" (Mal. 1:11). God speaks in a sarcastic tone here. An honest crook is better than a dishonest priest. They knew better, but they didn't act like it, bringing lame and sick lambs before a holy God and expecting Him to accept and approve the offering. What we bring to God is a reflection of what we think of Him.

How would you characterize your obedience in this area of your life? Are you giving God the best, or are you trying to see how little you can do and still curry God's favor? Worse, are you giving every indication that you're faithful in your giving, trying to keep up impressions, while hypocritically hiding your stinginess? I've seen this happen in giving campaigns where people have such disdain for God that they bring a blank pledge card and put it on the altar. If you'll lie to God, you'll lie to anybody. If you'll steal from God, you'll steal from anybody. Any attitude other than our best for Him is lame. It's a form of godliness without the power. And it's an ongoing hindrance to revival.

ANY ATTITUDE OTHER THAN OUR BEST FOR HIM IS LAME. IT'S A FORM OF GODLINESS WITHOUT THE POWER.

Personally I would avoid someone who doesn't tithe as much as I would avoid a convicted pickpocket or bank robber. Both are thieves. Neither can be trusted. For the opposite of generosity is not stinginess—it's robbery. "Will a man rob God? Yet you are robbing Me! But you say, 'How have we robbed

You?' In tithes and offerings" (Mal. 3:8). Look at these pointed accusations in Malachi: "'If you do not listen, and if you do not take it to heart to give honor to My name,' says the LORD of hosts, 'then I will send the curse upon you and I will curse your blessings; and indeed, I have cursed them already, because you are not taking it to heart'" (Mal. 2:2). The word "honor" in Hebrew meant something heavy or weighty. This wasn't just a casual oversight; this was a big deal in the eyes of a holy God. God says He will not share His glory with anyone, yet these people were keeping back some of the glory for themselves.

So why am I harping on this when we're talking about revival? I learned from Ron Dunn that "God always reserves something for Himself in the physical realm, where man obtains his living, to remind man that God is the sovereign owner." This truth is found over and over in the Scriptures. God reserved a tree in the Garden, the Sabbath in the work week, a rest for the land, the tithe, and so on. God owns it all, but our failure to acknowledge this fact is a resistance to surrender and a hindrance to revival. To rob God is to covet, defraud, deceive, or embezzle. It's pretending to be something you aren't. It keeps us far from surrender.

In the movie *Flywheel*, car dealer Jay Austin is seen putting an empty envelope in the offering plate as it passes by during the worship service. His life prior to an encounter with God was about self—stealing from others, ripping people off, and lying about the cars he sold. When he turned his life completely over to Christ, he not only did business with integrity, but he also gave money back to the customers he had wronged.

There is hope in surrender. There is a promise made to those who heed the warnings and surrender to Him completely: "Then those who feared the LORD spoke to one another, and the LORD gave attention and heard it, and a book of remembrance was written before Him for those who fear the LORD and who esteem His name" (Mal. 3:16). God remembers those who honor Him. In the midst of all those making excuses, justifying selfishness, and arguing with God, there was a remnant of those who feared Jehovah God.

Where there is a remnant, there is hope. This book is written for the remnant. The carnal will never seek revival, and we must not let them set the tone. We must set the tone if we are to see revival in our lifetime.

MAKE WAY FOR REVIVAL

I am reading a new biography of the late Manley Beasley, written by Ron Owens, entitled *Manley Beasley: Man of Faith, Instrument of Revival*. I've given a copy to every member of my staff. To me it's a must-read if you are sick and tired of religion as usual. But only read it if you are ready to surrender your life, your love, and your all to Christ.

I've had the privilege of being connected with the Beasley family over the past twenty years since Manley's death. His wife, Marthe, has spoken at our church. His son Jonathan and his daughter Debbie have both served on our staff here. Manley Jr. is a friend and fellow pastor. One of my great regrets is that we had Manley scheduled to speak at Sherwood in August 1990, and he died in July. Heaven's gain was our loss.

To meet Manley was to meet a man who walked by faith, a man who lived in perpetual revival. I had the privilege of preaching with him at the last "Faith Week" Camp for Eastwood Baptist Church. Talk about intimidation! But Manley was not one to intimidate. He had been places with God most of us have never been. Manley just wanted you to want what Jesus wanted for you—if you had enough sense to want it.

Manley was a rare man. He was one who really knew how to trust God for a meeting. He knew how to believe God for a work, regardless of what others might have thought. Manley described faith as "acting as if a thing is so when it is not so in order for it to be so because God says it is so."[2] He told his son Stephen one day, "Son, you can have all of God you are willing to pay the price for."[3]

Ron relates the story of a time when God moved in a powerful way in a church in Mobile, Alabama. Manley said, "There was such an awareness of the presence of God that night. It was so unusual that I asked the Lord to show me what was behind it. I knew from the study of the Bible and revival history that something had taken place—that in all probability someone had paid the price in prayer. You may not realize it, but when you see God manifest Himself in some unusual fashion, you can be assured that someone has been praying."[4]

You'll never see revival without prayer. You'll never see revival in a proud church or in a proud Pharisee. You'll never see revival if there is no repentance and turning from wickedness. You'll never see revival in the hearts of stingy people. Sin is what God says it is, not what the politically correct crowd might *want* to say it is. You'll never see revival if you think God has already done all He's going to do. Only when we meet God's conditions and break through the junk that clutters and pollutes our lives and our churches will we see a moving of God.

It's been too long since we've seen a visitation from God in our land. It's been too long since our altars were covered with tears over the carnality, indifference, and lukewarmness in our pulpits and pews. It's been too long since God broke through in a new dimension. We've justified our lack of revival for too long. The problem in America is not a lack of churches; it's the absence of the power of the Holy Spirit in our churches. We've settled for less than God's best. We've accepted the ways of the Pharisees as the way it has to be. We come to church expecting little of God or from God. We must wake up. We must get on our knees and push through anything and everything that keeps us from seeing God work.

Stephen Olford said, "Revival is that strange work of God in which he visits his own people, restoring, reanimating, and releasing them into the fullness of his blessing."[5] And as one believer to another, I tell you it can happen. We've seen it happen several times in the church where I serve. I've watched God set us free from legalism. I've watched Him use a back-door revival to make way for those who wanted to be part of a church where God was at work. I've watched Him be my defender and shield when Pharisees sought to control and discredit me. I've watched Him answer our fervent prayers for a movement of God. I've watched the devil resist us (and he is still resisting us) as we've sought to be a place where the Spirit is welcome.

It can happen. It can happen to you. It can happen in your church. It can happen today. If not today, maybe tomorrow. But it won't happen until you push through whatever and whoever is hindering you and keeping you from a fresh touch of God. Don't let anything keep you from revival.

CHAPTER 7

WE NEED ANOTHER JESUS MOVEMENT

I believe nothing so distinctly causes the people of God in any generation to "stand in awe" as when they hear of the great works of God in awakening his people powerfully.
—John H. Armstrong

LORD, I have heard the report about You and I fear. O LORD, revive Your work in the midst of the years, in the midst of the years make it known; in wrath remember mercy.
—Habakkuk 3:2

I WAS THERE. I was part of it. I witnessed it firsthand. It started on the West Coast with young people who were disillusioned by the war and hypocrisy and were turned off by life in general. It was God's answer to the countercultural movement. It was a divine intervention in a generation headed in the wrong direction. It was an opportunity for a sweeping movement of God.

It was called the Jesus Movement or the Jesus Revolution. It made the cover of *TIME* magazine and captured the attention of people around the nation. It revolutionized lives.

I've lived through a few revolutions in my life. The Sexual Revolution brought us rampant cases of venereal disease. The Reagan Revolution brought back American pride and led to the downfall of the Soviet Union. The Scientific Revolution has led to discussions on matters our parents would have never imagined, such as stem cell research, cloning, and other ethical and moral issues. But the Jesus Revolution changed me forever.

During a youth night revival in my home church, I surrendered my life to the lordship of Christ as Vance Havner preached. During the message the old preacher had been driving home his point to my heart. And during the invitation he said, "Now, I want us to turn to the hymn 'I Have Decided to Follow Jesus.' I'm going to call young people who are serious about God to come down in a moment. I'm calling you out to face this congregation and sing the words to this great hymn. I don't want any quartets, duets, or trios. I'm not looking for an aisle parade. I'm looking for a solo. I'm wondering if there is one who will stand up and come face this congregation and sing,

'The world behind me; the cross before me. No turning back, no turning back. Though none go with me, I still will follow.' God's not interested in your voice; He's looking at your heart."

I was the second person down the aisle that night—one of about eight students, if I remember correctly. For me it was a defining moment. The Jesus Movement was no longer something on the West Coast—it was in my heart. As I look back on it, that one moment has determined every other decision of my life.

I know that in recalling these days, they may sound old and faded. Much has changed since then, from clothing styles to car designs to technological savvy. We are no longer living in the days of rotary phones and eight-track tapes. But as I share some memories and recollections of that era in our cultural history, I hope you won't be distracted by the scenery. I just want us to start thinking about revival now the way we thought of it back then. What we need today, even more than in the 1960s and '70s, is a Jesus Revolution. This generation is in trouble. Depending on who you listen to, somewhere between 85 and 92 percent of teenagers do not belong to any church or religious organization. Of those that do, 92 percent will drop out of church after high school. God help us if we don't find some young Joshuas, Calebs, Davids, Deborahs, and Marys in these desperate days before us.

GOD HELP US IF WE DON'T FIND SOME YOUNG JOSHUAS, CALEBS, DAVIDS, DEBORAHS, AND MARYS.

Our schools have moved from problems with chewing gum to problems with guns. The issues are no longer simple. The halls of many public schools are patrolled by police officers and security guards. The Internet has given us a jaded generation that thinks nothing of posting inappropriate pictures, thoughts, and blogs for the world to see. There seems to be no shame, nothing to catch ourselves on the filter of conscience.

Our future is at stake. The future of the next generation is at stake. In the atrium of our worship center hangs a massive banner that states, "Whoever wants the next generation the most will get them." I want to see revival in our land. Don't you? The hope will be in a praying remnant and a spiritual revolution among our children and young people.

OPEN WIDE

I was playing the game. My parents made me go to church—or else! I didn't want to know what the "or else" meant, but I knew it wasn't good. I had a great youth minister, but I wasn't sold out to anything but myself. I went on witnessing trips just to get out of town.

One day that all changed.

God bombarded me with the awareness that I was a joke. I had the talk but no walk. There's a huge difference between knowing *about* God and knowing Him personally. Revival and revolution will come when people get to know God as He is, not as they want Him to be.

I recall those youth prayer meetings. That handful of adults, led by our youth minister James Miller, wanted more for both themselves and for us. I remember one youth fellowship when we were at a church member's home. We got a call that night from a guy named Leo Humphrey from a phone booth at the Washington Mall after Arthur Blessitt had finished his walk across America with the cross. I also recall the response of many churches regarding what God was doing. Many, not all, were resistant. They weren't willing to change and let these teenagers with the long hair, bell bottoms, sandals, and guitars into their sanctuaries.

One man I know was different. My friend John Bisagno tells the following story:

> In 1971, something big happened in America. It wasn't planned by a committee, created by a church, or structured by a denomination. It was a spontaneous movement of the Holy Spirit, and hundreds of thousands of young people were converted. The Jesus Movement received national attention. The face of Jesus was on the front page of *Newsweek* and *TIME* magazine. Judy Collins' rendition of "Amazing Grace" was #1 on the charts, #2 was "Put Your Hand in the Hand of the Man from Galilee," and #3 was "Spirit in the Sky." On the beaches from Galveston to Ft. Lauderdale, the kids were grooving on Jesus. They were wearing Jesus swimsuits and T-shirts, selling Jesus snow cones, and preaching and singing about Jesus.

First Baptist Church Houston quickly decided to join where God was working. We organized something called SPIRENO, which stood for Spiritual Revolution Now. It was a three-month youth revival structured as follows: Five men donated $15,000 each. The $75,000 budget was equivalent to three times that much today. Evangelist Richard Hogue and his singing group, Bill, Dave and Mary, were engaged for the three months. At that point in history, it was possible to book youth assemblies in the high schools. We were able to book Richard and his team in forty-five of Houston's fifty middle and high schools. He spoke on drugs, alcohol, and sexual purity. We asked no fee. We only requested an announcement be made that they could hear more from Richard that very night in a special rally in the same auditorium. We paid for those venues.

At the end of two months, we had Richard preach and the team sing every night for one month at Houston's First Baptist Church. Buses ran to the high schools. Each bus made four stops at a different school at 6:30, 6:45, 7:00 and 7:15. The church was more than packed every night, and a large percentage of the teenagers were unsaved. Some nights the worship service was so powerful that Richard gave an invitation with no sermon as hundreds poured down the aisle to receive Christ.

I remember talking to a little old lady one night who said, "I sure don't understand all this, Pastor, but it's wonderful to see all these young ones going forward." At the end of the crusade, we had a citywide rally in the coliseum with 9,000. At its conclusion at 9:00, we had a police escort and a Jesus March down the main street of Houston from the coliseum back to the church where we baptized for nearly three hours. At the conclusion of the three months, there were over 11,000 decisions for Christ, all by young people. 4,100 had been saved and 1,700 baptized. At that point, it was an all-time record in the Southern Baptist Convention.

Following the crusade, we booked the entire Galvez Hotel in Galveston for a retreat. Between Friday night and Sunday afternoon, Richard Hogue spoke to the 1,400 who attended twelve different times. He covered all the bases: holiness, Bible study, missions, witnessing, God's will, etc. At the conclusion, we organized SPIRENO Bible Clubs in every school. They met weekly, averaged twenty to forty in each meeting, and continued more than two years. To this day, I receive reports of young men and women who came to Christ during SPIRENO and who are active in their churches, many of whom are preaching the gospel and serving in foreign lands.

We are losing an entire generation. And if something desperate doesn't happen, there's no tomorrow for America. We must take desperate measures, and that means doing anything as pastor and people to reach today's youth. The apostle Paul said, "I have become all things to all men that I might by all means win some." The message is absolutely non-negotiable. The purity of the gospel must never change. But the means and the methods must be ever-changing.[1]

The problem of that time, instead of a lack of surrender, was the level of cynicism in the church regarding this movement. The enemy successfully worked his magic, and churches threw water on what could have been the fires of revival. Whereas the sign of the movement was an index finger pointed toward heaven, saying "One Way," there were those who said "No Way" when it came to letting these "undesirables" in the doors.

In the early '70s, *Look* magazine did a feature on the movement. "The Jesus Movement is upon us. . . . It shows every sign of being a national preoccupation." The article described how "thousands and thousands of young people, upper, middle-class kids and often formerly very spaced-out kids, had obviously found an inner, very real religion."

Soon, *LIFE* magazine followed with an article on the movement. One father said the movement "transforms its converts. These kids had already bugged us with every kind of classic adolescent rebellion. We'd been through long hair, peace marches, macrobiotic diets, meditation—drugs, too, of course. Now along comes this which seems to be solving all their problems from the cosmic to the trivial."

Following these articles, *TIME* ran a full-length article entitled "The Jesus Revolution." NBC's *Today* show spent an entire program on the movement. It was on the verge of being a national spiritual awakening led by young people.[2]

Everywhere you turned, you saw former hippies with Bibles in their hands. Stickers were the thing, and I had a softcover Bible with "One Way" stickers all over it. I was driving a blue VW Beetle at the time. I had a "One Way" sticker on each of the back windows. I put a little card on my dash that said, "Pray at the start, praise at the stop."

I heard it all from adults in those days. "You'll get over it." "You're too emotional; religion is a personal thing." "This will all go away in time; it's just a fad." For me, I've never gotten over it. It hasn't gone away. I long for the day when such a move of God happens in our country again. The youth culture needs it. The graying and dying church in America needs it. Maybe this time we'll have enough sense to know what to do with it.

NEW POINT OF VIEW

I can tell you what I experienced. It was all about Jesus. We didn't haggle over doctrinal differences. All we knew was that

Jesus was the answer to our questions. "Hey, man" was replaced with "Jesus loves you" when you met someone. Witnessing wasn't something you had to guilt the saints into doing; it was as natural as breathing. Transformation wasn't a theory.

I saw drug addicts set free in a moment. I saw people delivered from bondage, sin, and self. I saw people dead in trespasses and sin who were made alive in Christ. Prayer was a privilege, not drudgery. We had prayer meetings that would last for hours. We didn't pray for ingrown toenails, like most church prayer meetings. We prayed for power from God, for our lost friends to be saved, and for the church to realize what God was doing. The *TIME* magazine article said of the movement, "Their lives revolve around the necessity for an intense personal relationship with Jesus and the belief that such a relationship should condition every human life."[3]

I recall times when guys and gals I knew from school drove by the church while we were having a youth prayer meeting. Seeing the car of a friend, they would walk into the church not even knowing why they were coming in, except that they sensed something telling them to stop and see what was going on. I watched dozens never get all the way in the building before falling on their knees in conviction and crying out for someone to tell them how to be saved.

It wasn't organized or orchestrated. It just seemed to happen. The problem with most of us is we want to organize, and we've forgotten how to agonize. In those days before I understood anything about inerrancy or the infallibility of Scripture, I just believed the Bible was God's Word. I believed in miracles, power from on high, and a God who could melt the coldest heart. I still do. Do you?

It was in those days that I first began to understand the Holy Spirit. I don't recall one sermon my pastor had preached before on the Holy Spirit. Until then, it was as if God's Spirit was a ghost we were to be afraid of, or it was the third person of the Trinity those Pentecostals got that made them act weird. Little was said about the Spirit. If it hadn't been for my youth minister, I wouldn't have understood anything about the power of the Holy Spirit. He taught us and helped us understand that we couldn't live without Him. "'Not by might nor by power, but by My Spirit,' says the LORD of hosts" (Zech. 4:6). "For our gospel did not come to you in word only, but also in power and in the Holy Spirit and with full conviction" (1 Thess. 1:5). I believe the Spirit was at the root and core of the movement. Only the Spirit of God can set people free from the bondage of sin, sex, and drugs.

In the process new music came into the church. Boy, talk about something that turned people off! Thank God for folks like Andrae Crouch, Larry Norman, the Imperials, Roger Breland and TRUTH, and others who were on the forefront and cutting edge of contemporary Christian music. It became the music of that generation. My favorite song was probably one the Imperials recorded, but I heard it first in a TRUTH concert in 1971—"Jesus Made Me Higher." In a day when drugs were dominating and destroying a generation, those who were coming to Christ were discovering that the high they got with Jesus made any other experience pale in comparison.

It was the right movement at the right time. We were living in a day of questioning authority and government. It was a time of situational ethics. Premarital sex with multiple partners was advertised as sexual freedom. The movement for many brought a restoration of values, morals, and a commitment to being a disciple of Jesus Christ without apology. In evaluating these energetic days, Billy Graham had incredible insight. Regarding his generation, he wrote:

> We came through the depression and World War II. Hardship and death made us determined that our children would never have to go through another depression or another war. In pursuit of that goal, we chose the wrong means. Instead of turning to spiritual values, we turned to materialism. We collected things, hoarding them against want, constructing an affluent way of life that no one in the world had ever known. Technology burst upon us, and we began to step higher and faster. By the millions, we sent you to colleges and universities. Then we bought you cars and stereos and trips to Europe. And you threw it all back in our faces.[4]

Graham recognized, as few other religious leaders of his day, the tension of the culture. He visited with young people. He spoke at Expo '72 with hundreds of thousands of youth and college students in attendance. He sought to listen and learn. He invited those who sang the new music of the Jesus Movement to participate in his crusades. He understood the crisis that was taking place and sought to bridge the generation gap.

We need someone today who sees that conditions are similar to those in the days of the Jesus Revolution. The times are ripe for a movement of God. If the church doesn't pray, act, and reach out, we'll miss a window of opportunity. The bell bottoms and long hair of my day have been replaced by piercings and tattoos. A generation is marking their bodies because they have no sense of self-worth in and of themselves. While the church berates this behavior, we offer no alternatives. Even in the day in which we live, we want them to clean up and then come to church. Jesus, however, meets people where they are. You can't expect someone to clean up the outside until they've been set free on the inside.

YOU CAN'T EXPECT SOMEONE TO CLEAN UP THE OUTSIDE UNTIL THEY'VE BEEN SET FREE ON THE INSIDE.

Today we have study upon study by all kinds of sociologists, psychologists, therapists, psychiatrists, researchers, and institutions trying to figure out the current youth culture. Might I say that this has happened on my watch. As a middle-aged adult I've watched the church become gray and say nay. We have spoiled our kids by giving them everything but God to make them happy. We've pampered them like no generation before us, yet I find very few parents who spend much time on their knees in prayer for their kids.

I find it amazing the number of parents that defend their kids who are out of bounds, disrespectful, and playing with sin. I'm on Facebook and MySpace, and I can testify that there are kids on the Internet with pictures and blogs that no parent should be willing to tolerate. It's as if today's moms and dads have been duped by the devil into thinking this generation needs parents who are buddies. They don't. They need parents who are godly!

I've had parents get upset with me when I've challenged them to rein in their kids, or when I've told them their kids were too young to date. We've had parents get ticked at a youth minister when he told them to take the computer out of their kid's room because of the instant availability of pornography. They responded, "That would be an invasion of his privacy." We will not see a revival in this generation without first seeing repentance, brokenness, and desperation in parents.

Make all the excuses you want. Point all the fingers you want. The generational issues are spiritual. It begins with fathers not being the godly leaders in their homes. It continues with parents divorcing over "irreconcilable differences." It grows when the rules are abandoned because parents would rather be cool than have rules. It finds its culmination in parents who are hypocrites, saying one thing at church but living differently at home. As someone who served as a youth minister for fifteen years, I can tell you emphatically that the number-one issue I faced in talking with kids was the hypocrisy they saw in their parents. And many of their parents were deacons and Sunday school teachers.

If we want to see another Jesus Revolution, we've got to model it. Yes, the Jesus Movement of the 1970s happened without parental involvement, and it can happen that way again. But if we thought the home in America was in trouble in the 1970s, it's under hospice care today. If something doesn't change in the home, there is little hope for a movement of God among our students.

Teenagers are a modern phenomenon. Prior to the days of the Industrial Revolution, there wasn't really a teen culture. Now advertisers, music moguls, and companies market directly to them. Modern teen culture invites the advertising dollar. Programs geared to teens are filled with sexuality. Movies geared to teens would be nothing more than short films if you took out the sex and profanity. Potty humor is the mantra of the day. "Stupid is as stupid does" seems to be the theme of our hour.

When a former president says, "It depends on your definition of sex," it's hard to tell your kids to save themselves for marriage. When preachers, evangelists, politicians, and community leaders are in the news for sexual immorality, soliciting prostitutes, and having liaisons with homosexuals, it's difficult to shift the blame to our children. Forgiveness is available from Christ for every sin, of course, but something has to change in those of us who are supposed to know better.

It's not going to change by belaboring the point. It's not going to change by whining about it or throwing our hands up in frustration. We need a movement of God. We must find the remnant among our students and children and teach them to believe God for more than they are seeing and experiencing.

A HEART FOR TOMORROW

I was a part of a movement of God in my teenage years. And I want to be part of another one before I go home to glory. But if I'm going to see it happen, I need to be right with God. Then I need to find ways to connect with this generation before they are so jaded that they reject the church, the message, and the messenger. They are probably not going to read this book, but you are. You could join me in making a difference.

What young person could you take under your wing and choose to mentor? Who could be your Timothy? Who could you invest in, pray for, and believe in? Someone is going to have to do it. Why not you? Does your church foster an environment where young people are welcome and wanted? Are you interested in the next generation? Would you do whatever it takes to insure that your church does all it can to reach them?

We have a generation of Christian students who are abandoning the church. I know the church in many corners of our country is out of date, irrelevant, and boring. But you can't love Jesus and not love the church. The synagogues during Jesus' time were filled with hypocrites and legalists. Nonetheless, Jesus went to the synagogue to worship every Sabbath. He didn't let the hypocrites keep Him from going to church to meet God.

Trust me, I know the problem is with the church. Nothing has jaded my youthful zeal more than church people. They can be the meanest, most hateful people on the planet. Even today I find inexcusable prejudice. I see blatant materialism. I observe men, hungry for power, who have no desire to serve. I've seen it all. But I'm committed to the local church because Jesus is coming back for the church. You can't change something by abandoning it. In her book *Quitting Church*, Julia Duin writes:

> When church isn't relevant, the first out the door are usually the young. By mid-2006, evangelical youth leaders were complaining about this exact trend. At a series of leadership meetings in forty-four cities, more than six thousand pastors were told that at the current rates, only four percent of America's teens will end up as Bible-believing Christians, compared to 35 percent of the Baby Boomers and 65 percent of their World War II-era grandparents. . . .
>
> Youth are hardly pouring into church these days, certainly not at the level Baby Boomers did during the 1970s Jesus Movement. Churches then weren't any more seeker-friendly than they are today, yet there was a revival happening, and many churches were transformed by the arrival of legions of hippies and other young people driven to seek God.
>
> In March 2006 the National Association of Evangelicals passed a resolution bemoaning "the epidemic of young people leaving the evangelical church" and an "unacceptably low percentage" of young people who by the age of twenty have made a personal commitment to Christ.[5]

When church becomes therapy, when preferences prevail, you can see the end of a church in sight. When a church becomes driven only to reach a certain target group, they will ultimately die when that target group dies. This is the problem with the churches established twenty years ago to reach Boomers. Now they aren't relevant to the Gen X crowd.

What we need today are churches to rise up and say they are going to be multigenerational. They must be willing to die to preferences so that people different from them can be reached. We need churches that will say prejudice is unacceptable in any shape or form. We need churches that will refuse to align themselves along socioeconomic lines, churches where "whosoever will" may come.

Every Sunday I look out into a section full of young people. I look across the room and see very successful doctors, lawyers, and businessmen. I also see men saved and baptized who live in the streets of our community. We have blue-collar and white-collar. We have pharmacists and farmers. I see women who have been saved through our Crisis Pregnancy Center. I see marriages put together by the love of God. I see people delivered from a homosexual lifestyle. I see students saved out of drugs, and children being nurtured who have no father in the home. I see Hispanics, Asians, African Americans, Caucasians, and others. I see people from eleven different nations and twenty-nine surrounding communities. I see the church reflecting the community we serve.

One day maybe the church will take seriously the biblical mandate to make room for people of every nation, tribe, and tongue. A Jesus Revolution would put the nail in the coffin of racism in the church. We need revival because our churches are compartmentalized. I wonder if your church would have reached out to the Ethiopian eunuch? How about Rahab the harlot? Maybe we just don't want most of the folks God is leading us to reach. If we don't have revival, it'll be because our church is nothing like what the church is supposed to be.

How can we say we believe the gospel when our prejudices and preferences scream to the younger generation that we don't love people? Does your church reflect your community, or is it more about your preferences? The reason our churches are aging and dying is because we care only for ourselves.

Most of the churches in my denomination are lily white. Sunday morning is still the most segregated hour in America. We have an African-American missionary with the International Mission Board who came out of our church. He has spoken in churches where people got up and left when they found out the missionary was black! A church not far from us had a crusade several years ago. The crusade team was allowed into the public schools. Hundreds of students responded to the gospel, and over three hundred of them were African-American. But the church leadership threw away their decision cards. As one said, "We don't want their kind in our church."

We either need a revolution, or we need a few funerals.

God has allowed me to pastor in one community for two decades. During that time our population has declined, factories have shut down, and the demographics have changed greatly. But we have chosen to stay in our neighborhood. It is easier to move a church to a more convenient area than to change your heart and face the issues. I don't care where you are—you can run, but you can't hide. It would be hypocrisy for us to have our movies in nearly sixty countries and thirteen languages and then say, "We don't like the demographics of our neighborhood; we're going to relocate."

Do we really want the kid with the tattoos and the body piercings? Do we want the outcast kid, the one who's a little rough around the edges? Do we want the African-American, Asian, and Hispanic kids? Or do we only want kids that look safe? In revival we'll stop judging by externals.

Are we going to be risk takers, caretakers, or undertakers? Do we really care about what happens to this next generation? What opportunities have we missed because of preconceived ideas and prejudices?

This generation needs a touch from heaven. These kids have grown up in highly mobile, dysfunctional homes where divorce is the norm. They have grown up in an educational system that tells them they are nothing more than the product of pond scum. They are biblically illiterate, hostile to authority, and increasingly depressed. They make up the number-one age group for suicides. They are sensually driven, bored, disconnected, fractured, and easily deceived because they have no moral moorings. They can bypass your computer firewall, but they can't discern what's good to put in their minds.

If my generation of the 1960s was different from my parents, this generation is light years from mine. They have different assumptions, values, and goals. They speak a different language.

They are impacted and influenced by dozens of media options. The only hope is for us to go after them. But this requires us to think strategically. Things I did when I was a youth minister no longer work.

Let's not compartmentalize the next generation; instead, let's embrace them. Our youth group is not perfect, but for the most part they sit down front in the worship center. Many of them take notes. Dozens of them are my friends on Facebook. I may not like some of the things they do, but I love them. They are the future. They are looking for someone to love them. We must build bridges, not walls. When Paul went to a new city, he didn't say, "Okay, let's get the Jews over here, and the Gentiles over there." He didn't say, "White-collar folks go to this location, and blue-collar folks go to that location. Slaves in this corner, and masters up front." What Paul said in essence was, "You folks get together under the Spirit of Christ and figure it out." But we divide and, therefore, we do not conquer.

We need a God-given love for this next generation. We need a heaven-sent burden for them. We need to be the kind of people who gives them Jesus, or we'll lose them. When that happens, we'll have set our course for disaster. James A. Stewart identified the reason why we aren't seeing a movement of God among young people today:

> Let us stop dictating to the Holy Spirit. How remarkable it is to hear true gospel preachers declare that they long for an old-fashioned revival while they at the same time dictate to

God the direction and terms on which they would have the revival come. They insult the Holy Spirit by telling Him what kind of revival to bring! They want revival. But it must be one of their own understanding—a poor, puny thing that they can organize to death. They want a dignified revival or no revival at all. As I ponder on my knees before God this deep mystery of the suppression of the Spirit, I have come to the conclusion that people are afraid of something they do not understand—something they have never experienced.[6]

God give us men and churches like John Bisagno and First Baptist Church of Houston who were willing to get out of the box and out of their comfort zone to see God work among young people. God raise up men and churches who will stop dictating to the Holy Spirit what He should do and how He should do it. I pray we'll allow God to upset our apple carts. If we don't, I doubt if we'll have much fruit that remains.

CHAPTER 8

THE TEST OF REVIVAL

1 John 4

A revival may produce noise, but it does not consist of it. The real thing is a wholehearted obedience.
—Ernest Baker

Beloved, do not believe every spirit, but test the spirits to see whether they are from God, because many false prophets have gone out into the world.
—1 John 4:1

HOW DO YOU KNOW if revival has come to your heart or your church? This is an important question because the devil constantly strategizes to deceive the saints. Even within the church there are those who talk about revival. They use the term, but they don't use it biblically or in the context of how we have viewed revival historically. They have the right word, but they use a different dictionary.

The prophets of these so-called revivals tell us that in the last days, the office of apostles and prophets will be restored. They tell us that God now gives extrabiblical revelation. They speak of end-time anointing. You often hear them say things like, "God told me to tell you . . ." In our desperation to see God work, we've bought into the laughing revivals, healing revivals, barking revivals, and other manifestations that have no biblical basis.

Although God manifests Himself in different ways at different times, some of these "revivals" should concern us. As P. T. Barnum said, "There's a sucker born every minute." I am disturbed by the lack of discernment in the twenty-first-century church. Because of our biblical illiteracy, we sometimes fall for anyone and anything that claims to be from God.

I own two "Rolex" watches. Both of them are fake. I bought one on the streets of New York, and the other came from China. I can show them to the casual observer and pass them off as the real thing. But I can take them to a jeweler, and he will immediately be able to tell they are counterfeits. A lot of people buy knockoff Prada, Louis Vitton, or Gucci handbags. From a distance they look like expensive bags purchased at

Neiman Marcus. But upon strict examination they are found to be fake—two for $50. In 1 John we read:

> Beloved, do not believe every spirit, but test the spirits to see whether they are from God, because many false prophets have gone out into the world. By this you know the Spirit of God: every spirit that confesses that Jesus Christ has come in the flesh is from God; and every spirit that does not confess Jesus is not from God; this is the spirit of the antichrist, of which you have heard that it is coming, and now it is already in the world. (1 John 4:1–3)

John's problem is our problem. There are people today who claim divine inspiration and revelation but should actually cause us to raise an eyebrow. John not only tells us we are to test them (in other words, don't believe everything you hear), but he also gives us the principles by which they are to be tested. This is not a subjective test; it's a true or false test.

FACTS AND PHONIES

The problem of true and false prophets is as old as the Scriptures. How can you tell what's real? Who should you listen to? Some of the false teachers are obvious. For instance, one tells his listeners not to even entertain the thought that he might be a counterfeit. Another famous teacher says he wishes he could get a Holy Ghost machine gun and blow away his critics.

The true prophet doesn't fear being tested. The false prophet is the one who wants to keep pawning off counterfeit bills, hoping you'll buy them without any further examination. This is why Peter said we have the "more sure" word of the prophets (2 Pet. 1:19). Peter had incredible experiences. He had walked with Jesus for three years. He had been to the Mount of Transfiguration. He preached the first sermon at Pentecost. Surely we could rely on his experiences. But even Peter said the true test is the Scriptures.

Hank Hanegraaff writes, "Christianity is undergoing a paradigm shift of major proportions—a shift from faith to feelings, from fact to fantasy, and from reason to esoteric revelation." He calls this shift the "counterfeit revival."[1] The issue is not whether something supernatural is happening; the issue is the source. Is it of God, or is it a counterfeit? Remember, the false prophets of Pharaoh imitated almost every sign of Moses. I don't care how successful someone is in ministry or how many decisions they record. There's a difference between Elmer Gantry and Billy Graham. Marjoe Gortner was a fake, and thousands missed it until he finally admitted it himself.

In the 1 John passage, we are clearly commanded to be discriminating in our acceptance of someone's claim to be a Christian. It is not sufficient to reason that since only God knows the heart, we cannot—and should not—judge the validity of someone's claim to be a Christian. Quite the contrary! If we have sufficient reason to suspect that someone's profession of faith may be false (based on the tests John provides), we are to reject their profession of faith. John primarily had Gnostics in mind, but his words are applicable to any profession of faith, "because many false prophets have gone out into the world." For while the Scriptures do speak to a specific audience, they also speak to today. Every generation must discern between those who speak for God and those who don't.

Remember King Ahab? He had four hundred court prophets who lied to him and said what he wanted to hear. Ahab's counterpart in Judah, Jehoshaphat, was not convinced. He asked, "Is there not a prophet of the LORD here that we may inquire of him?" (1 Kings 22:7). Ahab mentioned Micaiah, but Ahab didn't like him because he told the truth. People who tell the truth are often rejected because we want our ears tickled rather than our hearts turned.

We need a Micaiah today—someone who will risk raining on the parade of the popular trends to say what God says. The trend today is toward the subjective and experiential. There is little in the way of sound, exegetical preaching that would give us the mind and heart to discern what we are hearing from these so-called prophets, or seeing in these so-called revivals. Satan is most effective in the church as an angel of light. We can spot a roaring lion, but it's much harder to discern a false spirit. We must not be ignorant of his devices. Wolves are among the sheep to lead away the fold and march them off the cliff of their own feelings.

We often fail to address dangerous issues or question something that seems out of order for fear we might offend someone. But if we wait until false teachings are entrenched, it's too late. The time to operate on cancer is when you first find it. If you see a wolf coming, warn the sheep. I'm not talking about a witch hunt. I'm talking about being a guardian of the gate.

We are drifting toward a Christianity inconsistent with sound doctrine. We are drifting toward worshipping celebrities instead of Christ. We are drifting toward embracing anything and everything because we fail to understand that biblical principles cannot be violated or ignored in true revival.

Vance Havner wrote, "Some of us lived through the theological controversies of the 1930s when we had everything from William Jennings Bryan to Harry Emerson Fosdick. Today new personalities and new terminologies are among us, but the same virus merely sports new names. What we used to call rheumatism is now arthritis, but it hurts just the same. Putting poison in a new bottle and calling it ginger ale makes it all the more dangerous. False doctrine always uses a plausible gimmick to get its foot in the door—and it is always the back door! If you take a stand against it, you are 'not Christ-like.'"[2]

> **PUTTING POISON IN A NEW BOTTLE AND CALLING IT GINGER ALE MAKES IT ALL THE MORE DANGEROUS.**

I'm thinking right now of famous television preachers who have prophesied of their abilities to do the supernatural. Where's the evidence? The test of a true prophet is this: everything he says comes to pass. These false prophets of our day have predicted everything from the second coming to raising the dead. They fail to deliver on what they claim. But the biblical test we are to use on them is not subjective. It's not "if they get it right 90 percent of the time." If they claim something—anything!—and it doesn't come true, they are a false prophet. This is clearly stated in both the law and the prophets. "When a prophet speaks in the name of the LORD, if the thing does not come about or come true, that is the thing which the LORD has not spoken. The prophet has spoken it presumptuously; you shall not be afraid of him" (Deut. 18:22). "The prophet who prophesies of peace, when the word of the prophet comes to pass, then that prophet will be known as one whom the LORD has truly sent" (Jer. 28:9).

Every now and then one of these false prophets of a counterfeit revival will get something right. But the Bible warns, "If a prophet or a dreamer of dreams arises among you and gives you a sign or a wonder, and the sign or the wonder comes true, concerning which he spoke to you, saying, 'Let us go after other gods (whom you have not known) and let us serve them,' you shall not listen to the words of that prophet or that dreamer of dreams; for the LORD your God is testing you to find out if you love the LORD your God with all your heart and with all your soul" (Deut. 13:1–3).

James Montgomery Boice says that "behind every prophet stands a spirit, either the Spirit of God or the demonic spirit of antichrist."[3] Paul noted, "Therefore I make known to you that no one speaking by the Spirit of God says, 'Jesus is accursed'; and no one can say, 'Jesus is Lord,' except by the Holy Spirit" (1 Cor. 12:3). God has not left us in the dark on these matters. The test of a genuine preacher or movement is an objective one, based on proven biblical principles.

These leaders of false revivals have exalted themselves above the Scriptures and above the Lord. They may use Scripture "to support the legitimacy of the phenomenon, although Scripture plainly offers no support for the phenomenon as something to be expected in the normal Christian life."[4]

> You are from God, little children, and have overcome them; because greater is He who is in you than he who is in the world. They are from the world; therefore they speak as from the world, and the world listens to them. We are from God; he who knows God listens to us; he who is not from God does not listen to us. By this we know the spirit of truth and the spirit of error. (1 John 4:4–6)

In his commentary on 1 John, Boice points out that the pronouns in the passage are crucial:

> Verse 4 begins with "you." It is a reference to those who are of God, that is, to Christians. John says two things of these persons. First, he says that they have overcome the false teachers. . . . The false teachers had been seeking to deceive these believers, but they had not succeeded. Merely by testing them and refusing to be taken in by their lies, the Christians have conquered.

Verse 5 begins with "they." This refers to the false teachers who, John says, are of the world because what they say is of the world. It is the world's philosophy even though it may be dressed in Christian language and be presented by those who claim to be Christian teachers.

Verse 6, begins with "we." This "we" is not the same as the "you" who "are from God" in verse 4. In verse 4 the "you" is all Christians. In this verse "we" must refer, not to all Christians, but to the apostles, as the direct counterpart to the false teachers of verse 4. . . . What does this mean? It simply means that those who are of God and those who are of the world may be distinguished by their response or lack of response to the apostolic teaching.[5]

Although some claims of revival may seem real on the surface, they often fall short when held up to the light of Scripture. Though we can be understandably desperate for a moving of God and eager to see signs of spiritual renewal, we can chase a rabbit down the road and fall into a trap. Better to wait on the Lord than to be baited by the devil.

The manifestations may be different, but the principles of true revival are always the same. Manley Beasley said, "In any revival, the first thing is that people see themselves as they are. Then brokenness comes. As the brokenness comes, there is deep sorrow. That could be considered the measure of brokenness.

There is a change of mind about self and God. Then comes holiness, righteousness."

I am troubled by all the commotion and motion that abounds in our land that distracts and perverts genuine revival. Most of what I hear and see, especially on religious television, promotes the preacher, not the power of the Spirit. There is little sense of knowing God and walking with Him.

Why are people so easily deceived? Let me give you several reasons. First, we have a generation looking for someone who sounds authoritative. With the demise of the family and of respect for authority, there is a sense in which we will listen to anyone who sounds like a leader. Smooth words can sway many. Second, since the early part of the twentieth century, believers have become obsessed with the *gifts* of the Spirit rather than the *fruit* of the Spirit. We've bought the lie that "a miracle a day keeps the devil away." Third, I believe American Christianity is the most susceptible to the prosperity gospel. Most revivals are born out of suffering. The "you can have it all" approach is appealing to our materialistic, self-centered mind-set. A rule of thumb for me is just to preach Jesus. If you can't preach your message in a third-world country or inside a mud hut, it's not the gospel.

(For further study on this matter, you should read Hank Hanegraaff's *Counterfeit Revival* or *Christianity in Crisis*. These books and others deal with the perversions and substitutes of the Word and revival. It is essential that we know truth if we are to detect error. We must not buy the lie of signs and wonders when the Spirit and the Word are our tests.)

The preaching of many today is soulish. It involves psychological manipulation. It plays on the emotions. God never does His deepest work in the shallowest part of our being. While emotions are certainly a part of our faith and revival, emotions ebb and flow. Revival is as much a change of mind as a change of heart, agreeing with what God says about sin and self. That's why the true test of revival is repentance. Vance Havner said, "I doubt whether we shall see deep repentance in a shallow and superficial generation, in this affluent age when the church is rich, increased in goods, and has need of nothing. . . . Real repentance produces confession and forsaking of sin, reconciliation and restitution, separation from the world, submission to the Lordship of Christ and the filling of the Holy Spirit."[6]

PENTECOST LIVING

Those who were present at Pentecost were amazed and asked, "What does this mean?" Peter answered, "This is what was spoken of through the prophet Joel" (Acts 2:16). As I look at the programs, promotions, and props we depend on for church today, I believe I can safely say this is *not* what was spoken of through the prophet Joel. Surely Jesus died for more than we are experiencing. Surely the Holy Spirit empowered us to live better than we are living. This can't be all there is.

At the same time we can't try to reproduce Pentecost. Lacking fire, we buy flame throwers. Lacking power, we buy generators. But what is painfully lacking in our churches is the wind, breath, power, and sense of presence of the Spirit of God. People drive by our churches and think nothing of us. The only time they might even glance our way is if they see a new sign out front.

Again, the first order of business is to repent. The church can be involved in many things *after* repentance, but she has no power and can do nothing *until* she repents. At Pentecost, Peter quoted the prophet Joel, who called God's people to repent:

> Gird yourselves with sackcloth and lament, O priests; wail, O ministers of the altar! Come, spend the night in sackcloth, O ministers of my God, for the grain offering and the drink offering are withheld from the house of your God. Consecrate a fast, proclaim a solemn assembly; gather the elders and all the inhabitants of the land to the house of the LORD your God, and cry out to the LORD. Alas for the day! For the day of the LORD is near, and it will come as destruction from the Almighty. . . .
>
> "Yet even now," declares the LORD, "return to Me with all your heart, and with fasting, weeping and mourning; and rend your heart and not your garments." Now return to the LORD your God, for He is gracious and compassionate, slow to anger, abounding in lovingkindness and relenting of evil. . . .
>
> Gather the people, sanctify the congregation, assemble the elders, gather the children and the nursing infants. Let the bridegroom

come out of his room and the bride out of her bridal chamber. Let the priests, the LORD's ministers, weep between the porch and the altar, and let them say, "Spare Your people, O LORD, and do not make Your inheritance a reproach, a byword among the nations. Why should they among the peoples say, 'Where is their God?'" (Joel 1:13–15; 2:12–13, 16–17)

Vance Havner said, "Preaching repentance is the loneliest and most thankless business in the world. . . . Stand in a local church where everybody knows everybody and call deacons, Sunday school teachers, and choir singers to repentance, however, and you will understand what Joseph Parker meant when he said, 'The man whose sermon is repentance sets himself against his age. . . . There is but one end for such a man: off with his head! Better not preach repentance until you have pledged your head to heaven.'"[7]

Pentecost was preceded by forty days of waiting and praying. They didn't rush out from the Ascension and start printing tracts and T-shirts. They knew they couldn't give what they didn't have. Repentance and prayer are the tests of a genuine and deep work of God.

R. A. Torrey preached a message entitled "Keep Praying Until God Answers." He preached the sermon to address the issue, "What sort of praying is it that prevails with God and obtains what it seeks from Him?" He said:

When we pray, if we do not obtain the thing the first time, pray again; and if we do not obtain it the second time, pray a third time; and if we do not obtain it the hundredth time, go on praying until we do get it. . . . Our Heavenly Father delights in the holy boldness that will not take no for an answer. The reason why He delights in it is that it is an expression of great faith, and nothing pleases God more than faith. . . . For example, in many churches and communities there are those who are praying for a revival. The revival does not come at once, it does not come for some time, but they keep on praying. They have nearly prayed through. They are right on the verge of attaining what they sought, and if they would pray a little longer, the revival would break upon them. But they get discouraged, throw up their hands and quit. They are just on the border of the blessing, but they do not cross into the Promised Land."[8]

We have caved into feverish, frustrating, and futile events as our witness to the world. Not being energized by prayer, we entertain. Not being purified through repentance, we back away from declaring the true Word. Even the world can tell the difference between a sideshow and the main event. We seem to be wearing ourselves out trying to produce the results of revival . . . without the revival.

THE WORK OF THE SPIRIT

The test of a true work of God is a blessed balance between Spirit and truth. It's not wildfire. Nor is it the absence of fire altogether. It's not a legalistic approach where we seek to box in the Holy Spirit. Nor is it "anything goes as long as we put the Holy Spirit label on it." The problem with some fundamentalists is they aren't any fun. The problem with some charismatics is that all they want to have is fun. There must be a balance. The danger for those who are solely committed to truth without any emotion or power is that they are so afraid of the Holy Spirit, they never let go of dry doctrine.

The Spirit has chosen to reveal Himself to us in the Word. He is the author of the Word. He came to glorify Jesus. Therefore anything and everything born of the Spirit is consistent with the person and work of Jesus Christ. It is consistent with both the living Word and the written Word. If someone claims to be speaking on behalf of the Holy Spirit, there are biblical guidelines.

The problem for me personally is that when I talk about the Holy Spirit, the first question some folks ask me is, "Do you have the gift?" Yes, I do. I've got the gift. I got the gift of the person of the Holy Spirit when I gave my life to Jesus. I don't need a secondary gift because I've got the primary one. I refuse to emphasize the least and minimize the best. Once after I had finished speaking on the Spirit-filled life, someone came up to me and said, "You finally got it. You got the Holy Ghost." It's pathetic to me that if someone speaks about the filling of the Spirit, all the extremists on that subject want to adopt you.

In 2008, I gave two messages from the book of James on healing. We had a prayer service for those who were sick. We didn't slay anyone in the Spirit, and I didn't breathe on anyone. I clearly stated what I understood the Scriptures to say about healing. (By the way, the best book on healing is the one written by Ron Dunn, *Will God Heal Me?* It's the best because it's based on Scripture, not on subjective and wishful thinking.) You won't believe the number of e-mails and letters I got from folks who had heard I was going to speak on the subject. People drove from other communities to hear what I had to say.

Their response was fairly consistent, many of them disappointed that I wasn't "enlightened" and had not taught healing as part of the atonement. Yes, God heals, but He is also sovereign. He is not a cosmic bellhop at our beck and call. It's sad to me that if you testify of healing, all the faith healers want to claim you for themselves and put you in their camp.

Jesus didn't heal everyone. If Jesus didn't do it while He walked this Earth, how can any faith healer claim *he* can? If healing is a sign of a last days' revival, will all be healed? I don't think so. Even of those Jesus healed, He didn't heal everyone the same way. He certainly didn't set up healing lines and blow on people or smack them on the head. Such methods have trivialized and distorted a true understanding of how we're to pray for those who are sick. As my friend Bill Stafford is fond of saying, "When the Spirit touches you, you don't fall backwards; you fall forward on your face before a holy God."

And what about speaking in tongues? Paul, writing to the most carnal, self-centered group of believers to grace the planet, said, "Yet even lifeless things, either flute or harp, in producing a sound, if they do not produce a distinction in the tones, how will it be known what is played on the flute or on the harp? For if the bugle produces an indistinct sound, who will prepare himself for battle?" (1 Cor. 14:7–8). Obviously in this passage Paul was dealing with tongues. But let's look at the larger picture and the importance of Paul's illustration. Let's talk not just about how revival is supposed to look and feel, but how it's supposed to sound.

I'm not musically inclined, although I do have a 160-gig iPod loaded with music. I have enough of an ear to know when someone is singing off pitch or when a piano is out of tune. We used to own my grandparents' piano. We inherited it when they died, and it was in our family for more than fifty years. As best I can recall, it was never tuned. You could play it, but it didn't sound great. We also used to have a large pipe organ at Sherwood. We finally sold it for next to nothing. It was useless because we couldn't keep it tuned. No matter what we did, it wouldn't stay in tune with the piano. What good is an instrument that is out of sync with the others?

I've preached a number of funerals for men and women who have served in the Armed Forces, and often someone plays "Taps" at the graveside. What if the bugler didn't know what to play? What if he played "Charge!" or "Retreat!" instead of "Taps"? There would be confusion and chaos.

Revival brings with it a certain sound. What God says about holiness, repentance, confession, and prayer are not obsolete—they are absolute. One preacher said, "I'd rather know a few things for certain than be sure of a lot of things that ain't so." We can be certain about what God says, even though we can't always be certain about some of what we hear being trumpeted as revival. That's why we need discernment. We need to know what's true so when we hear something questionable, we can go back to what we know for sure.

Revival contains the certain sound of the lordship of Christ. Any revival that exalts anything or anyone above Christ is not true revival. The reason we need revival is because we've created a dichotomy between Christ as our Savior and Christ as our Lord. In the New Testament, He is the Lord Jesus Christ. The term "Lord" is used more than four hundred times. So following Jesus is not like a buffet line where you take what you want and pass up the rest. Someone committed to lordship will take seriously the three invitations of Christ: "Come to Me," "Follow Me," and "Abide in Me." If you obey those commands, you'll walk in personal revival.

Another certain sound of real revival is the filling of the Holy Spirit. Call it what you will—the surrendered life, the victorious life, the deeper Christian life—it is lacking in the majority of believers. I for one don't want to get in an argument over how to express it and thereby miss the person of the Holy Spirit. Sometimes we fail to notice a work of God while arguing over secondary things. It's like a bunch of beggars debating what a wallet is, when all of them are broke. The Spirit-filled life is the revived life. We walk in the fullness of the Spirit when we come thirsty. Don't drink from the broken fountains of experiences— sooner or later you'll forget that experience. Don't drink from

the bottled water of this world—you'll only have to keep finding more bottles to drink from. Drink from the artesian well of
living water that only Jesus can offer. When I look to Jesus as
my source, I can overflow in perpetual revival.

The certain sound of a true work of God will also ring true with
the remnant, the church within the church. They have been
called the faithful few, or the Master's minority. They know the
difference between a sermon and a message. They can discern
between true and false fires, and they can smell a pretender from
a mile away. God has always been in
the remnant business. In every church
there are true believers who long for
the "much more" of God. They live
with holy dissatisfaction toward the
status quo. They don't want to be pampered; they want to be challenged.
They aren't interested in the superficial because they judge everything in

FOLLOWING JESUS IS NOT LIKE A BUFFET LINE WHERE YOU TAKE WHAT YOU WANT AND PASS UP THE REST.

light of eternity. A. J. Gordon said, "A few Spirit-filled disciples
are sufficient to save a church. The Holy Spirit acting through
these can bring recovery and health to the whole body."

These are the sights and sounds of true revival.

RELYING ON A REMNANT

I never expect everyone to get it. Most of the church doesn't
even bother to show up on Sunday morning. Those that do
often fail to make it back on Sunday night. If you are waiting
on the majority, you'll never see real revival. Revival starts in

the core, not in the masses. We might feel more confident if we had Gideon's 32,000, but God can do more with three hundred who are sold out than with 32,000 who just show up. One way or another, revival or persecution will trim the crowd and show us who really means business with God.

The remnant are not focused on revival, as such. They are focused on the Lord of revival. Isaiah said of Messiah, "Therefore, I have set My face like flint" (Isa. 50:7). Luke said of Jesus, "He was determined to go to Jerusalem" (Luke 9:51). Along the way Jesus met those who made excuses, but He kept moving toward Jerusalem. His own disciples tried to discourage Him, but He maintained His focus. Jesus avoided the easy road and the shortcuts during His life. He rejected the alternatives offered by the devil on the Mount of Temptation. He rejected the popular ideas of what Messiah might do. Those who seriously want revival will not settle for counterfeits or substitutes.

The remnant possesses the commitment of Caleb: "I followed the LORD my God fully" (Josh. 14:8). Caleb waited a long time to see the Promised Land, and it was worth the wait. The remnant stands with the steadfastness of Joshua: "As for me and my house, we will serve the LORD" (Josh. 24:15). The remnant lives with the boldness of Elijah: "If the LORD is God, follow Him; but if Baal, follow him" (1 Kings 18:21). The remnant has the heart of David and the focus of Paul. They don't dabble in forty different things. They have only one thing that drives them: Jesus.

Duncan Campbell was speaking at a large convention in Britain when God gripped his heart to leave immediately and go to the island of Berneray. The chairman tried to convince him not to leave because he was scheduled to deliver the closing address, but Campbell left the next morning. Two planes, a car, and a ferry boat ride later, he finally landed on the island where God had called him.

"On arriving," he reported, "I said nothing to the man who ferried me across. I was never invited to the island, and to my knowledge no one on the island had ever met me." Finding the first person he could, he asked, "Would you direct me to the nearest minister?"

The man replied, "We have no minister on the island. Just now both churches are vacant."

"Would you then direct me to the nearest elder?" he asked, instructing the man to go up and tell the elder that Mr. Campbell had come to the island. If the elder asked "What Campbell?" the man was to say, "The Campbell that was on the island of Lewis."

After a few minutes the man came back and said, "Hector McKennon was expecting you to arrive today. And he asked me to tell you that he has initiated a meeting at the church at 9:00 tonight, and he expects you to address it." This elder had prayed earnestly for God to send Duncan Campbell to his island, saying, "God, I don't know where he is, but You know, and You send him." Soon the man sensed that God heard his prayer and started preparing for the meeting.

On an island of five hundred people, about eighty people had gathered. At first Duncan Campbell wondered if he was supposed to be there because nothing out of the ordinary happened.

The elder said to him, "I hope you are not disappointed that revival has not come to the church tonight. But God is hovering over us, and He will break through any minute!"

As they were walking away from the church, the elderly man said, "Stand, Mr. Campbell! God has come! God has come! See what is happening!" All along the road people were falling on their knees, crying out to God. The meeting was actually starting outside—after the organized meeting—and it lasted until 4:00 in the morning. Duncan Campbell said, "An awareness of God, a consciousness of God, seemed to hover in the very atmosphere . . . charged with the power of Almighty God! That is Revival! There was at least one man on that island who fulfilled the conditions of 1 Chronicles 7:14, and God being a covenant-keeping God, must be true to His covenant engagements. God, to vindicate His own honor, had to listen to the prayers of the parish postman [the elder] who knelt in prayer that day."[9]

Every true revival begins in the hearts of a few. Like the Marines, I'm looking for a few good men and women. The remnant will pray in faith, believing that God will send revival. The old revival preachers used to call the remnant "kindling wood," the small pieces of dry wood used for starting a fire. When my dad was growing up, his job every morning was to stoke the fire in the fireplace. He would take the smoldering embers of the previous night's fire and add a little kindling wood to it, fanning it until the flames came. That's the role of the remnant.

When real revival comes, we will have the praying, faithful remnant to thank for it. As Winston Churchill said of the

British airmen who saved London during the German blitz-krieg, "Never was so much owed by so many to so few." Let the Holy Spirit come and take control and send a great revival in my soul! Lord, we surrender to Your timetable—if not today, maybe tomorrow. Lord, rend the heavens and come down that Your people might rejoice in You, that we can once again have seasons of refreshing from the Lord, that we might know one more time before Your return what it means to walk in revival.

CHAPTER 9

THE PERSON GOD USES

2 Kings 18, 2 Chronicles 28–29

Revival is the exchange of the form of godliness for its living power.
—John Bonar

He trusted in the LORD, the God of Israel; so that after him there was none like him among all the kings of Judah, nor among those who were before him. For he clung to the LORD; he did not depart from following Him, but kept His commandments, which the LORD had commanded Moses.
—2 Kings 18:5–6

AS A RESULT of great movements of God in our nation, we have seen significant social impact: the abolition of slavery, child labor laws, the building of hospitals and orphanages, increase in mission work, even revivals among armies in times of war. Revival does more to transform the moral character of a people than any law or program.

When revival comes, the rules change. Status quo is not acceptable. Things once justified, pampered, or even exalted to a godlike status are laid aside. Jonathan Edwards, leader of the first Great Awakening, once said in a sermon, "What the church has been used to is not a rule by which we are to judge, because there may be new and extraordinary works of God."

As you study the writings of Edwards and his accounts of how God moved in the 1700s, you can trace the extraordinary things God did in churches and communities. One thing Edwards emphasized was the influence of example. "It is agreeable to Scripture," he said, "that people should be influenced by one another's good example. . . . This way of people holding up truth to one another has a tendency to enlighten the mind, and to convince reason."[1]

We all know the power of example and the influence a leader can have. Someone has said, "As the pastor goes, so go the people." We need leaders to point the way. Whether it's Moses leading Israel through the wilderness, or our Lord leading His disciples, or the leaders of the great revivals and awakenings, we look to leaders. As our world grows increasingly secular and pagan, leaders raise the hope that revival can come—those who realize that this is our great need of the hour.

Politics will not bring revival. Programs will not bring revival. *People* are God's instruments of revival. People influence people. Mentors pour into their followers.

As I write this chapter, I'm sitting at my computer at home. There is a picture on my left of the heroes who have impacted me in the developmental years of my ministry. Much of who I am is because of their influence. And all of them were influenced by the message of revival. All of these men have marked me. They instilled in me a desire for "something more." I've mentioned their names throughout this book, but I never tire of thanking God for them. They remind me that one person can be used of God to make significant changes in others' lives. These men have certainly made a difference in mine.

James Miller was my youth minister. He saw what God was doing in the Jesus Movement in the late 1960s and early '70s and got on board. We had youth prayer meetings two nights a week where hundreds of students would come to pray. We would go street witnessing in the French Quarter of New Orleans. James was the first person to help me see that there was more to the Christian life than just showing up for church.

I met Lehman Strauss in 1990 when he came to Sherwood for a Bible conference. Lehman was a great Bible teacher and a true student of the Scriptures. His kind and gentle manner, blended with unapologetic proclamation, is something I'll never forget. He took an interest in this young preacher and was always willing to spend time with me.

Ron Dunn was a hero and one of the best friends I've ever had. I first heard Ron at a Bible conference in Kansas City in

1975 right after his oldest son had died. I subscribed to his tape messages through the years and prayed I could preach like him one day. We became friends in 1987, and no one has influenced my preaching and life more than Ron.

Vance Havner was one of a kind. I've never known a more interesting and distinctively different person. He had a nasal, Southern accent that was as distinctive as any you would ever hear. Someone asked Vance how he could preach so much and not have throat trouble. He said, "It's not hard when you preach through your nose." He was cut from a different cloth. He was a modern-day Amos. Billy Graham said he was the most quoted preacher of the twentieth century. Once you heard Havner, you could never forget him. He performed surgery on the heart without anesthesia. For the last fifteen years of his life, he and I enjoyed a close, fruitful relationship. About nine months before he died, we prayed together in his apartment. He laid hands on me and asked the Lord to give me a portion of his mantle. That moment was my real ordination.

GOD PLACES PEOPLE ALONG THE JOURNEY TO CHALLENGE THE STATUS QUO OF OUR LIVES.

Manley Beasley was the greatest man of faith I've ever met. I only knew him for a couple of years, but those years had a powerful influence on my life. It was during a time of transition and testing that Manley came into my life and taught me about faith. I had the privilege of preaching two meetings with him.

Roger Breland founded the contemporary Christian group TRUTH, which traveled the world for more than thirty years.

Regardless of the church I was serving, TRUTH came to per-form each year. Roger is a friend, encourager, and one of the greatest mentors I've ever had.

God uses people in our lives to stir us and stretch us. He places people along the journey to challenge the status quo of our lives. They make us want to do better, be better, pray more, love more, and serve more. Each of these men have pushed me beyond myself. They've all had a passion to see a great work of God in the church, and they've all prayed for a mighty moving of the Spirit.

You could probably name a few people yourself who have had such a significant impact on your life. May we step into their shoes as people God can use.

SOMEONE LIKE ME, SOMEONE LIKE YOU

In 2008 God moved in our church during the annual ReFRESH™ Conference on revival. Each year God meets us in a unique way. Prior to the conference I sent an e-mail to several praying friends, asking them to join us in believing prayer that God would have His will and way with us. My friend Alan Stewart sent me a text with these words: "Go up to the mountain and view the path to lead us in. Spy out the dangers. Find the pure waters and secure the hiding places. Find God's pace. Press in, my brother, a generation awaits your entry."

I'm the last guy I believe God would pick to do such a thing. I am overwhelmed by the seasons of revival we've experienced in the church I pastor. God has moved in our midst countless times to take us to new heights. But unfortunately there seems to be little hunger in the laity or leadership for revival in many churches. In the last several years I've preached all across this land, and I can tell you that revival is considered an "old" message. It has become so old that it would sound new if we would preach it!

I have friends with a heart for revival who have been told when they minister in other churches, "We can't have you back. We are moving in a new direction. We need a different message." That statement alone should tell us how much trouble we are in. These are desperate times, and yet the saints are yawning. The crying sin of the church is her laziness after God. We are content to be lukewarm. And if we are going to be helped out of this, it's going to take a prophet who is not satisfied and cannot be silenced.

We are at a fork in the road. America is either going to have revival, or we'll most likely have a riot. The only options for us are apathy and anarchy if we do not become the recipients of divine intervention.

But let me be quick to say: while you are waiting for a corporate revival, you don't have to wait for a personal revival. It's easy to talk about wanting things to be different. It's easy to complain about whose fault it is for why we've gotten ourselves into this kind of mess. It's quite another thing, however, to set our hearts on seeking the Lord with all our might. God is looking for a person or a people He can trust with revival.

One of those people is you.

The Old Testament is full of stories of revival and return, occurring in times of deep moral darkness and wickedness. As you study these accounts, you find that each revival was based on the Word of God and a return to the authority of Scripture or the law. They all resulted in a return to true worship and a cleansing of idols from the land. Rightful sacrifices were again offered to the Lord, resulting in great joy and blessings among God's people.

But these revivals had one other thing in common as well: they usually began in the heart of one person.

I read a clipping out of *The Wall Street Journal* from 1954 that said, "What America needs more than railway extension, Western irrigation, a low tariff, a bigger cotton crop, and a larger wheat crop is a revival of religion, the kind that our fathers and mothers used to have, a religion that counted it good business to take time for family worship each morning right in the middle of the wheat harvest, a religion that made men quit work a half hour earlier on Wednesday so that the whole family could get ready to go to Prayer Meeting."[2] Will you be that kind of person? Will you let revival start with you? Will you set an example that others can follow?

THE VOICE OF CHANGE

One of the great revivals in history occurred during the reign of Hezekiah, one of the kings of Judah. He reigned for twenty-nine years, but it's how he began that marks him as a revival leader. God used him to lead the people of God into a time of refreshing and renewal. Oh, that we might have kings, leaders, and politicians who could see the real issue behind our problems and get us back to God!

The name Hezekiah means "the Lord strengthens." And this king's story certainly gives evidence of that in the biblical records. God enlightened him as a young man to the real problems in the land. He empowered him to boldly address them and enabled him to lead, endearing him to the people who were willing to follow his godly leadership.

God is looking for fit vessels He can use—faithful, available, teachable vessels through which He can pour out His power. There is no personality type for a revival leader. There is no "one, two, three" formula. God is not going to work according to our planned-out, prearranged ideas about who He may use.

I can say with much assurance that I'm the last person many would have expected to be a pastor. I don't have many of the gifts that the great communicators and preachers have. I have only average intelligence, and I haven't "worked the system" in my denomination. Vance Havner taught me, "You don't have to chase key men when you know the One who holds the keys." My calling is to be faithful and available.

When my dad died in 1998, a number of people from our church came to support our family and attend the funeral. As we were standing around prior to the service, my Aunt Hazel was talking to my assistant, Debbie Toole, and to Shirley Horne, a longtime secretary at our church. She asked them, "Who are all these people here?" They told her they were members of the church. Aunt Hazel asked, "Well, how many members are in that church?" They said about three thousand. Then my Aunt Hazel (who definitely had the gift of discouragement) said, "Hmm, we never thought he would amount to much."

I'm sure those who knew of the wicked King Ahaz assumed his son Hezekiah would never amount to much. "We can't put any hope in him. He'll be like his father—or worse." Never try to predict or underestimate the person God might use. Walter Kaiser noted, "Hezekiah is one of the best refutations of the oft repeated but badly understood warning that the sins of the fathers visit the children to the third and fourth generation. That is only true when the children agree in the evil of their fathers and decide to walk in their footsteps. . . . In this case, Hezekiah saw the wickedness of his father and refused outright to imitate it."[3]

But no matter what anyone thought about Hezekiah, there came a day when he stepped to the throne as God's man for God's time.

He had a lousy father figure who could best be described as evil personified. Ahaz was an ungodly man who made idols to Baal, worshiped Molech, and burned incense to idols. He also sacrificed his children to Molech. Not exactly a candidate for "Dad of the Year." He was the national leader in an era when all restraint was gone. Godlessness was on the throne. Evil abounded on every corner. He might have liked his image to be cleaned up over time, but the Word of God does not provide us with a revised version of history. The Scripture chisels the truth in granite. It tells us exactly how depraved and decadent Ahaz was.

> The LORD humbled Judah because of Ahaz
> king of Israel, for he had brought about a lack

of restraint in Judah and was very unfaithful to the LORD. So Tilgath-pilneser king of Assyria came against him and afflicted him instead of strengthening him. Although Ahaz took a portion out of the house of the LORD and out of the palace of the king and of the princes, and gave it to the king of Assyria, it did not help him.

Now in the time of his distress this same King Ahaz became yet more unfaithful to the LORD. For he sacrificed to the gods of Damascus which had defeated him, and said, "Because the gods of the kings of Aram helped them, I will sacrifice to them that they may help me." But they became the downfall of him and all Israel. Moreover, when Ahaz gathered together the utensils of the house of God, he cut the utensils of the house of God in pieces; and he closed the doors of the house of the LORD and made altars for himself in every corner of Jerusalem. In every city of Judah he made high places to burn incense to other gods, and provoked the LORD, the God of his fathers, to anger. (2 Chron. 28:19–25)

The temple of God had been shut down and gutted. There was no worship. But under Hezekiah, the nation was about to experience a great reformation. His actions reveal his character.

THE PERSON GOD USES

They also show us the steps toward revival and the person
God can use. Let's look at the parallel passages in 2 Kings and
2 Chronicles to see how it all took place.

> Now it came about in the third year of Hoshea,
> the son of Elah king of Israel, that Hezekiah the
> son of Ahaz king of Judah became king. He was
> twenty-five years old when he became king, and
> he reigned twenty-nine years in Jerusalem. . . .
> He did right in the sight of the LORD, accord-
> ing to all that his father David had done. He
> removed the high places and broke down the
> sacred pillars and cut down the Asherah. He
> also broke in pieces the bronze serpent that
> Moses had made, for until those days the sons
> of Israel burned incense to it; and it was called
> Nehushtan. He trusted in the LORD, the God
> of Israel; so that after him there was none like
> him among all the kings of Judah, nor among
> those who were before him. For he clung to
> the LORD; he did not depart from following
> Him, but kept His commandments, which the
> LORD had commanded Moses. And the Lord
> was with him; wherever he went he prospered.
> (2 Kings 18:1–7)

Hezekiah's father was a wicked king, but he didn't use a
bad home situation as an excuse. He was young, but he didn't

use that as an excuse either. Instead he served as an example to both young and old.

> He did right in the sight of the LORD, according to all that his father David had done. In the first year of his reign, in the first month, he opened the doors of the house of the LORD and repaired them. He brought in the priests and the Levites and gathered them into the square on the east. Then he said to them, "Listen to me, O Levites. Consecrate yourselves now, and consecrate the house of the LORD, the God of your fathers, and carry the uncleanness out from the holy place. For our fathers have been unfaithful and have done evil in the sight of the LORD our God, and have forsaken Him and turned their faces away from the dwelling place of the LORD, and have turned their backs. They have also shut the doors of the porch and put out the lamps, and have not burned incense or offered burnt offerings in the holy place to the God of Israel. Therefore the wrath of the LORD was against Judah and Jerusalem, and He has made them an object of terror, of horror, and of hissing, as you see with your own eyes. For behold, our fathers have fallen by the sword, and our sons and our daughters and our wives are in captivity for this. Now it is in my heart

> to make a covenant with the LORD God of
> Israel, that His burning anger may turn away
> from us. My sons, do not be negligent now, for
> the LORD has chosen you to stand before Him,
> to minister to Him, and to be His ministers and
> burn incense. (2 Chron. 29:2–11)

It didn't take a rocket scientist to realize change was needed. But it took the courage of one man to make it right. Hezekiah had a discerning mind and heart. He knew what was wrong, and he wasted no time getting it corrected. In the first month of the first year of his reign, he started to work to restore the land and the temple. Like a good doctor he quickly diagnosed the disease and wrote the proper prescription. The problem could be fixed, but there was no time to lose.

Hezekiah called the priests and religious leaders together with his plan for restoring the worship and honor of God in the land. The degradation had certainly happened under their watch. Maybe they had simply been afraid of Ahaz. Maybe they had been willing to look the other way. We don't know what their attitude had been or if they had cautioned Ahaz about such evil. But when Hezekiah proposed reforms, the priests and Levites set about getting things in order.

Hezekiah's discernment led to a fixed determination. He was stirred to act. He put feet to his prayer. "It is in my heart," he said (2 Chron. 29:10). And if we are going to be people God can use, we must be like Hezekiah. We must stop waiting for the crowd to catch it. We must be willing to stand alone.

There is a leadership void in our churches today, as well as in our nation. People are crying out for leaders. Fear of man is a snare in the church, just as compromise is rampant in the world at large. Hezekiah didn't make such excuses; he just went to work. He was willing to pay the price to get the nation back on the right track.

Notice he didn't launch an economic stimulus package. There was no infrastructure resurgence. He didn't promise to improve the educational system or rebuild the defense fund, although the nation was in danger by threats on all sides. Instead he called the politicians and priests together and said, "Listen to me and do what I say. I'm not going to debate you over this. I expect you to do it and do it without delay. My agenda is to get right with God."

Hezekiah was a man whose faith was focused. He didn't have time to waste on secondary issues, as important as they might have seemed to others. He simply "trusted in the LORD" (2 Kings 18:5). His confidence was in God, and it showed through in his character. Like David, he was a man after God's heart. There are three indicators of his character: he clung to the Lord, he did not depart from following the Lord, and he kept God's commandments.

God is looking for a man or woman, a church or denomination that He can use to bring revival. He's watching and waiting. The lack of revival is not because God is disinterested. Rather we have come to believe we can exist without it. We need leaders today who are driven by opinions rather than convictions, people who are willing to die for what they believe. We need a leader who will stand and say, "Get back to God. Get right with God." That voice is strangely silent in our land today.

A CHURCH RESTORED

What happens when a leader sets his heart on these things? In Hezekiah's case "the house of the LORD" was put in order (2 Chron. 29:3). He opened the doors of God's house and repaired them. He got the place of worship back in shape. He removed the clutter and repaired the facilities.

The church today is in a mess. We have people arguing over styles. We have preachers minimizing substance. Some folks continue to argue over translations yet still don't love their brother, the way every translation says. We have remote sites, satellites, and multiple campuses, but I'm wondering, "Do we have God?" Are we seeing His manifest presence? As one Russian pastor said of America's churches, "You have everything except God."

If we want revival, we need to clean out the gimmicks in God's house. Technology cannot replace a commitment to truth. Programs will not fill the gap left by prayerlessness. Honesty must replace hypocrisy. Committees must be replaced or at least staffed by people crying out to God. Power groups must give way to prayer meetings.

We need revival. Immorality abounds in the culture. We even see it increasingly in the church. There is an all-out attack on the moral fiber of our land. Divorce is easy. Prenuptial agreements have taken the place of "till death do us part." Sex is casual, drugs are recreational, and what used to be hidden is now parading in the streets. The pollution of evolution has turned the minds of our kids into pond scum. No wonder their self-image is so lousy.

But there is still hope. As long as there is one pastor, one church, one believer who wants to see God move in powerful ways, we have a chance. I've been in several meetings in Washington, D. C., and in my own state capitol in recent years, and there are politicians and major players asking what they can do.

Today we need the voice of one empowered by the Holy Spirit that resonates with "thus says the Lord." If we want revival, it will demand our full focus and undivided attention. It cannot be optional on our calendar or a multiple choice selection between television and church, between prayer and play. Revival is not about getting the pagans in the world to shape up. Revival is about God's people getting right. The term "revive" indicates a return to consciousness or life. It is moving from a form of godliness to a godly life. It is moving from a cluttered life to a focused life.

We need to think about all the things we've let slip in recent decades. There is much debate, for example, about whether or not churches should have Sunday night services. I'm not wanting to be legalistic about this, but I would like to ask why we've done away with it. I hear pastors say things like, "God delivered me from having to preach on Sunday night." Well, what were you called to do? Should you draw a full-time salary for doing one "talk" a week? Wesley and Whitefield preached multiple times a day, almost every day, often after traveling on horseback to get there. Maybe the difference is they had a Word from God and we don't. There's no fire in our bones. There's no passion to present "every man complete in Christ." We'd rather work on our golf game than our prayer closet.

Some say, "My people won't come." I say people follow leaders. If it's important to the leader, it will be important to the people. As many as 50 to 60 percent of our Sunday morning crowd at Sherwood returns on Sunday night, even though many of them are families with young children. They've discovered this is a better place than the den sofa to have "family night." Besides, it's not about the size of the crowd; it's about discipling the saints and keeping the remnant stirred up. If we've decided to cancel things because they lack support, then Jesus should have canceled the cross because almost all of His followers forsook Him there. As a wise sage once said, "Never move a fence until you find out why it was put there." I won't debate this, but I can tell you it's hard to see revival in a Sunday morning crowd. Our greatest services and the greatest movements of God have happened on Sunday nights. It's the perfect way to end the Lord's day.

> **REVIVAL IS NOT ABOUT GETTING THE PAGANS IN THE WORLD TO SHAPE UP. REVIVAL IS ABOUT GOD'S PEOPLE GETTING RIGHT.**

But take a look in any local paper or any church ad in the phone book, and note the number of churches with no Sunday night activities. In Muslim countries and Communist China they do all they can to stop the church. In America we stop it on our own. We are our own worst enemy, and even applaud ourselves for our lack of commitment and the "freedom" we derive as a result.

The sliding of commitment and faithfulness will result in compromise and unfaithfulness in the people of God. And whenever these hit our doorsteps, the gospel is inevitably watered down, prevailing prayer is silenced, and the prayer meeting crowd becomes nothing more than praying for the physically sick while ignoring the spiritually sick.

If there is going to be a great revival, the person God uses must demand that others in leadership follow his lead. He can't wait for consensus. He must stand without hesitation or reservation and say, "This is what we are going to do, and I expect you to join with me."

WHERE IDOLS GO TO DIE

Hezekiah called in the priests and Levites and told them to consecrate themselves. No one got off the hook or hid in the tall grass. Everyone was called out and called on the carpet. The king didn't care what position they held or how long they had been in that position. He expected them to step up to the plate.

Not only did he call out the leaders: he went even deeper than most of us are willing to go. He started dealing with the idolatry that had become embedded in the land—not just the obvious idols but the idols others might have ignored. Sometimes we let people off the hook when it comes to idolatry because we don't want to offend them.

Second Kings 18:4 says he "removed the high places and broke down the sacred pillars and cut down the Asherah." Those were the obvious pagan images. Everyone would have agreed on that. Destroying the high places, the pagan idols, and the false images was the right thing to do.

But Hezekiah saw beyond the obvious. He saw another idol, one that might have gone unrecognized even by the priests and Levites. "He also broke in pieces the bronze serpent that Moses had made, for until those days the sons of Israel burned incense to it; and it was called Nehushtan" (2 Kings 18:4).

I've been in church long enough to know there are relics. We start something, God uses it, and then we start to worship it. The bronze serpent had been used 750 years earlier by Moses as an instrument of deliverance (see Num. 21). Moses had lifted it up and said, "Look and live," and the people were delivered. By the time of Hezekiah, however, they worshipped it and burned incense to it. A sacred relic—an instrument used mightily, miraculously, and appropriately by God at one time in history—had now become an idol. They took a genuine spiritual experience and turned it into an object of worship.

I've seen this happen more times than I can count. Churches start a program and, before you know it, it's the Seventy-Fifth Annual Singing Christmas Tree or Easter Pageant. There's no more power in it. The glory is not there, but they've always done it. We could miss a fresh work of God by hanging onto a dead experience.

We used to do the Singing Christmas Tree at Sherwood. It was a tradition. It didn't take me long, however, to realize we were spending a lot of money, time, and energy and seeing few results. We were entertaining the members of other churches, but we weren't reaching the lost. The program was no longer accomplishing its original purpose.

So I cut the tree down. Not literally, but I cut it out of the church program. I declared one Sunday that until we started using certain events to reach the lost, we weren't going to do them. Our job is not to entertain the saints; it's to see the lost come to Christ. The singing Christmas tree had become a "thing of brass" we had to get rid of.

I was speaking in a conference a few years ago to about six hundred ministers of music. I asked them the question, "Are you willing to get before God and ask Him if He wants you to continue doing your Christmas and Easter programs? Are you willing to die to your big event?" I doubt if many went back and changed anything. After all, what do you do if you don't have a sugar stick and a carrot to bait people to serve God?

The form has taken the place of the force. The power is gone, but we're still singing the song. The joy is gone, but we are gutting it out for Jesus. We worship the secondary and miss the primary.

That's why we need revival.

Today's churches and believers can still have their bronze serpents. We can worship lots of things—buildings, pageants, events, names of organizations, titles, classrooms, people, pastors, and many more. You walk into some churches, and there are "off limits" signs on furniture, pews, programs, or positions. They waste the present by worshipping the past. Now certainly we are told to remember the past, but we aren't supposed to worship it. Remembering the past encourages us to build on the things God has done in generations before. It's a memorial stone that cries out for us to press on. But worshipping the past allows us to make excuses and justify our ruts. We begin to substitute the stories of the good old days for trusting God in the here and now.

I served a church in the 1970s where we shuffled some of our Sunday school classes. One class had actually bolted their chairs to the floor. They even called a local TV station and said they were going to boycott the services and take over the pulpit if they didn't get their room back.

One time in my home church, we did an Easter pageant called "The King Is Coming." The first time it was presented, it was great. People worked together to build sets and learn songs, and God used it in a mighty way. But after a few years, it was just a bathrobe and a bale of hay. People would fuss and gripe and then get on stage and tell the story of the cross. It was complete hypocrisy!

I pastored a church in Oklahoma in the 1980s where the auditorium desperately needed to be reconfigured. Time will not allow me to tell you all that was wrong with that facility, but I finally pushed to get some work done to make the place more conducive to worship. The last night before the renovations were set to begin, the lady who had chaired the original committee walked around the room crying and patting her hands on the walls as if we were going to destroy the Holy of Holies. It would have been funny if it hadn't been so pathetic.

I tell you all these stories to remind you that if you are going to see revival—if you are going to be a person God significantly uses—some things must go. You must lead people to die to things that don't matter or events that are no longer being used of God. If the horse is dead, dismount.

I saw this happen when I was a youth minister. I went to a church in Texas that had held youth camp in the same location since five years after the crossing of the Red Sea, I believe. They did camp the same way every year. And if we didn't go to that one place and do camp that one way, we weren't really having camp. Their events had become institutions. Certain things had to happen at a certain time. And when I suggested changing some things up. a few people fought me as if I were trying to tear the first five books out of the Bible.

They were arguing for their tradition, not for truth. They cared more about their initiations, plays, and softball leagues than they did about seeing kids come to Christ. I had to hold the line. Nothing I was trying to change had anything to do with the spiritual aspect of camp. It was all about the pranks and jokes, when in reality, this once great *camp* had become a joke because Jesus wasn't the center of attention.

They bucked when I added more Bible studies to the experience. They bucked when I said no more initiations of new kids at the camp. They bucked when I breathed. But with the changes we made, God broke through and we had an outpouring of the Spirit they hadn't seen in years. Sometimes the devil doesn't have to fight us; we provide our own fleshly opposition to the work of the Spirit.

The people and priests had come to believe that this antique bronze serpent had some mysterious power in it. They weren't spiritual; they were superstitious. One thing I try to emphasize in our annual ReFRESH™ Conference is that each year be different. God will deal with us in different ways at different times. We can't waste this year's conference hoping God will do exactly what He did in last year's conference. We have to avail ourselves to God and let Him work!

It's not right to try to recreate a moment, an event, or an experience. We are to bring ourselves before the Lord whose mercies are new every morning and see what He says to us in the here and now. We can say we are seeking the Lord when in reality we are settling for the secondary. We take the detour of tradition, denominational service, experience, holding an office, serving on an important committee, or being the lead soloist—and we miss Jesus. God doesn't bless methods. He looks for people who are like Jesus and blesses them.

BE THAT PERSON

The person who hinders revival could be just as sincere as Simon Peter on the Mount of Transfiguration, where he said something to the effect: "Let's build an altar here, us four and no more. Let's just have church 24/7 and stop worrying about the rest of the world." Peter wanted to camp on the mountain of a great experience.

But there is a cost in revival. And the person who leads it pays a price. It's never easy, but it's always right. Real revival is never cheap. The bronze serpent had to be destroyed. The leaders named in 2 Chronicles 29 were told about the problem. They had to lead the way. They had to answer the questions, deal with the concerns, and confront those who wanted to justify keeping an antique. They probably even heard, "You are grieving God. Don't you know God is the one who gave us this bronze serpent?"

If you are waiting for someone else to lead, it may not happen. Everything rises and falls on leadership. If a supposed leader sits out a call for revival, he disqualifies himself as a leader.

Hear me clearly: I don't hate tradition, but I do despise the worship of tradition. When we worship chairs, rooms, buildings, hymnals, or quarterlies as if they were built or written by God Himself, we are in danger of worshipping a bronze serpent. It's just Nehushtan, a piece of bronze.

Some things have to be destroyed. There can be no peaceful coexistence. It can't be shipped off to the Smithsonian or given to a Bible college or seminary. It just has to go. Otherwise we could find ourselves prostituting and perverting the blessings of God.

There is far more to Jesus than most of us are experiencing. There is more to what the Lord wants to do in our churches than what many of us are seeing. Surely Jesus didn't give His life so that we could build brick and mortar with no power inside. Surely He didn't die for programs and methods. Surely there is more to the Spirit-filled life than some of us are experiencing in our churches.

We need a person God can entrust with the message and ministry of revival. It will be a person who is willing to be misunderstood and even resisted within his own congregation. Jonathan Edwards was one of the great intellectual minds in American history. As pastor of the Congregational Church of Northampton, Massachusetts, he was burdened about the condition of the clergy and the church. In 1734 he began a series of sermons on "Justification by Faith Alone." He told them that their membership, rule keeping, and observance of the Lord's Supper were worthless to obtain entrance into heaven. It was as if Edwards was saying, "Your good works, your membership, and your taking of the Lord's Supper are just things of brass. They mean nothing unless you have met God and given your heart to Him." The reality was that a lot of the church members in his day needed to be saved, just as they do in our churches now. That in itself would bring a wave of revival.

"With no let-up Edwards hammered home an awe-inspiring concept of God's sovereignty. As sinners they deserved instant damnation if not for God's intervention. There was nothing they could do but to throw themselves on the mercy of God, who showed His overflowing goodness in giving His Son to die for them. The Holy Spirit used the sharp edges of this great preacher's sermons to cut deep. People couldn't sleep on Sunday nights. The next day they could talk of nothing but the amazing upheaval in the pulpit."[4]

Eventually the stirring of revival and awakening was in the air. Edwards made a covenant with God to preach the truth and to call people to repentance. The results changed his church and set in motion the first Great Awakening. God had found His man. One man's commitment to the truth led to conversions and impacted communities from miles around. The nation in her early days was touched by a movement of God.

May God raise up His next generation of leaders in our day, people He can use to usher in a sweeping new wave of heaven-sent revival in this time and place.

May one of them be me. May one of them be you.

CHAPTER 10

SURRENDER DEMANDS A TURNING ASIDE

2 Kings 18

When all that you are is available to all that God is, then all that God is is available to all that you are.

—Ian Thomas

"Do not come near here; remove your sandals from your feet, for the place on which you are standing is holy ground. . . . I am the God of your father, the God of Abraham, the God of Isaac, and the God of Jacob."

—Exodus 3:5–6

I SET ASIDE TIME every year to go to conferences. I need the time away. I need the input from other people to speak into my life and challenge me. Many of my peers in the ministry don't seem to share my enthusiasm for turning aside and getting away. For me it is a non-negotiable priority.

For nearly twenty years Terri and I have made a point of going to The Cove, the Billy Graham Training Center in Asheville, North Carolina. I've had the privilege of speaking there twice, but my most memorable times have been those conferences where we've gone to sit and soak. It's a relaxing, first-class facility where we can get away. Through the years we've heard Warren Wiersbe, Howard Hendricks, Erwin Lutzer, and Calvin Miller. I've read these men for years, but to hear them and meet them makes their books come alive. Now I can hear their voices as I read their books.

Most of those who attend these conferences are laymen. Unfortunately very few pastors attend. I was asked by one former director of The Cove why pastors didn't come. I told him, "The problem is, for many pastors, if we aren't on the program, we aren't attending. Too often I find my peers are no longer putting themselves in the position of a learner. But I've discovered I've never learned anything when I'm talking!" I always leave with pages of notes, fresh insights, new ideas, and areas that I need to ponder—as opposed to most preachers' conferences, where we mainly just get together and hang out.

Every year I also take at least three two-week study breaks. I pack a box of books and my computer and head to our mountain retreat to think, pray, write, and work on sermons. I need this time to stay ahead as a pastor. The day-to-day responsibilities of pastoring and the demands of ministry are too much to prepare sermons on the fly. I need time to let God speak to me. I need a fresh environment, a new view, and time alone. These times have been some of the most enriching of my life.

Moses was a busy man—a leader among the Egyptians, a mover and a shaker. Yet a casual observance of his first forty years reveals that he knew about Jehovah but hadn't gone deep enough to know God's ways. God had to take His man to the desert for forty years—certainly a humbling experience. Herding sheep was a far cry from the splendor and glory of Egypt, but it was necessary for Moses to remain usable.

> Now Moses was pasturing the flock of Jethro his father-in-law, the priest of Midian; and he led the flock to the west side of the wilderness and came to Horeb, the mountain of God. The angel of the LORD appeared to him in a blazing fire from the midst of a bush; and he looked, and behold, the bush was burning with fire, yet the bush was not consumed. So Moses said, "I must turn aside now and see this marvelous sight, why the bush is not burned up." When the LORD saw that he turned aside to look, God called to him from the midst of the bush and said, "Moses, Moses!" And he said, "Here I am." Then He said, "Do not come near here; remove your sandals from your feet, for

the place on which you are standing is holy
ground." He said also, "I am the God of your
father, the God of Abraham, the God of Isaac,
and the God of Jacob." Then Moses hid his
face, for he was afraid to look at God.
(Exod. 3:1–6)

Think about Moses' beginning. He had a godly birth mother,
Jochebed, whose name means "Jehovah is glory." Spared from
death by his parents and raised by Pharaoh's daughter, this
guy had the touch on his life. He was blessed, protected, and
favored. There were few like Moses.

His birth would have to be considered one of the most
remarkable in all of human history. His life changed the course
of a nation. His story resonates through history. He was a man
born at a time when God needed a man. Read what Stephen
said about Moses in Acts 7:

But as the time of the promise was approaching which God had assured to Abraham, the
people increased and multiplied in Egypt, until
there arose another king over Egypt who knew
nothing about Joseph. It was he who took
shrewd advantage of our race and mistreated
our fathers so that they would expose their
infants and they would not survive. It was at
this time that Moses was born; and he was
lovely in the sight of God, and he was nurtured

three months in his father's home. And after he had been set outside, Pharaoh's daughter took him away and nurtured him as her own son. Moses was educated in all the learning of the Egyptians, and he was a man of power in words and deeds. But when he was approaching the age of forty, it entered his mind to visit his brethren, the sons of Israel. And when he saw one of them being treated unjustly, he defended him and took vengeance for the oppressed by striking down the Egyptian. And he supposed that his brethren understood that God was granting them deliverance through him, but they did not understand. On the following day he appeared to them as they were fighting together, and he tried to reconcile them in peace, saying, "Men, you are brethren, why do you injure one another?" But the one who was injuring his neighbor pushed him away, saying, "Who made you a ruler and judge over us? You do not mean to kill me as you killed the Egyptian yesterday, do you?" At this remark, Moses fled and became an alien in the land of Midian, where he became the father of two sons. (vv. 17–29)

Notice that Moses was "lovely in the sight of God." Other translations say "well pleasing" or "most beautiful in the sight of God." The word was used of one who was a city dweller and was well-bred, polite, and eloquent. In Acts 7 and Hebrews 11 it is used of Moses to mean elegant in external form. Moses was a stud—stunning to look at. He had it all . . . but he was still lacking something. D. L. Moody wrote, "Moses spent his first forty years thinking he was somebody. He spent his second forty years learning he was a nobody. He spent his third forty years discovering what God can do with a nobody."[1]

Note how God had to humble Moses. After all, for the first forty years everyone around him served at his beck and call. He was royalty, raised to be the best. He had everything going for him and the power of Egypt behind him. But he was rejected by the Jews. His own people didn't respond as he had anticipated when he killed the Egyptian. His act of indignant courage didn't lead the people to rally behind him. Instead they rejected him, forcing Moses to run for his life.

Some have speculated that Moses knew a deliverer had been prophesied. Maybe he figured, "I'm the guy. I can handle this. I've got the background, training, and expertise to take on this task." He was both right and wrong. Yes, he was the man. But Moses had to be pruned before he could be used. God had to take him out of Egypt to get the worldly way of doing things out of his system.

His spiritual DNA needed to change. He had been trained in the proper life; now he needed to be pruned. Josephus says that the reigning Pharaoh had no sons, so Moses would have been in training to possibly take the throne. He was "educated in all the wisdom of the Egyptians." He was qualified to be a

Pharaoh but unqualified to lead God's people into a new dimension of faith.

Isn't that the way God always chooses to work? He bypasses our methods and ideas, working in such a way that no one can take the credit or the glory. God is looking for people like Paul described in 1 Corinthians 1:

> Where is the wise man? Where is the scribe? Where is the debater of this age? Has not God made foolish the wisdom of the world? For since in the wisdom of God the world through its wisdom did not come to know God, God was well-pleased through the foolishness of the message preached to save those who believe. For indeed Jews ask for signs and Greeks search for wisdom; but we preach Christ crucified, to Jews a stumbling block and to Gentiles foolishness, but to those who are the called, both Jews and Greeks, Christ the power of God and the wisdom of God. Because the foolishness of God is wiser than men, and the weakness of God is stronger than men.
>
> For consider your calling, brethren, that there were not many wise according to the flesh, not many mighty, not many noble; but God has chosen the foolish things of the world to shame the wise, and God has chosen the weak things of the world to shame the things

which are strong, and the base things of the
world and the despised God has chosen, the
things that are not, so that He may nullify
the things that are, so that no man may boast
before God. But by His doing you are in Christ
Jesus, who became to us wisdom from God, and
righteousness and sanctification, and redemp-
tion, so that, just as it is written, "Let him who
boasts, boast in the Lord." (vv. 20–31)

Paul reminds us that the people God uses have been called
and chosen not because they have degrees or eloquence or eti-
quette. This is a paradigm shift from many conferences you'll
attend, books you'll read, and speakers you'll hear these days.
They tell you preaching the Word is old-fashioned. But it's the
strength of our flesh that hinders us.

Most people are too big for God to use because they want to
be somebody. To be used of God, you have to be willing to be a
nobody. That's what servants do. God is not looking for celebrities; He's looking for servants.

BACKSIDE OF THE DESERT

Back in the early days of the Jesus Movement and contemporary Christian music, there was a sense of celebration if a
celebrity or singer proclaimed their faith in God. We all went
crazy when Bob Dylan came out with his album *Slow Train
Coming*. People were ecstatic when B. J. Thomas, who recorded
"Raindrops Keep Falling on My Head," began singing songs like

"Home Where I Belong." There were others, though most of them have waned or washed out.

My daughter, Erin Bethea, was the female lead in *Fireproof*. One day I asked her how she wanted people to pray for her. She said, "Pray I'm not another one of those 'Christian girls' who claims to be a believer but becomes more sensual as her career grows. Those girls have lost their ability to be role models and have embarrassed all of us with their provocative CD covers, photos in magazines, and compromised lifestyles."

Think it through: who influenced your life? Probably not a celebrity. Most likely it was someone "of whom the world is not worthy"—a nobody in the eyes of the world, perhaps, but a somebody in the kingdom.

We will not see revival when we give preachers rock star status. When the entourage for the TV preacher is greater than the number of original disciples, that's a pretty good indication you've got an ego working. We've confused size with sort, quantity with quality. God can do much with little. He doesn't need us, our stuff, our gifts, or our programs. He needs our availability and yieldedness. We need to turn away from man's ideas of what works. We need to look to the old, old story to see how God can (and will) do fresh and new things when we avail ourselves to Him. The problem is not the gospel. The problem is that we are too wise in our own eyes. We aren't desperate. We aren't hungry for revival. We're satisfied with status quo.

> **TO BE USED OF GOD, YOU HAVE TO BE WILLING TO BE A NOBODY. THAT'S WHAT SERVANTS DO.**

Moses was a man of power and persuasion. It's interesting to note, as we will see later in this chapter, that when he met God at the burning bush, he said he couldn't talk. Here was a charismatic personality, a man's man. But he wasn't in a position to be God's man yet. He needed to step back. He needed to get alone with God. Moses may have thought "getting away" meant a cruise down the Nile, but God's idea was to eat dust in the desert.

For forty years Moses was a forgotten man. Apparently no one came looking for him. He became a persona non grata. People moved on. Pharaoh found someone else to invest in. The Hebrews went back to building the pyramids. It's a long fall from the palace to a desert tent, working for your father-in-law. But I'm sure that over time Moses felt this was the way life would be until he died.

For God to do all He desires in us, however, there must come a time when we find ourselves on the backside of the desert, when we die to self, when we die to doing God's will on our own terms. F. B. Meyer said,

> Such experiences come to us all. We rush forward, thinking to carry all before us; we strike a few blows in vain; we are staggered with disappointment and reel back; we are afraid at the first breath of human disappointment; we flee from the scenes of our discomfiture to hide ourselves in chagrin. Then we are hidden in the secret of God's presence from the pride of

> man. And there our vision clears; our self life
> dies down; our spirit drinks of the river of God;
> our faith begins to grasp His arm, and to be the
> channel for the manifestation of His power;
> and thus at last we emerge to be His hand to
> lead an Exodus.[2]

Have you ever felt God has forgotten you? Have you ever found yourself on the backside of the desert? Did you have high aspirations for your life only to discover life has not turned out like you thought it would? Have you convinced yourself that your failure is final? It doesn't have to be. Brokenness can lead to blessings. Abandonment to *your* plans can position you to follow *God's* plans.

As long as you think you can help God out, you can't be what God wants you to be. Revival is not about helping God out; it's about surrender and abandonment. It may be that time has not passed you by but that you've been running ahead of God. You need to turn aside and get alone with Him.

Moses thought it was over. But it was just beginning. Only when his goose was cooked was he in a position to hear from the Lord. He had to find out that his strengths were actually his weaknesses. God didn't need his strengths. God wanted his availability.

A TURN FOR THE BETTER

So we come to Exodus 3. Moses was pasturing the flock of his father-in-law in the boondocks, the backwoods. He probably spent many days thinking about what he had been, even while God was working on what he would be. He was shepherding sheep for his father-in-law while God had plans for him to shepherd the flock of God.

You may have tried every method known to man. You've spent time, money, and energy trying to fix your life. You know there's something more, but honestly you wonder if it's for you. You find yourself with a bankrupt business, a dead-end marriage, or a miserable life in general. You may be a single parent and think God has forgotten you. You may feel like you've missed God, resigning yourself to being less than He intended.

Then you are in a good place at a good time for God to renew your life. He's just waiting for you to turn aside and surrender to Him.

There is no indication Moses was expecting a life-changing encounter that day. After forty years you just resign yourself to being a lowly shepherd. You shuffle along through life, making ends meet and making sure you check all the boxes. I doubt if Moses thought he was going to meet Jehovah God on that day, but he did. I can imagine that the sun rose that day, like every other day. There was probably a dull haze in the air as the mountains cast their normal shadows over the land. There was nothing new on the agenda. Just get up, get dressed, get the sheep moving, look for green pastures, and make sure no predators are on the horizon.

But suddenly things changed. The hour had arrived. There was going to be a voice, a turning aside, and a surrender to God. It was going to be a day that changed the life of Moses, the life of the people of God, and even the nation of Egypt forever. Nothing would ever be the same after this day.

I believe God is looking for a man, a remnant, a church that will expect the unexpected. Not long ago I was preaching on the presence of the Holy Spirit in the church. I am convinced one thing that is killing our churches is our attempt to do God's work on our terms. We are serving in the flesh, not in the spirit. I am weary to the point of exhaustion hearing the lame things God's people say. It's painfully apparent that they don't read their Bibles or pray persistently. They aren't desperate. They're operating in the flesh. As I travel around the country and speak in churches I hear:

"I'm doing the best I can."
"I'm trying harder."
"I'm going to do better."
"That's just the way I was raised."
"That's the way it's always been."

I want to cry out, "What worldly philosophies of life!" God never told us to try harder or do better. That's the flesh talking, and the flesh can't please God. He is looking for surrender, not your help.

God is looking for a church that is sick and tired of being sick and tired. We've done the one thing the enemies of Christ could never do to His church: we've made it boring. One thing I know from reading the accounts and activities from the book of Acts is that it wasn't boring! There was power. There was a presence of God that attracted the lost and struck down liars and hypocrites. Now *that* might bring revival!

Unfortunately most of us try to achieve spiritual means by carnal methods. We check the political winds to see if it's expedient. But a person without focus will never surrender. A person who worries what others think will never turn aside to meet God. Chuck Swindoll writes, "If you manipulate and connive and scheme and lie to get yourself to the top, don't thank God for the promotion!"

If we are going to have revival, there must be abandonment to God. Otherwise we'll fall prey to worldly and fleshly methods. We can't achieve spiritual things with worldly thinking. My fear is that we measure success in terms of money, buildings, budgets, and size, not prayer, faithfulness, holiness, and other kingdom-focused standards.

Moses could have stayed in Egypt. He could have been a great leader from the world's perspective, but he wouldn't have been God's man to deliver the people. He had to turn away before he could turn aside. The reason we fail to surrender is simple: pride. Until pride is gone, men will not humble themselves in tears at an altar. There will be no movement during the invitation. There will be resistance to any "thus says the Lord" preaching. The preacher who calls people to repentance will often be on the receiving end of more brickbats than bouquets.

If you want revival, you must be willing to pledge your head to heaven for the gospel. The carnal and the comfortably contented will resist it, but the remnant will stand with you. The question is: Will you surrender to the whims of whiners, or will you set your sails to catch the wind of the Spirit? Will you listen to God or to man? Moses listened. God spoke suddenly and broke forty years of silence. It could have been the first time Moses heard His voice. With one calling of his name, things changed. His life would never be the same.

Could it be that God has something on the horizon of your life that could change your direction and destiny? No matter how much you feel like you've failed, God knows where you are. He has not forgotten you. Get up every morning and expect the unexpected. Anticipate and pray that God will do a new work in you. Avail yourself to Him, abide in Him, and remember that apart from Him you can do nothing. Zero. Zip. Nada. Anything done by an individual or a church apart from the indwelling and overflowing of the Holy Spirit is nothing in God's eyes.

> **COULD IT BE THAT GOD HAS SOMETHING ON THE HORIZON OF YOUR LIFE THAT COULD CHANGE YOUR DIRECTION AND DESTINY?**

SACRED SURPRISES

Is anyone expecting revival today? Or have we lived so long without it that we don't expect it? The reason many don't meet God is they aren't expecting to meet God. Will you turn aside and see?

In John 12 we find that powerful phrase, "Sir, we wish to see Jesus" (v. 21). Del Fehsenfeld III tells us there are four things necessary to see Jesus: we must embrace His crucifixion; we must follow His example; we must join Him in His work; we must pay the cost of discipleship.[3] Isn't this in a sense what Moses did? He turned aside to see God and joined Him in His work. He was willing to pay the price to go back and deliver the people of God from slavery. Can we ask God to give us the ability to see what He sees and join Him in that work?

I remember Ron Dunn talking about how Manley Beasley could trust God for a meeting. Manley would get with God, and God would speak to his heart about the direction and even the results of a meeting. During most revival meetings the church expects nothing but a schedule interruption. Rarely am I in a church where they prepare, pray, and expect God to move.

I'm at a point in my life where I don't want to get on a plane or drive to someplace where they just want a speaker. If they aren't interested in hearing from God, why should I take the time to go? If they aren't believing God for the meeting, will I be casting pearls before swine? I'd rather be in a small meeting where the pastor believes God than in a big church where they see the meeting as an interruption or inconvenience planned by the pastor instead of an opportunity to encounter the Lord.

My friend Alan Stewart pastors outside Chattanooga, Tennessee. Several years ago I did a meeting in Alan's church. In those days he had a man who was giving him fits. This person wanted to run the church, run the preacher, and ruin everyone's life. But I quickly found the church also had a remnant ready for God.

On Tuesday night of the meeting, this man confronted Alan at the end of the service. First he tried to get me to agree with him. I told him he was acting in carnality and out of God's will and that he should submit to the pastor's authority. Then he turned on Alan. People stood around and watched this god-less man in absolute disgust. It was the breaking point.

The next night I showed up forty-five minutes early to pray with Alan. When I got there, dozens of folks were around the altar and in the pews, crying out to God. Their hearts were broken by what they had seen and heard, realizing they had allowed a carnal man to have his way for too long. They came, they wept, they prayed, they repented, and they asked God to move.

He did. That night we had an incredible moving of the Spirit. Today there are many in that church who still pray, seek, and long for a true heaven-sent revival. They are no longer content with business as usual.

Alan said he would rather resign than pastor a people who didn't want revival. I don't find many pastors with that kind of gumption, gut, and grace. We need more like him. I'm praying for God to raise up men who will hear from God, turn aside, and then get up and go out to do the will of God.

When's the last time you opened God's Word expecting Him to speak to you? When's the last time you walked into church expecting something to happen? When's the last time you were overwhelmed by the awareness of the presence of God? Are you really expecting Him to do anything in your life?

The good news is that if you've read this far, you must know there is something more for you than you are seeing right now.

HOLY GROUND MOMENTS

When God works, He probably won't work according to your preconceived ideas. You'll quickly realize you aren't in control. He won't fit into your thoughts, ideas, and ways. The psalmist said, "He made known His ways to Moses" (Ps. 103:7). The Lord spoke to the prophet Isaiah and said, "'For My thoughts are not your thoughts, nor are your ways My ways,' declares the LORD. 'For as the heavens are higher than the earth, so are My ways higher than your ways and My thoughts than your thoughts'" (Isa. 55:8–9).

We will never turn aside until we get beyond the notion that our lives are compartmentalized. There is no such thing as a Sunday theology that doesn't match a Monday-through-Saturday philosophy. What God says on Sunday works during the week. We have to turn aside from our worldly, wicked ways of thinking and begin to appropriate the mind of Christ. We must surrender all our selfish thoughts—our "I know better or more than God knows." We must surrender any notion that we can help God out. Only in an environment of surrender will we begin to expect the unexpected and look for God in even the mundane things of life.

Do you recall Jesus meeting the two travelers on the road to Emmaus, the men who later recognized Him when He broke the bread for them? It was just an ordinary event. But Jesus met them unexpectedly in the midst of their normal routine. Some of the greatest surprises in my life have come at unexpected times. My friend Roger Breland says he often prays, "Lord, today would be a good day for You to surprise me."

So don't miss the power of this phrase in Exodus 3:4—
"When the LORD saw that, he turned aside." Suddenly the sovereign took precedent over the sheep. The Hebrew word for
"when" indicates it was at the same time. In other words, God
started speaking *when* Moses turned aside; it was not until he
turned aside that God spoke. Vance Havner said:

> We face three tests in our journey here below.
> There is the test of the miraculous, the mar-
> velous, the great days when we are on the
> mountaintop of great success. It takes special
> grace for that because we tend to grow proud
> and drunken with the wine of victory. There
> is the test of the monotonous, the daily grind,
> and it takes great grace for the weeks and
> months when nothing much happens and life
> sinks into routine. But the greatest test is the
> mysterious chapter, when things happen that
> don't make sense, when God seems to have
> forgotten us, when nothing works out accord-
> ing to all our little plans—and when instead of
> a storybook ending, all crashes in unexplain-
> able confusion. Paul knew all three chapters—
> the third-heaven exaltation, daily care of the
> churches, the thorn in the flesh. Blessed is the
> man who is fortified by a double dose of Divine
> grace for the marvelous, the monotonous, and
> the mysterious.[4]

Moses also knew all three of these chapters. He certainly had the mountaintop experiences: meeting God on Mount Sinai to receive the Ten Commandments, seeing the backside of the glory of God. There was the monotonous: herding those sheep for decades, walking in the wilderness knowing the Promised Land was just over the horizon. And finally the mysterious: Why didn't the people of God embrace him when he slew the Egyptian? Why was he in the desert? Why was all his training being wasted herding sheep? In a moment there was a burning bush that got his attention. And he responded to the revelation.

Maybe the Spirit of God is seeking to get your attention. He's longing for you to stop your hectic pace long enough to realize that holiness is lacking in your routine. He wants to use you, but you won't slow down long enough. You're missing the burning bush while putting batteries in your flashlight.

When's the last time you had a holy ground moment? God may not work according to your agenda, but that doesn't mean He's not working. I'm sure over those forty years, Moses wondered if God would ever come through for him again. But as Jack Taylor said, "If you intend to go on with God, prepare for those times when he chooses to wean you from his having to always come through at your appointed time. If he can trust you to trust him, he will put you in tight places where your soul is enlarged and your vision is widened. Then you will be able to delight more in who he is than in what he does."[5]

When God gets your attention, He will in one way or another remove from you that which hinders you. He will impoverish you to show you His riches in Christ. He will take what you have trusted in and either give it new meaning or show you it is no longer necessary.

That's because we can miss holy ground moments by being self-absorbed. Face it: most of us live dull lives. We won't be featured on television. Our lives won't be made into a movie. No one is going to write a biography about us. But God wants to meet us, speak to us, and reveal Himself to us. To hear Him, however, we have to turn aside and turn to Him.

God called Moses personally by name. God knows your name too. He knows your gifts, talents, and weaknesses. He knows the baggage you carry and the possibilities you hold. Not only did God know Moses, but He also knew Moses' father: "I am the God of your father, the God of Abraham, the God of Jacob." Please don't miss this. God was saying to Moses, "I knew your daddy. I know your family. I know how your life was spared. I was there. I orchestrated it. I'm totally aware of you and your life."

David testified to God's omniscience in Psalm 139: "You scrutinize my path and my lying down, and are intimately acquainted with all my ways. Even before there is a word on my tongue, behold, O Lord, You know it all. You have enclosed me behind and before, and laid Your hand upon me. Such knowledge is too wonderful for me; it is too high, I cannot attain to it" (vv. 3–6).

Don't think God doesn't know and see. God told Moses, "I'm the God your father served. Not only do I know you and your family, but I'm also very aware of what's going on with

My people. I have seen. I have heard. I am aware of their suf-
ferings." God is not indifferent to our needs. He is touched by
what touches us. Don't think for one moment that God is not
aware of our culture wars, godless hedonism, abortion, same-sex
marriages, watered-down gospel, and dying churches. He knows
it all. He knows better than we know, and He is not surprised,
unaware, or indifferent.

One thing I know about revival: it involves a restoration
of understanding regarding the holiness of God. In true revival
and surrender, people aren't chummy with Him anymore.
Today's spirituality is too chummy. We've lost the awe, reverence, and respect He demands and deserves. There is no revival
among a flippant and casual people. God is not interested in
making Himself more user-friendly. He is looking for people
who understand who they're dealing with. We're talking about
the Holy One of Israel, the Lord God Almighty. If we will bow
before Him in glory, I doubt we should be chest-bumping and
high-fiving on Earth.

Where's the respect? Where's the awe and the wonder? God
may be the God of my father. He may be the one who knows me
by name. But that doesn't mean I can get overly familiar. I still
have to take off my shoes. I still need to reverence His holiness.
I'm a sinner; He is sovereign God of all. There's still a difference
between God and man.

If we ever got a grip on the holiness of God, I doubt we'd
have a mosh pit. We'd more than likely try to hide our faces
in a pit out of fear and reverence. Moses hid his face, but we
strut into church. As I look around, I don't see many who walk

humbly before God. The fear of God is a missing element. In our attempts to be warm and intimate in our worship, we may have missed the awe of God. We sing personal songs and sometimes forget the great songs filled with doctrine and truth about His majesty. We must avoid the temptation of modern Western Christianity to be casual in approaching the God of glory.

Mike Minter, in his excellent book *A Western Jesus*, writes, "Statistics show that professing believers live no differently than the world. Something is clearly wrong when followers of Christ are not following. Something is clearly wrong when believers don't really believe. . . . We have diluted, watered down and compromised Jesus in our western culture to the point that he is hardly recognizable. We have made Jesus fit our culture to the point that he follows us. We call the shots. We direct his steps."[6]

I would also add that we can't have a sweeping move of God as long as we dictate the time or the look of it. Vance Havner often said, "Churches talk about holding a revival. Someone needs to turn one loose." When God is in control, you're not. Where there is surrender, you will automatically reconsider who Jesus really is and what He expects.

God basically said to Moses, "I may be the God of your father, but don't get cute with Me." Two other accounts in Scripture also illustrate this point. When John was exiled on the Isle of Patmos—a long way from those intimate days during Jesus' earthly ministry—He saw God and fell on his face "like a dead man" (Rev. 1:17). Similarly, when Peter had fished all night and caught nothing, Jesus came to him on the shore and told him to cast the nets again. When their nets were miraculously filled to overflowing, Peter said, "Go away from me, Lord, for I am a sinful man!" (Luke 5:8).

Turning aside is an act of deliberate obedience. It is an event followed by a process. It may be an experience, but it continues with an abiding relationship. It may be a moment in time, but it is a timeless moment. It may be a step, but it's the beginning of a walk. When you turn aside, expect God to give you a specific assignment.

IT'S YOUR TURN

God revealed Himself to Moses to reveal His mission. Look again at Exodus 3:10: "Therefore, come now, and I will send you to Pharaoh, so that you may bring My people, the sons of Israel, out of Egypt." God gave Moses an assignment. The turning aside is never just about you going deeper with God. It's also about God using you to make a difference. Surrender leads to something God wants you to do. Moses was an old man, but God still had something for him to do. Paul reminded the Ephesians that "we are His workmanship, created in Christ Jesus for good works, which God prepared beforehand so that we would walk in them" (Eph. 2:10).

If I am in Christ, I expect to be serving.

If I am His workmanship, there's work to be done.

While we are justified by faith alone, we are not justified by a faith that *is* alone. Faith works, not only *for* salvation but *because of* salvation. The reason people in the church don't serve and use their spiritual gifts is because they've never surrendered. They still think they are large and in charge. They haven't taken up their cross and died to self. In reality, they may not be saved. We may be trying to get lost people to act like saved people. And we'll never see revival and surrender until the lost turn aside from their sin. Our greatest opportunity for evangelism will probably first be within a revived church when lost church members get saved.

God didn't tell Moses to go start a church or have a Bible study at the burning bush and invite all his friends over for a wiener roast. Nor did God listen to Moses when he started making excuses. The good news after forty years in the desert was that Moses had torn up his résumé. He had forgotten all about his press clippings and his scrapbooks. He had come to an honest confession: "Who am I?" He was stripped of all his pride and self-sufficiency, his ego and impetuous nature. Now he was reduced to size—the size of a man God could use.

> Moses said to the LORD, "Please, Lord, I have never been eloquent, neither recently nor in time past, nor since You have spoken to Your servant; for I am slow of speech and slow of tongue." The LORD said to him, "Who has made man's mouth? Or who makes him mute or deaf, or seeing or blind? Is it not I, the LORD?"
> (Exod. 4:10–11)

I love the fact that God kept this exchange in the Scriptures. Moses wrote it himself, and it's not very complimentary (yet another sign to me that the Bible is inspired). Most of us would never allow our frailties and failures in print for all to see. Every time Moses made an excuse, God answered loud and clear. He said, "I made you the way you are. I know what you can do and can't do. Where I guide, I provide. You can't give Me an excuse that I can't meet. Here's what I need done, now go do it."

The Scriptures remind us over and over again that our God is sufficient—and that He uses surrendered people:

"My God will supply all your needs according to His riches in glory in Christ Jesus." (Phil. 4:19)

"For when I am weak, then I am strong." (2 Cor. 12:10)

"I can do all things through Him who strengthens me." (Phil. 4:13)

"And it is no longer I who live, but Christ lives in me." (Gal. 2:20)

"My grace is sufficient for you, for power is perfected in weakness." (2 Cor. 12:9)

Is it time for you to turn aside? Have you been making excuses too long? What's in your hand? What has God given you that He wants to use for His glory? He took Moses' staff and used it as an instrument of deliverance. You've got more available to you now than you are using. You know more than you are living up to. Turn aside. Look to Jesus. Let Him use your surrendered life as a powerful tool for His glory. You may be just the person He is looking for to lead the next great movement of God.

When you surrender, God will take what you already have and use it for greater glory. He said to Moses, "'Take in your hand this staff, with which you shall perform the signs.'. . . So Moses took his wife and his sons and mounted them on a donkey, and returned to the land of Egypt. Moses also took the staff of God in his hand" (Exod. 4:17, 20).

God has done something for us; now He wants to do something *to* us, *in* us, and *through* us. But we've got to turn aside. If we fail to turn aside, we may spend our entire lives in a mundane existence and never experience all God has for us in Christ Jesus.

The story is told of an old Indian chief in the 1800s who was forced off his land and pushed west. He came to a mountain pass, but he was too old and weak to climb the mountain, so he sent some of his young warriors to climb it. He told them to try to get to the summit and to pick up things along the way that would help the old chief know what was up there. When they came back, they had nothing in their hands, but there was great joy on their faces. When the old chief asked why they brought nothing back, they said, "We saw the sea."

What have you seen on your journey? Have you spent your life picking up a rock here and there, or have you seen the sea? Have you seen beyond what you know right now? Have you gotten a glimpse of what God might have for you just over the horizon?

God may or may not allow you to see revival. But you can surrender, turn aside, pray, and believe Him for it. Even if it doesn't come to our nation or to your church, it can come in your heart. What are you waiting for? Turn aside. You've been on this journey long enough. It's time to stop making excuses and start expecting the unexpected.

You may be walking around in a desert feeling deserted. You may feel as if God has forgotten you and His people. But wait— just over the next hill, there may be an opportunity for God to use you as an instrument of revival. Keep your eyes open, your heart sensitive, and your ears in tune with what He might be trying to do. The times are tough. The terrain seems impossible. But all is not lost.

CHAPTER 11

REFLECTIONS ON REVIVAL

Let God have your life; he can do more with it than you can.
—D. L. Moody

Let Your hand be upon the man of Your right hand, upon the son of man whom You made strong for Yourself. Then we shall not turn back from You; revive us, and we will call upon Your name.
—Psalm 80:17–18

THE FACT YOU HAVE READ this book is an indication that you know we need revival. And that's good—because until revival becomes a personal issue, it will never become a corporate reality.

Yes, in our desire to see revival in our churches, we could miss it in our own hearts. It's much easier to pray for God to change our churches and nation than to ask God to change *us*. There is a difference between a sovereign move of God across the land that in some sense is unexplainable and irresistible, and the revival of the heart, soul, and mind. This kind of revival may not change a nation, but it can change us. It has happened among the remnant in past days, and it can happen in you if you'll make yourself available to Him today.

In April 2009 Anne Graham Lotz was speaking in Jacksonville, Florida, sharing about a time in the 1990s when her life was bombarded by one attack after another. She said that in the midst of those multiple storms, "the cry of my heart was, 'Just give me Jesus.' I want a fresh touch from heaven." In an interview with *Baptist Press* during that meeting, she said, "We need to experience old-timey revival. We need to talk about hell. We need to talk about heaven. We need to talk about the fact that there's only one way to God—through faith in Jesus. We need to get back to some of the basics of the gospel and God's call in our lives and how He would use us."[1]

With this personal appeal in mind, I've asked a few friends to help me answer some questions about revival in this final chapter of the book:

- *Jimmy Draper* is the former president of LifeWay Christian Resources and a former president of the Southern Baptist Convention. He has been called a pastor's pastor.

- *Junior Hill* is an evangelist who has traveled America speaking in churches and conferences for nearly fifty years. His heart for the church and for the lost is known across the land.

- *Roy Fish* is professor emeritus of evangelism at Southwestern Baptist Theological Seminary. He is known for his commitment to evangelism and revival. His book on the revival of 1858, *When Heaven Touched Earth*, is a classic, comprehensive work on the subject.

- *Mark Bearden* is a revival historian and student of revival who has served with Life Action Ministries for more than twenty years.

- *Sammy Tippit* is known across the world as an evangelist with a great heart for a revived church. He has spoken around the globe on the subject of revival.

- *Ronnie Floyd* has been a pastor for more than thirty years and has a true heart for revival. He currently pastors First Baptist Church in Springdale, Arkansas.

- *Alan Stewart* is a pastor who has been used of God to do a deep work in Soddy Daisy, Tennessee. For years he has traveled to India as an evangelist, seeing tens of thousands come to Christ. His heart for revival and a deeper work of God is what motivates him.

When you think about revival, what comes to mind?

"A sovereign intervention of God in which His presence is demonstrated, our sins are made clear, and a renewed hunger for His likeness falls upon us."—JH

"Personal revival is a deep work of the Holy Spirit in the heart of the believer that brings change to his or her life and results in making them more like Christ. Revival in the church is what happens when God visits His people in such a way that the church is transformed and has a transforming affect on the community."—ST

"Revival is the manifest presence of God. It is when God unveils His power and glory to a point in which it is witnessed by most and experienced by many."—RFloyd

"The power and presence of God so evident that nothing else matters except being in harmony with Him and His purpose in our lives."—JD

"When I think about revival, my thoughts go both to local church revival and revival of a more general nature, as far as its extent is concerned. When I think of local church revival, the first thing I think of is extended worship services lasting for several hours as the Spirit is permitted to freely work in a congregation. Time means very little in a real work of the Spirit. During this period personal testimonies regarding what God is doing in one's life are usually shared. This includes discreet confession of sin, words of praise and thanksgiving for victories won—even in that service—and requests for prayer. Generally if this occurs, lost people are brought under deep conviction, and most of them are saved in the service. When I think of more general revival, I usually think in terms of an unusual God-consciousness gripping an area and producing the same results as mentioned above. It really cannot be revival unless large numbers of people are being saved."—*RFish*

"I think of the life-changing presence of God. (I take that phrase seriously! If what we call His 'presence' isn't changing us, we are missing something.) It is God manifesting Himself in such a way that His glory, power, and love become our overwhelming awareness. In light of these things, our sin becomes loathsome to us."—*MB*

"First and foremost, I think of a conscious awareness of the Lord's presence. Secondly, with the awareness of His presence, change is inevitable. It is impossible for a man to perceive the holiness of God and remain the same. He will go away either tender at heart or thicker at heart. In the history of genuine moves of God, the holiness of His presence—like throwing a pebble into the river—was at the center of a multitude of ripple effects of change."—*AS*

What do you believe is keeping us from experiencing revival in America?

"The insatiable hunger for self-gratification—the desire for comfort, pleasure, and almost total disregard for God's holiness. The need for prominence and earthly praise."—*JH*

"Pride and selfishness, which is expressed through materialism, prayerlessness, and busy lifestyles."—*ST*

"The impotent, indifferent condition of the church. The number-one religion in America is self-worship. We engage in self-exaltation, self-preservation, and self-relaxation, loving ourselves and pleasures more than God."—*RFloyd*

"The most obvious one to me is that we have a large percentage of our people who are not saved. This robs the church of the spiritual unity and passion necessary for real revival to come. The second is the spirit of self-confidence that makes God unnecessary for the work of the church. We can do it ourselves! We don't need God because we are smart and capable and know what is best for our church and our lives. The most important reason is that we have no passion for revival. Revival is a historical term for most of us, and we don't know what it is and why we need it. Revival can only come out of a severe judgment of God, as in the Old Testament, or out of a deep spiritual hunger in the hearts of people to experience it. We have neither right now. At least we don't recognize the hand of God's judgment, so we are not driven to the desperation necessary for revival."—*JD*

> **IF AMERICA IS EVER LAID TO WASTE, MUCH OF THE BLAME WILL LIE AT THE DOORS OF THE CHURCH.**

"Material prosperity which breeds a strong sense of self-sufficiency is probably doing as much as anything to keep our nation from experiencing revival. Materially prosperous, self-sufficient people don't sense a need for God or what God can do."—*RFish*

"There is a quote from the Welsh Revival: 'Once you've experienced the fire, you are never content with the smoke.' We have become content with the smoke. We throw water on the altar, not so we can allow God to prove Himself like Elijah, but simply to produce more smoke: the smoke of numbers, excitement, emotional experience, being relevant, etc. As long as we are content with these, we will never see Him. We must become like David in Psalm 63, recognizing we are in a dry and barren place, passionately longing for Him, remembering what it is to behold His power and glory."—MB

"While I realize that revival is a sovereign work of God, it is increasingly obvious that leaders have failed to turn the sails to capture God's wind of revival. It is a matter of being in the right position, but the lights of truth and conviction have been dimmed to such a degree that few know where that position is any longer. We have grown comfortable to the dark, and the following consequences have resulted: 1) God is put on display in the "house of Dagon" and mingled with other gods in the land for the sake of being politically correct. 2) Shallow and sinful interpretations of the Word being preached have created a deep chasm of unbelief. 3) Emphasis upon the cross has diminished and has opened other avenues to salvation. 4) In boasting of tolerance, we have utterly forfeited convictions. To state it simply, I believe the one thing that is keeping us from experiencing revival is the fact the Lord cannot trust us with revival!"—AS

"If America is ever laid to waste, much of the blame will lie at the doors of the church. We have the answer to the needs of man, but are we understanding of the times in which we live?"—*Vance Havner*

What is the role of prayer in revival?

"Prayer is obviously essential—however, strange as it may seem, many of the real moves of God I have been blessed to see arrived on the unexpected wings of His sovereignty. Many of them came without much human fanfare or earthly preparation. While there are principles in His Word that must always be honored, there seems to be no magic formula that assures us He will always show up when we ask Him to."—JH

"It is vital. When God gets ready to move among His people, He looks for those whose hearts are hungry and thirsty. Such hunger and thirst will always be manifested through people seeking His face. When a deep thirst for revival takes place through prayer, that often *is* the revival. We encounter Christ, and that is revival. He moves in our hearts and transforms our lives."—ST

"Prayer is the means of communicating with God our honest condition, appealing to Him for a new, fresh movement in our lives. Prayer coupled with fasting is God's means to humble His people. Prayer, fasting, and the Word of God result in a dynamic trio that can usher us to the point of being where God wants us to be, but revival is a sovereign work of God, and He alone gives it. We cannot jump through hoops to get it, but we must be where He wants us to be personally and as a church."—RFloyd

"Prayer is the key to revival. It is not so much our asking God for revival as it is placing ourselves before God for Him to use as He sees fit and longing for His presence. Without this spirit of surrender and desperation, revival will not come."—JD

"Prayer is the one indispensable factor in revival. I heard Edwin Orr say there has never been a revival of any proportion which did not begin with prayer. Prayer is essential for the beginning and also the sustaining of revival. Matthew Henry said, 'When God designs a mercy, He sets His people praying.' True prayer by its very nature is a recognition of our need. God set His people praying so that when He comes, He has a prepared people who will give Him proper glory for His arrival."—MB

"Prayer seems to be a significant ingredient in every revival throughout history. The depth of our praying reveals the true pursuits and motives of our heart. It was the earnest and genuine 'prayer requests' that paused Jesus amidst the crowds, rewarding the one who dared to believe Jesus could answer their prayer. I once heard it said, 'It was the angel that fetched Peter from prison, but it was prayer that fetched the angel.' How often do pastors or churches even ask the Lord for revival any longer? Perhaps we 'have not because we ask not.'"—AS

What are the indicators that most concern you regarding our need for revival, specifically within the church?

"One of the most obvious is the strange disappearance of Holy Spirit conviction. That which once made us weep now makes us laugh. Sin is no longer offensive, and any mention of man's failures are viewed as negative and unwholesome. The disdain of strong biblical doctrine has brought the American church dangerously close to apostasy—and the tragedy is that most church attendees are not even aware of it."—JH

"Busyness is the biggest culprit of this day. We have worked and played God out of our lives. We are now reaping the fruit of such frantic lifestyles. The moral decline within the church runs parallel to the busy lifestyles of her members."—*ST*

"The church is impotent. The church is stuck in structure, and the wineskins need to be discarded. The church is so time-conscious, it is difficult for even God to have an opportunity to give a divine interruption. The church's indifference concerns me greatly. We have churches more excited about being cool and dead than being biblical and alive. We are more bent on having crowds than building a church. Success is determined more by numbers of people and dollars than by whether or not God showed up and moved mightily."—*RFloyd*

"The confusion and chaos and contention within most churches. I preach in many churches each year, and it is rare to find a church that has harmony and passion for God's presence and power. Also, the power struggles that take place with most churches, people, lay people, and pastors and staff alike, striving for control. Lack of respect for the pastor and ministers of the church. Lack of understanding for the role of the pastor and deacons in the church. Both are servants of God."—*JD*

"I am most concerned about a lack of brokenness on the part of God's people. General indifference to the spiritual dearth in which we are living is a matter of deep concern."—*RFish*

"Simply put: powerlessness. Where are the changed lives? Where are the transformed communities? Where are the young men and women selling out to the mission field? Where are the Jim Elliots and Amy Carmichaels of our next generation? When we lose our power, we lose the respect of the world. Anyone will associate with us, and no one holds us in high regard. You can point to any number of sins in the church, and the solution is the power of God changing lives."—MB

"Churches all across America are empty. Not just in numbers, but primarily in substance. Over the last fifteen years I have observed these indicators that concern me with how far away my generation is from genuine revival: 1) Worship is no longer about pleasing God but rather pleasing ourselves through personal preferences in worship. Worship is more about 'getting' than 'giving' anymore. 2) Our generation would rather be entertained than exhorted. 3) Leaders are more interested in numbers and accomplishments than holiness. 4) Prayer is given little emphasis and exercised mostly out of formality. There are so few willing to wait, watch, and wail in the upper room until power comes from on high! Old timers called it 'praying through,' but our generation appears to be 'through praying!' 5) A lack of brokenness and desperation in our lives. We have become the Laodicean church—'rich and increased with goods and have need of nothing.' Our dry eyes are an outward evidence of an inward void. 6) The church has lost respect and its voice of authority to the world. We are no longer the measuring stick the world looks to for the standard of living."—AS

"A revival is a work of God's Spirit among God's people when they get right with God, themselves, and others. It means conviction of sin; repentance of sin; reconciliation and restitution; separation from the world; submission to the lordship of Jesus Christ and being filled with the Spirit."—*Vance Havner*

What are the key elements of a movement of God?

"It wasn't manufactured. It was a work of God. But there were people asking God to do something out of the ordinary. There was an acute awareness of sin among the people, and with it an intense desire to realign themselves with God. It was repentance driven, not worship driven. However, the kindness of God that produced repentance freed hearts for glorious worship! There was lasting fruit. I recently had a woman approach me, telling me that twenty years ago God changed her and her husband's life in a Life Action Summit. The change affected their own relationships with God, their purity, their marriage, how they raised their children, everything. That's the result of a real move of God."—MB

"Over these past forty-two years, I have had the joy of seeing a number of what I believe to be authentic revivals. In every single one there was marked awareness of His presence, the absence of frivolity, and a keen personal examination of our hearts."—JH

"My ministry was born in a revival in a local church. It began with a praying pastor. He refused to believe his circumstances, but believed that God would send revival among the young people, even though they were not interested. He called for public meetings in the church to seek God for revival. The revival broke when a leader publicly repented of sins. When he confessed before the church his failures, the Spirit of God fell on that small congregation. Brokenness and repentance swept through those in attendance. The crowds grew daily until we had to move out of the church and on to the college campus.

They continued to grow until we finally ended up in the civic center. There was racial reconciliation among the young people. Notorious drug dealers were converted to Christ. Christ was honored in the secular media."—*ST*

"In 1995 I saw and experienced our church moving through a season of major revival. Coming off my first forty-day time of fasting and prayer, God broke me, and the church got a new pastor. Also on that day, June 4, I got a new church. The service went almost three hours on Sunday morning. Sunday night, 70 percent of the Sunday morning crowd was back for four hours before God in confession of sin and restitution. All of this led to several weeks of a major movement of God. If someone were to ask me, I'd say that everything we do at our church today goes back to those moments in 1995. The key elements: the pastor became broken before God through fasting and prayer, responsiveness of the people to the Holy Spirit, confession of sin, restitution, and major prayer."—*RFloyd*

"Key elements in what I have seen of revival are brokenness, a willingness to be totally clean with God, and relationships which have been broken made right and restored to love."—*RFish*

"At best I can only say I have seen a gentle stirring of the Lord. I was only five years old, but there are some significant things that stand out about it in my memory: strong conviction, repentance of sin, multitude of salvations, and demonic interruption. The revival was strong in emotions but wasn't lasting in duration."—*AS*

I thought it was important to ask these men what the role of the pastor is in revival. If you are a pastor, read carefully. If you are not, pray diligently for your pastor. Come alongside him in believing prayer.

"I used to think more that he was to avoid 'touching the ark' and fade into the background. I now believe in the necessity of his continuing to shepherd in the midst of what God is doing. Revival does not mean instant maturity and wisdom. Especially today, when our people are so biblically illiterate, there is more of a danger of falling into excesses, or as Manley Beasley put it, 'chasing the tangents.' Particularly during testimony times, there is a need to give biblical correction and input. I remember being in the midst of a genuine move of God among college students. As they sincerely shared what God was doing, I was struck by how many unbiblical statements they made. I would say to the pastor that Spurgeon's words hold true: 'The true preacher should be *more* holy than his people, lest he be unfit for office. He should be *as* holy lest he be a hypocrite. Depth of walk with God is the most essential qualifier for the responsibility of God's presence.'"—MB

"The pastor must openly preach and challenge his church to live in the constant hunger for revival. A pulpit that has no call for personal repentance and holiness will be ignored by the congregation. Few churches will ever rise above the desperation of their leaders. Satisfied pastors produce indifferent saints."—JH

"The pastor should be a model of hungering and thirsting for revival. People will follow strong pastoral leadership which

is characterized by humility and holiness. If the people see the
pastor genuinely crying to God for revival, they will be more
likely to seek God for revival."—*ST*

"The pastor's burden for revival, transparency about his own
life needing revival, and his leadership to the people to enter
on that journey with him are absolutely imperative. The role of
the people is to be under the leadership of that pastor, praying
diligently for God to reveal His direction to them through him.
If he has no interest in revival, then they have to intercede
mightily for God to work in his life."—*RFloyd*

"Before a shepherd would take his sheep on their yearly
pilgrimage, the shepherd would walk
down the paths where he would lead
his sheep. He did so in order to recognize enemy hideouts, to clear waters
of pollution, to remove poisonous
plants, and to determine the most fertile pastures. A pastor sets the tone of

FEW CHURCHES WILL EVER RISE ABOVE THE DESPERATION OF THEIR LEADERS.

the spiritual atmosphere, and it is difficult to lead people somewhere you are not willing to go yourself first. It is interesting
that a church takes on the heart, personality, and vision of its
pastor. In the history of revivals, they rarely began with a multitude of people. Clovis Chappell once wrote: 'The great awakenings of the past have not been begun by the gathering in of
the many, but by the deeper consecration of the few.' A man
or woman full of the Spirit of God is such a rare oddity. Others
take notice and are drawn to the work of God in unsuspecting
servants."—*AS*

"I have never seen local church revival where the pastor did not support what God was doing. Both the people and the pastor must reflect the things I have already mentioned."—*RFish*

"Revivals in history have generally risen from the people. The great awakenings were essentially lay movements. There were some notable preachers during those times, but mostly the Spirit of God moved in the hearts of the lay people to place themselves before God in a way that He could move in their midst. I personally believe that God uses the pastor to lead the church, but few pastors seem to feel the need for a great revival. Revival would surely come if pastors and people became burdened and passionate about the need for revival."—*JD*

VANCE HAVNER

The greatest revivalist I ever met was Vance Havner. He preached to call out the remnant, to stir the saints. He understood that a revival would not solve all our problems, but it would give us something we haven't had before or something we've lost. Pentecost didn't result in the conversion of all of Jerusalem, but Jerusalem was never the same after Pentecost. God is calling out a people for Himself, and revival furthers that purpose.

Havner believed that revival never started with singing but with sighing. Revival always begins with conviction, prayer, and repentance at the altar on our knees. God's house needs to be a dreadful place before it can be a delightful place. When the carnal are comfortable and status quo is the order of business, there is no revival. Repentance always precedes rejoicing. God is knocking at the door of the church as the Divine Disturber, and we've got "Do Not Disturb" signs on our doors.

Here we are in the twenty-first century, upset because of the cultural decay. We bemoan the policies of Washington but do not rebuke the backslidden in our churches. We complain about the prevalence of worldly thinking and its affect on the family, but the family of God has divorced itself from the Father. We have more prodigals than prophets. Havner would say of us what he said of a previous generation: "It does little good to wring our hands and lament the inroads of television, ball games and other attractions on our church attendance. If we do not have enough vitality to compete with all this, maybe it doesn't matter much whether we have our meetings or not. If the gospel means so little to us that it can be sidetracked by every sideshow that blows into town, it wouldn't mean much if such people did gather to go through the hollow motions of a dead faith. It is certain that the answer does not lie in stubbornly holding on to the form when the power has departed. We seem to be preaching and promoting something while most of its adherents wouldn't miss it much if they lost it! There is something frightfully wrong when we have to beg most of our crowd to come to church to hear about it."

I remember Dr. Havner saying, "If I were a non-Christian who dropped into the average church during a so-called revival and saw a fraction of the membership trying to get more recruits for the army of the Lord when most of the outfit had already gone AWOL, I would conclude either that Christianity is not what it is supposed to be or else we have been sold a cheap and easy brand, inoculated with a mild form until we are almost immune to the real thing."

Outside of his family, nothing influenced young Vance more than the church and revivals. Even in his eighties you could see the longing in his eyes and hear it in his voice—the desire for one good old-fashioned, Holy Ghost revival. At Corinth Church they always had their revival meeting the last week of July. In fact the Baptists had their meeting in July, and the Methodists had theirs the first week of August. Havner would say, "Some of us Baptists got revived in July and went over to the Methodists the next week for a second blessing. If a revival had broken out at some other time, it would have been postponed until the last week in July!" He noted:

> During those horse and buggy days, preaching
> through a summer revival in the country was
> a herculean task. That night in the crowded
> church, where screens were unknown, kerosene
> lamps flickered, babies slept on pallets, dogs
> barked, and horses neighed outside. In spite
> of all the competition, those faithful exhort-
> ers managed to get the message across. There
> was loud preaching and off-key singing. People
> got happy and shouted. Nowadays I never see
> such shouting unless someone wins an automo-
> bile or a mink coat on a TV show. Plain folks
> who could never have made a speech before a
> congregation were so filled with happiness that

they lost all their inhibitions. We could use some of that joy that swept England with the Wesleys, Wales in the great revival of the early 1900s, and the Colonies in the great American Awakenings.

I remember one dear lady who could go up and down the aisles with her eyes shut and never run into a bench. I don't know what kind of radar she had, but I wish we could recover the explosive as well as the expulsive power of a new affection that sent rural saints out church doors with heaven's glow on their homely faces. There may have been some extremism but what passes for worship in most of our cold sanctuaries today is nothing to brag about in comparison.

In his book *Three Score and Ten* he wrote:

Such revivals have been caricatured and made the subject of jokes that approach blasphemy. Those shouting sessions had their faults and failings, but there was one tremendous difference between them and the imitations worked up these days: they were genuine; there was nothing phony about them; they were not simulating something. Nobody dreamed of that under the preaching we heard in those days!

Nobody was in the mood for cheap, superficial ham acting—they were facing sin and hell and judgment, and there was nothing funny about it. What I saw in old Corinth was not a show—it was an encounter with God. Some of it was crudely expressed and imperfectly demonstrated but it was not a masquerade. It was understood then what we highbrows have not discovered apparently, that the gospel was never meant for entertainment. In those days, believers talked about a blessing, not a religious experience.

Havner described the preaching as more of a filibuster than something to impress the saints with eloquence. An old saying from the turn of the century went something like this: "If you are preaching in town, take your best suit; if you are preaching in the country, take your best sermon." The revival preachers of Havner's influential years preached the Bible without apology. They didn't care if it offended a particular listener. They would let God be true and every man a liar.

MORE REVIVAL REFLECTIONS

During the Albany ReFRESH™ Conference in 2008, we had a panel discussion on the subject of revival, which included Tom Elliff, Bill Stafford, Ken Jenkins, Daniel Simmons, Allen Atkins, and myself. What follows are the stories these men shared during the discussion.

- *Tom Elliff* is now in itinerant ministry, having served as a pastor and foreign missionary. He is a former president of the Southern Baptist Convention and believes the only hope for our nation is a sweeping revival. He is a featured speaker at all our ReFRESH™ Conferences and is in demand around the world.
- *Bill Stafford* picked up the mantle from Manley Beasley, heading up the International Congress on Revival in Budapest and South Africa. Bill has been a pastor and has traveled the world for many years, preaching the message of Christ, the Spirit-filled life, and abandonment to Christ.
- *Daniel Simmons* is my "co-pastor" who now serves as pastor of Mt. Zion Baptist Church here in Albany. Daniel is a dear friend and has been a featured speaker at the conference from day one.
- *Ken Jenkins* is an author and *National Geographic* award-winning photographer. He travels the country using his photography to teach spiritual truths on the deeper life. He speaks at all our ReFRESH™ Conferences and has been with us since its inception.
- *Allen Atkins* is a pastor who was deeply influenced at an early age by the ministry of Ms. Bertha Smith, renowned missionary to China. His heart for revival is lived out in his preaching on the subject.

What is your first remembrance of revival?

"It occurred back in the early 1970s. I was kneeling in prayer with a group of eleven men, deacons, and other leaders in our church in Mansfield, Texas. I heard the phone ring. On the other end was someone asking if I would come do a revival in Buena Vista, Colorado. I asked, 'What churches are involved?' The lady said, 'No churches, just come up here and preach.' I replied, 'When are you planning on doing this?' and she said, 'Next week.'

"I was reluctant, but one of the men said, 'I think you ought to go, and I want to go with you.' So four of us traveled to Colorado and were met by this lady in a VW microbus. She led us up to a cabin, and when we opened the door, folks were all over the floor, stretched our before God, praying for revival. We prayed through the night with them and had no idea what form this would take.

"The next morning at 6:00 a.m. an elderly gentleman knocked at the door of the cabin and said, 'Would you men come help me move chairs down at the high school gymnasium? Aren't you meeting there tonight? We'll need chairs.' I was amazed and asked, 'Do you have bleachers? Don't you think that will be enough? We haven't announced anything.' He said, 'Oh no, we'll need to have chairs.' So we went down there and set up chairs. I remember putting a chair in the center of the gym, right on the head of the mascot—the Buena Vista demons. And I thought to myself, 'I wonder who's gonna sit here?'

"That night in the snow when we came to that school, people were standing outside trying to get in. No newspaper ads. No concerted church efforts. The place was packed. I spoke very briefly, maybe ten to fifteen minutes. People literally ran forward. I was amazed. I asked if there were any pastors present.

Five pastors were there, and I asked for their help to follow up with these people. In the course of three days, more than half of the high school students came to know the Lord. God touched homes, businessmen, and leaders in that community. You would walk down the street at night, and if you saw a light on in a house and knocked on the door, chances are you'd find yourself in the middle of a prayer meeting. It was an amazing visitation of God on a town.

"Michael, you've said this so often. You can't live at a state of that kind of spiritual energy all the time. Even Jesus said this about bringing His compatriots back down from the mountain to the valley. But I'll tell you, the remnant of that revival can be found today in Buena Vista, Colorado. That's been years ago, and you can still find people whose lives were touched by that revival."—TE

"I never shall forget the first time I was invited to do a meeting in Louisiana in a place where Bill and Eddie Smith took juvenile boys from the courts, kept them, raised them, and taught them the things of God. We did a meeting in the Catholic dance hall in the backwoods of Alexandria, Louisiana. The home housed thirty-two boys, and I stayed in a beautiful guest room in the same house. We were going to do a meeting Monday through Sunday. When we got to Friday night of the first week, a young man by the name of Milton Johnson got saved. Milton got so saved, in fact, that he couldn't help but go home and share with his wife. As a result, his wife became belligerent and hateful. She would hit him while he would do his devotions and pray. She made fun of him and was very hateful.

THE POWER OF SURRENDER

"Ed Smith asked me if I would stay another week. I said, 'I'll go home, and if the meeting continues without me and God keeps showing up among the people, we'll see what happens.' Well, it continued. People kept coming, and Ed Smith preached that week. It was the first time I had ever seen God capture an audience and a group, where people just driving down the road would get saved. So I went back for the second week.

"On Thursday of the second week, we were in the afterglow in the boys' home, and a pick-up truck pulled up in the circular driveway. Milton came walking in and said, 'Brother Bill, my wife, Carolyn, is in the pick-up under deep conviction. She wants to see you.' I walked out and opened the door. She leaped toward me and said, 'I'm lost, I'm lost, I'm a pagan. Can you help me?' I took her inside. It didn't take much to lead her to Jesus. As a result of that night and her relationship in the community, she became the center of reaching many people. One night after the service, so many came to get saved, we were up till 4:30 in the morning. That meeting went five weeks in the backwoods in a Catholic dance hall.

"By the way, Bill Anderson was in college at Louisiana Baptist College during that time. A bunch of those boys got in on that meeting, and Bill became an object of the whole thing, hungering for revival. He set it up for me to go to the college, and students swamped to the meeting to hear the truth, many of them coming to know Christ. The influence spread so far that Bill called me not long ago from Jena, Louisiana. He now works for the state convention. He said, 'We've had revival break out here. We've had to move out of the churches and into gymnasiums. In Jena! Four of the "Jena Six" have gotten saved. I need some help; I don't know what to do.' [*The Jena Six are a group of African-American youths convicted in the beating of a white high-school student in 2006, a case which drew national media coverage.*] I told him to share his desperation from his heart and God would show up. Four black pastors joined that meeting, and it went ten weeks. Years later, from that first revival, Bill had become an instrument for another revival."—BS

"As a child, being a preacher's kid, I saw a couple of true revivals from the outside, but never personally until I was older. As a college student at Albany State, I did an internship in Charleston, South Carolina. There was a revival in Orangeburg, about an hour and twenty minutes away, and people that I worked with had been . . . and had caught the fire. They started recruiting folks from the job to come, so I went. When I walked in, I was initially turned off because of my background. It was a Baptist church, but not a traditional Baptist church. They were already into contemporary music. I was used to "What a Friend We Have in Jesus," and they were rocking "O, Happy Day!" But I went in anyway.

"Something happened in that meeting. I had been in church all my life but never experienced anything like that. This is what revival looks like to me—people who are already in the church and call themselves church members, but for some reason they're not on fire for God. The fire has gone out. They're not living up to their true calling. They catch on fire first, and then they go out and impact the world. Something happened to me, and I caught on fire like never before.

"While I was in the church, I was indulging in some things I shouldn't have been. And I was able to sit in the church and still be comfortable doing those things. But in that meeting that night, I got delivered on the spot from the things I was involved in. It's like the hand of God touched me. I use this language: the taste for it left me. And I've never had another desire since that day.

"As a result of that revival, people in the church went out and began to evangelize, and people were saved. I was living in a boarding house with college students from all over the country. I had never shared the gospel with them, but I went back and shared with a young man and he confessed Christ, asking where he could be baptized. This was repeated over and over by many of us in that revival. It was scheduled for one week, but it just kept going."—DS

"As a layman I may have had much less exposure to revival. I've seen a lot of what I know is *not* revival. But as far back as I can reach and remember of true revival, it happened in my home church. I grew up in a small country town in east Tennessee—roadhouses, gambling, moonshining. I was surrounded by some godly people—my great-grandmother and grandmother and great-uncles who were deacons in the church. My great-grandmother was the most godly person I've ever known. She would pray over me at night and read Scriptures over me. Revival came to our church. The speaker had a boy my age—twelve years old. We played together all week, and every night we'd go to the services. His dad was a powerful man of God who preached so wonderfully yet so simply. It was really impacting my life.

"About the third night in the revival, I saw that second row where my great-grandmother always sat, and I saw her get up and make her way to the front. Both my great-uncles got up and went forward. I was confused—these were the most godly people I had ever been around. Some of the deacons and my Sunday school teachers got up. I thought just the mean people were supposed to get saved during revival. But I saw the transformation, the weeping, the desire to be all God wanted them to be. And I saw the enthusiasm that spread through the church.

"By the following Sunday morning God had gripped my heart, and I told my mom, "I'm going to get saved today because I'm giving my heart to Jesus." During the first note of the first song, I went flying down the aisle and sat on the front row. And down the row from me was my best buddy. He didn't know I was coming, and I didn't know he was coming. But in the following weeks many people got saved because the godliest people in that church allowed God to move again in their heart in the most powerful way to draw them to the foot of the cross and say, 'Lord, cleanse me.' The impact of that to a little boy was true revival because I realized that God had come down and met with His dearest saints first, and it had spread and touched my heart, and I wanted that."—*KJ*

"I was thirteen years old, and our youth minister was planning a youth camp. We went to the most rustic place you could imagine in North Mobile County. While kids today are blessed to hear a best-selling author or Dove award-winning band, our speaker was a retired missionary from China, a little lady in her seventies. That'll get you fired up, right? But that little lady was

Ms. Bertha Smith. With her flannelgraph characters and her stories from China and her little bony finger, what power and presence of God fell on that campground!

"One morning she said, 'I want you to take your Bible, notebook, and pen, and go out into the woods. Don't talk to anyone else.' She talked about how sin could block not our *relationship* with the Lord but our *fellowship* with the Lord. We needed to confess those sins, and she talked about a sin list. She told us to ask the Holy Spirit to remind us of every single sin we hadn't yet confessed to the Lord and to write them down. 'No wholesale confession. You committed them one by one; now you confess them one by one,' she said. 'As you repent of those and confess and ask forgiveness, receive forgiveness from the Lord and mark through that sin.'

"They had set up a fifty-five-gallon barrel in the middle of the campground and had a fire going in it, and we were supposed to throw our sin lists in there. I went out into the woods and—like I said, I was thirteen—so how much trouble could you get into by thirteen? A lot, actually! I didn't walk out of the woods with a sin *list* but a sin *notebook*. I felt such a weight from the load of those sins on me. It was about the most miserable I've ever been. And I was under such conviction that I began to think, 'There's no way I'm saved.' Long story short, my youth minister helped me walk through all that. But I can still remember to this day how clean I felt after doing it. That's about the most clean I've ever felt in my life.

"Another thing the Lord did that week: One night after the session, a girl from another church came up to me with a friend of mine, broken in tears. The girl said, 'Please pray for the kids in my youth group. A lot of them are lost. They were talking and passing notes, not listening to Ms. Bertha. Would you please pray for them?' I thought to myself that I'd do it before I went to bed that night. But my friend, who was a few years older than me, grabbed my arm. He took me to a prayer closet by the chapel and opened his Bible to Matthew 18:18–20. He looked at me and said, 'Do you believe that?' So we believed with all our heart and prayed and asked God to change those kids. Still in my mind I thought they'd get right two weeks later. But not twenty minutes had passed when we walked out of that chapel, and I couldn't believe it—there were twenty to thirty teens wailing on their knees, crying out to God. That was a powerful learning experience for me that God is ready to move and work if we'll just take Him at His Word and believe."—AA

"I grew up in a really dead Baptist church. The preacher's sermons were basically whatever he read in *Reader's Digest*. He had one sermon on tithing, and we heard that one a lot. But one thing he did right was bringing Vance Havner to preach, and it about killed the church. The crowd got smaller every service, but I remember the power and authority of that frail old man. I had never heard someone talk to church people like that. I had never heard anyone preach in such a way that people wanted to avoid him after the service. That was a turning point in my life. He came two years in a row. (I can't believe we had him back!) That was a time when God really turned my heart and helped me understand that normal Christianity as we defined it in the typical church was not New Testament Christianity. It was dead religion, lacking power. It stunk in the nostrils of God.

"I recall some great moves of God in the Jesus Movement days. The church wasn't ready for it. I remember Leo Humphrey coming to our church and saying, 'We're going to the beach to witness.' The first time I ever shared my faith was on the beach. A few weeks later my youth minister said, 'We're going down to the beach club.' He gave us tracts to hand out and told me to go to the bathroom and put them in all the stalls. So I unrolled the toilet paper and put about fifty tracts inside.

"I have seen God do a work. I have seen God deliver people and bring them in off the streets. I've seen them walk into a church and fall on their knees. I've had personal times of revival that didn't have anything to do with a church. Walking with God costs you. Sometimes we think revival removes problems, but it brings problems of its own. With all of that said, I'd rather have the problems of revival."—MC

I want you to talk about Ms. Bertha and what we can learn about revival from what she said and taught.

"Bertha Smith said she believed one-third of the people in our Baptist churches were lost. I believe it's much more than that—well over half. Billy Graham said 85 percent of those who come down the aisle at his crusades are members of an evangelical church. You can't revive something that has no life. So the call for revival in our setting falls on deaf ears. What really needs to happen is—people need to be saved. There needs to be evidence in their life of what it means to be born again. Sometimes we'll come to a place in a meeting when God comes down. But if you take that event and begin to extrapolate it, how many people in the church actually experienced it? The answer is to realize that if God really comes down in our lives, we're going to look at those folks as the harvest field.

"The time is right for those whose names are on the roll of a church but are not born again to come to Christ and get honest. I remember seeing Bertha Smith in a prayer meeting with some men I thought were pretty big dogs. We were all praying, and I thought, *I'd better make this good when it comes my turn.* I was praying a pretty good prayer. I had thought it through. But in the middle of that prayer, I felt her bony finger on my shoulder, and Ms. Bertha said, 'Young man, why don't you quit lying to God?' She was right, and it was no laughing matter. I believe that is a characteristic of revival. People get honest before God. They begin to realize we need Him so He can work His works through us.

"Incidentally, I believe there's a second reason why it is so difficult for churches to experience revival. I was watching a newscast recently, and my attention was caught by the trailer: 'In a few minutes, we're going to visit the home of the world's largest man.' When I saw this man, I began crying. I felt so sorry for him. He was trapped in a body that weighed a thousand pounds or something like that. He couldn't roll over or get up. It was a picture of a man who had a great appetite but no activity.

"I thought to myself, *That's the reason many people will never experience revival.* Activity generates a thirst, a hunger, a need.

He just had an appetite but no activity, so he was getting larger and larger and larger. And what a picture that is of many of us and our churches. Second Kings 7 talks about the four leprous men who sat at the gate when Samaria was delivered. They found these tents after the army had fled due to the sovereign work of a holy God. And they started eating and drinking and went and hid the gold and silver. Then they started eating and drinking again. But one of them said they shouldn't be doing such a thing, that they should go tell the king's household. That's our personal responsibility in the midst of God's sovereignty.

"What's it like to have an appetite with no activity? After a while you get picky—'I don't like that music or that preaching or the way we're doing that.' We're in it more for taste than for nourishment. Issues in church become a matter of taste, not satisfying a hunger in my soul. So we become bigger and bigger. I thought, *How is that man going to be delivered?*

God's got the answer for us. But that's one of the reasons it's difficult for churches. We have so much, we see so much, we have such a buffet in front of us. But if you have it all without activity, you're sure to get fat and unusable. The greatest books on spiritual life weren't written by people doing conferences but by people serving God in the trenches who had to serve God or die.—*TE*

"I preached a meeting, and Ms. Bertha was there with me. She was ninety-eight. I preached from the gospel of Luke about Simon Peter's transformation—the first time I had preached that message. When I gave the invitation that night, people came by the droves. And one of the people on their face was Ms. Bertha. At ninety-eight she was still repenting. God tore me up, and I fell on my face on the platform and said, 'God, help me to remember that repentance is my best friend next to Jesus.' I'm still repenting to this day, partly because that dear lady touched my life at ninety-eight."—BS

"I remember a meeting when I was on staff in Spartanburg, South Carolina, in 1979. Jack Taylor was preaching, and Ms. Bertha would come down from Gaffney. He did noonday sessions on how to be filled with the Spirit. I knew Ms. Bertha was in the room and that she had written a book called *How the Spirit Filled My Life*. I was working the sound that day, and Jack said, 'If you want to be filled with the Spirit, slip into this side room and I'll pray with you.' Ms. Bertha was the first one up. I thought, *Lord, help me. If Ms. Bertha's got to figure out how to be filled with the Spirit, I may not have it.*

"We have had giant oaks walk this land, and we've replaced them with shrubs. We've got shrubs claiming to be giant oaks today under which we try to shade our lives. But if we don't remind the generations behind us, we'll be like the book of Judges when a generation arose who didn't know the Lord. We're the last generation of people to know some of these giants like Ms. Bertha and Ron Dunn and Vance Havner. I had a friend who had breakfast with Duncan Campbell, the leader of the Hebrides Revival. He asked Duncan Campbell, 'What is it that you see we're missing in the American church?' Duncan Campbell never hesitated. He said, 'You have buildings and programs and preachers. The one thing the American church doesn't have is God. You've got everything but God, and you think you're okay.'"—MC

"Let's go back to something Tom said about the barriers to revival. One of the things that brings revival is the true preaching of the Word, when people get the unadulterated gospel of Christ. It offends you, makes you mad, holds up a mirror before your face. There must be a true preaching of the Word, and so many times this is missing. When that happens, the fault isn't in the pew; it's in the pulpit. The second reason has to do with the fact that people have to sense a need for revival. People don't sense that need. One thing that helps us sense the need is the preaching of the Word.

"Another is crisis in a community. When you can't look anywhere else, we typically look to God. Crisis is what brought black and white pastors together in Jena, Louisiana. The flood of '94 in Albany, Georgia, brought blacks and whites together. Personal crisis will also bring us to revival. But here in America, we think so highly of ourselves, our buildings, and our programs, we don't think we need revival. We just want to get the bad people saved. We don't think we need the Lord. But those of us in the church need Him, and we need to sense that need."—DS

We have all been in situations where there have been false revivals or excesses or imitations. Talk for a minute about the things you need to watch for when God is really beginning to move in the hearts of people.

"Attendant with revival is a great sense of freedom. But we all know freedom can very quickly become license. This is nowhere more evident than when freedom in a person's mind begins to eclipse the Word of God, the doctrinal parameters. Many people think doctrine becomes unimportant during revival. No, doctrine is to the body of Christ what the skeleton is to the human body. You've got to have it. It's not always visible, but it's what gives your body cohesion and leverage. You've got to have doctrine.

"In the early '70s when we had the Jesus Movement, those were incredible days. I was at Southwestern when the Asbury Revival came. But it was not the equivalent to what we so desperately need, which is a Great Awakening. We've had some mercy drops, but what happened to them? Maybe I can describe it this way: I can take a pitcher of water, go into the middle of the road, and set the pitcher down in the hot sun, then come back this afternoon or even tomorrow morning and still find it there. Due to evaporation, the level of water will be slightly less, but because there's a framework—a container—everything that is good in the pitcher will still be there. However, if I take the same amount of water and throw it in the street, ten minutes later you'll never know it was there. Why? Because there's no framework.

"One of the things that I believe is a danger to us is when we begin to live in such freedom that we ignore not just the teachings of Scripture but also the parameters and the doctrinal principles. We also fail to raise up a generation that is strong in the knowledge of the Word of God and why they believe it and how to defend it. Every great move of God has died in the throes of excess. Heresy is not the lack of truth; it's just any truth out of balance."—*TE*

"Every time God does show up in real revival, there's always a copy of it among people who want it but aren't willing to submit and surrender. They think we're just going through a light process of feelings and emotion, and everyone can get in on it. Revival is literally dying to self, realizing our nothingness. We all think we have something good, but there's none good—not one. Those who understand this can experience true revival. And the rest who want it so badly will copy it with a reproduction of self and flesh."—BS

"I think we see this in the life of Christ. And this happened more than once. Here's this lady in the crowd who's had an issue of blood for years. She's tried many things and has never gotten better. She heard about Jesus and His healing power. So she pressed through the crowd, touched the hem of His garment, and was healed. So Jesus said, 'I want to know who touched Me?' Why did He want to know this? This lady came forward and Jesus basically said, 'Let me correct what may be a misunderstanding so you don't go around telling people the wrong thing. Lady, it's not about touching the hem of My garment. Your faith has made you whole.' The Lord said this on numerous occasions. It was His way of seeing that they didn't take the good news and twist it. It wasn't just 'get to Jesus and touch His garment!' In revival we sometimes take a little part of the message and pervert it, and then revival dies."—TE

"The people who get off track are people who are trying to keep their emotional level high. With emotionally and spiritually immature people, if they're not rooted and grounded in the Word, something or someone will whisper, 'Try this.' We know people who started out right and got diverted by the extremes and tried to push the boundaries beyond Scripture, tried to make the Holy Spirit act inconsistently with Christ and the Word. The Holy Spirit is never beyond Jesus; He's always consistent with Jesus. The excesses we see have scared Baptists, at least, because we're afraid we're going to get into some crazy movement. But that's not the Holy Spirit. One of His fruits is self-control."—MC

"I don't want to be defamatory here. But I think a lot of this overdose we have through popular Christian television, a non-stop parade of gaudiness, is a detriment to us. The messages are twisted and erroneous. They say, 'If you get right with God, look how you can dress and live and what kind of chairs you can sit in.' The truth is, that's an aberration. That kind of approach to the Christian life will destroy us. We think we're big because we've got seventeen million Southern Baptists. There are seven different evangelical groups on mainland China that consist of *hundreds* of millions of people. In one convention, two thousand new churches started last month. There's no gaudiness or arrogance or poofiness. I'm not saying there's no sin or aberration there. But this nonstop portrayal of what Christianity and the Holy Spirit are all about is probably more a hindrance than a help."—*TE*

"As we send groups from our church to India, Nicaragua, and Romania, we're seeing God move in awesome ways. And I think the key is the desperation. I was talking to a pastor friend in India, and he said that one of the states in India had seen six hundred churches destroyed in one week, with pastors and believers persecuted and killed—hacked to death or burned alive. Some of the guys I was teaching were going back to that place. I said to this friend, 'I'm so sorry you're having to live through this severe persecution.' He said, 'Oh brother, don't be sorry. Without it, the church would get too soft.'

"You can go to some of these places and see hundreds of people saved in a few days. What we've noticed, especially in one country in particular, is that you can go out into some of the most remote areas and find satellite dishes on top of a hut. One of the things they watch is certain Christian television from the United States. We've tried to lovingly and humbly address it from the Word, but they're copying what they are seeing. We've seen the differences in some of the worship services, and that's where the devil comes in to distract and counterfeit. There's always emotion and weeping, but when the Holy Spirit's in control, it's orderly."—AA

What's the point of all this? God is stirring among His people to return to the message of revival. It's our only hope. We can deliberate as to the issues of our day, but most of them would be settled if we were to have revival. We have seminars and discussions on what the church needs to do. We discuss methods more than the Master. We look at the symptoms and not the root problem. The message of revival is needed more today than any time in the last 150 years.

Islam is on the march. Secularism is on the rise. Every form of mass media is flooded with pornography. Our schools are not safe. Our children are at risk from sexual predators. Meanwhile the church is having services that start on time and dismiss on time because we don't have time to wait on God. Something has to change or we're sunk.

Revival is not the way to Christ. Christ is the way to revival. Doctrine is not the way to revival. Experiences are not the way to revival. No, revival is when we look for the person of Christ to show up.

I don't know about you, but I'm past ready.

Just give me Jesus.

BIBLIOGRAPHY

Ablaze with His Glory, A Plea for Revival in our Time
   —Del Fehsenfeld Jr.
America Is Too Young to Die—Leonard Ravenhill
The Calvary Road—Roy Hession
Campus Aflame—J. Edwin Orr
Can We Pray for Revival?—Brian H. Edwards
Christianity in Crisis—Hank Hanegraaff
Counterfeit Revival—Hank Hanegraaff
The Cry for Revival—Robert Murray M'Cheyne
A Diary of Revival—Kevin Adams
Downpour—James MacDonald
Eight Keys to Biblical Revival—Lewis Drummond
Finney Lives On—V. Raymond Edman
Fresh Wind, Fresh Fire—Jim Cymbala
Great Revivals—Colin Whittaker

Heartcry, A Journal on Revival and Spiritual Awakening
    —quarterly publication of Life Action Ministries
Heritage of Revival—Colin Peckham
In Times Like These—Vance Havner
Invasion of Wales by the Spirit through Evan Roberts
    —James A. Stewart
It Is Time—Vance Havner
Jonathan Edwards on Revival
    —compiled by Banner of Truth Trust
Lord, Open the Heavens—Stephen Olford
The Nature of Revival—John Wesley
One Divine Moment—Robert Coleman
Open Windows: The Church and Revival—James A. Stewart
Personal Declension and Revival of Religion in the Soul
    —Octavius Winslow
Portraits of the Great 18th-Century Revival
    —Paxton Hood
The Reformation—Owen Chadwick
Repent or Else—Vance Havner
Revival—Andrew Murray
Revival—Brian H. Edwards
Revival—Martyn Lloyd-Jones
Revival—Richard Owen Roberts
Revival and You—James A. Stewart
Revival Fire—Wesley Duewel
Revival God's Way—Leonard Ravenhill
Revival in the Rubble—John Kitchen
Revival Praying—Leonard Ravenhill

The Revival We Need—Oswald J. Smith

The Shantung Revival—C. L. Culpepper

Sounds from Heaven: The Revival on the Isle of Lewis, 1949–1952
     —Colin and Mary Peckham

The Spiritual Awakeners—Keith J. Hardman

We Would See Jesus—Roy Hession

When God Comes to Church—Raymond C. Ortlund Jr.

When Heaven Touched Earth—Roy Fish

Why Not Just Be Christians?—Vance Havner

ACKNOWLEDGMENTS

I'm filled with gratitude to God for sovereignly seeing that I was adopted and not aborted as a baby. I'm grateful for Christian parents who raised me in a church where I was able to see a genuine move of God in my late teens. Had I not been in that home and in that church, I may have never known the message of revival.

I'm grateful for the influence of Vance Havner, who was the first New Testament prophet I ever met—a man who had a passion and longing for a genuine work of God in the church. I'm grateful for the remnant I've met along my spiritual pilgrimage who refuse to settle for less than God's best, a small but significant core within every congregation that believes God for "much more."

I'm grateful for a church willing to listen to their pastor week after week calling them to believe God for revival. I'm grateful that in my twenty-plus years of pastoring Sherwood Baptist Church in Albany, Georgia, we've seen significant mercy drops of blessings. I'm grateful for their support of the annual ReFRESH™ Conference both in Albany and Pigeon Forge. I'm grateful they understand that revival will never come if we don't position ourselves to catch the wind of the Spirit.

Because I am a pastor I have the opportunity to talk about revival in the same church every week. I have a lot of ears and friendly faces who listen, pray, take notes, and support this continual call to surrender. They have helped me develop these messages and truths. As several preacher friends have said about Sherwood, "Your people listen well."

I'm grateful for those who have written the countless books in my library on the subject of revival. These books are among my most cherished possessions. With all the books on revival out there, it's hard to imagine that I have anything new to say. I'm just picking up the mantle of saints who have gone before. At times I know they felt like a voice crying in the wilderness. I've heard their voices, sensed their hearts, and longed for similar awakenings and revivals.

I'm grateful for those who help me in the writing process. The staff at Sherwood understands the broader ministry that God has given me, and they cover the bases without ever complaining. They are the finest team on the planet, and I'm honored to serve the Lord with them. They, too, know of the need for revival!

I'm grateful for the many people who pray for me in the writing process—my prayer partners and friends who know when I'm writing and ask God to give me divine direction in what I say. These people are unknown to you, but I know them and the Lord knows them.

I'm grateful for Debbie Toole who has served with me for nearly twenty years. She manages my schedule, travel, and appointments. I'm old-fashioned in that I don't keep up with my calendar on my Blackberry as much as I depend on paper and pen. She reminds me of where I need to be and when I need to be there. Debbie is the consummate administrative assistant.

I'm grateful for Stephanie Bennett, my research assistant. She takes my writings and gives them the grammatical tweaking they need. She also keeps up with the Web sites I oversee, like 2ProphetU.com and my blog (michaelcatt.com). I love to write, but having a writer in the office next to me sure helps me look like I'm a better writer than I am. Her diligence has no limits. She has chased down quotes to make sure I was giving proper credit. She has consistently put the manuscript in the hands of the folks at B&H right on time.

I'm grateful to all the team at B&H Publishing Group. They have listened to me as I've shared my heart and given me a platform to reach people I probably would have never reached this side of eternity. Their support of my vision and ministry is humbling. I pray I've been half as good an author as they have been a publisher.

I'm grateful for Jim McBride, my executive pastor, who has at times cared more about my writing than about his own schedule. He has traveled with me, helped me set up book tables, encouraged me, and stood by me through my best and worst days. He's a friend that sticks closer than a brother. I'm also grateful for Jim and his partnership with Bill Reeves, who together act as my literary agents. I hate the business side of writing, and they cover those details for me so I don't get bogged down in things I know nothing about.

I'm grateful for my bride, Terri. She has been with me when I didn't think I had a voice or anything to say. She's believed in me when no one else did. She has stood with me through thick and thin, in the ups and downs of church life. We have weathered many storms and seen the blessings of God. God has allowed us to raise two incredible, beautiful, godly girls. I'm grateful that my PKs love Jesus and love the church. That may be the best legacy I have.

Most of all I'm grateful for the Lord Jesus, who allowed me to get a glimpse of revival during the days of the Jesus Movement. He put a burden for revival in my heart that I cannot shake loose. He has allowed me to fulfill my dream of starting a conference on revival. He has opened doors this boy from Mississippi could have never imagined. To Him be the glory. My prayer is that God would use this book in your life so that you would join me in praying, "Lord, rend the heavens and come down . . ."

Michael Catt
Albany, Georgia

NOTES

CHAPTER 1

1. "A Revival Account: Asbury 1970," *The Forerunner*, March 2008, http://www. forerunner.com/forerunner/X0585_Asbury_Revival_1970.html, accessed on July 28, 2009.

2. Charles Finney, "Breaking Up the Fallow Ground," www.firesofrevival.com/ fground.htm, accessed on August 14, 2009.

3. Warren W. Wiersbe, *The Bible Exposition Commentary: The Prophets* (Colorado Springs: David C. Cook, 2002), accessed via WORDsearch on August 14, 2009.

4. Finney, "Breaking Up the Fallow Ground."

5. A. W. Tozer, *Paths to Power: Living in the Spirit's Fullness* (Camp Hill, PA: WingSpread Publishers), accessed via WORDsearch on August 14, 2009.

6. Alexander MacLaren, *Expositions of Holy Scripture: Ezekiel, Daniel and the Minor Prophets, St. Matthew Chapters I to VIII* (Charleston, SC: BiblioBazaar, 2007), 111.

7. Quoted in a sermon by Greg Gordon, "Revival at Any Cost," http://www. sermonindex.net/modules/articles/index.php?view=article&aid=19431.

CHAPTER 2

1. John Blanchard, *The Complete Gathered Gold: A Treasury of Quotations for Christians* (Darlington, England: Evangelical Press, 2006), 528.

2. Leonard Ravenhill, *Revival God's Way* (Grand Rapids, MI: Bethany House, 1986).

3. Michael Horton, *Christless Christianity* (Grand Rapids, MI: Baker Books, 2008), 68.

4. Ibid., 69.

5. Ibid., 79.

6. Sammy Tippit, *The Choice: America at the Crossroads of Ruin and Revival* (Chicago: Moody Press, 1998), 80.

7. Vance Havner, *Repent or Else* (Grand Rapids, MI: Fleming H. Revell, 1958), 58.

8. J. Edwin Orr, *The Church Must First Repent* (Basingstoke, Hants, UK: Marshall, Morgan & Scott, 1937).

9. Manley Beasley, from the transcript of the Revival Forum with Life Action Ministries, 1989.

10. Ron Dunn, Lifestyle Ministries, 2001.

11. Frank S. Mead, ed., *12,000 Religious Quotations* (Grand Rapids, MI: Baker Book House, 1989), 376.

CHAPTER 3

1. Walter Kaiser, Jr., *Revive Us Again* (Nashville: Broadman & Holman, 1999), 101.

2. Ray Stedman, *Our Riches in Christ* (Grand Rapids, MI: Discovery House, 1998).

3. Warren Wiersbe, *The Bible Exposition Commentary: Old Testament* (Colorado Springs: David C. Cook, 2001), accessed via WORDsearch on July 30, 2009.

4. A. W Tozer, *God Tells the Man Who Cares* (Camp Hill, PA: WingSpread Publications, 2003), accessed via WORDsearch on June 12, 2009.

CHAPTER 4

1. Ron Dunn, *Any Christian Can* (Kalamazoo, MI: Master's Press, 1976), 22–23.

2. Blanchard, *The Complete Gathered Gold*, 528.

3. Roland Bainton, *Here I Stand* (New York: Mentor Books, 1950), 144.

4. John Wesley, *The Works: Volume 5* (Grand Rapids, MI: Zondervan, authorized edition of 1872), 3–4.

5. William Young Fullerton, *F. B. Meyer: A Biography* (Basingstoke, Hants, UK: Marshall, Morgan & Scott, 1929).

6. Vance Havner, *Pepper 'n' Salt* (Grand Rapids, MI: Baker Book House, 1987), 58.

7. Ernest M. Wadsworth, *Will Revival Come?* (Chicago: Moody Press, 1945), 54, 59, 60.

CHAPTER 5

1. Del Fehsenfeld, Jr., *Ablaze with His Glory* (Nashville: Thomas Nelson, 1993).

2. James A. Stewart, *Come, O Breath* (Asheville, NC: Gospel Projects Inc., 1969), 38.

3. Richard Owen Roberts, *Revival* (Carol Stream, IL: Tyndale House, 1982), 21–23.

4. Vance Havner, *It Is Time* (Grand Rapids, MI: Fleming H. Revell, 1953), 57–58.

5. Ibid., 59.

6. Ibid., 61.

7. Stewart, *Come, O Breath*, 44.

8. Paxton Hood, "Singers of the Eighteenth Century Revival," www.lifeaction. org/revival-resources/heart-cry-journal/issue-20/singers-eighteenth-century-revival/ (accessed August 4, 2009).

9. http://www.sermonindex.net/modules/newbb/viewtopic php?topic_id=2428 &forum=34&9 (accessed August 4, 2009).

10. James A. Stewart, *Revival and You* (Asheville, NC: Gospel Projects, 1969), 87–95.

CHAPTER 6

1. Havner, *Repent or Else*, 58.

2. Ron Owens, *Manley Beasley: Man of Faith, Instrument of Revival* (Garland, TX: CrossHouse Publishing, 2009), 38.

3. Ibid., 50.

4. Ibid., 64

5. Jack Taylor and O. S. Hawkins, *When Revival Comes* (Nashville: Broadman Press, 1980), introduction.

CHAPTER 7

1. Personal interview with John Bisagno, April 27, 2009.

2. Billy Graham, *The Jesus Generation* (Grand Rapids, MI: Zondervan, 1971), 14–15.

3. Ibid., 17.

4. Ibid., 24.

5. Julia Duin, *Quitting Church: Why the Faithful Are Fleeing and What to Do About It* (Grand Rapids, MI: Baker Books, 2008), 37.

6. Stewart, *Come, O Breath*, 106.

CHAPTER 8

1. Hank Hanegraaff, *Counterfeit Revival* (Nashville: Thomas Nelson, 2001), 9.

2. Vance Havner, *In Times Like These* (Grand Rapids, MI: Fleming H. Revell, 1969), 81–82.

3. James Montgomery Boice, *An Expositional Commentary: The Epistles of John* (Grand Rapids, MI: Baker Books, 1979), accessed via WORDSearch on August 4, 2009.

4. Stanley M. Burgess and Gary B. McGee, eds., *Dictionary of Pentecostal and Charismatic Movements* (Grand Rapids, MI: Zondervan, 1988), 790–91.

5. Boice, *An Expositional Commentary: The Epistles of John.*

6. Havner, *In Times Like These*, 84.

7. Vance Havner, *Living in Kingdom Come* (Grand Rapids, MI: Fleming H. Revell, 1967), 27.

8. R. A. Torrey, "Keep Praying Until God Answers," www.swordofthelord.com/onlinesermons/KeepPraying.htm

9. Adapted from "The Nature of a God Sent Revival" (Vinton, VA: Christ Life Publishers, 1993), 9–11.

CHAPTER 9

1. Mark Water, ed., *The New Encyclopedia of Christian Quotations* (Grand Rapids, MI: Baker Books, 2000), 869.

2. Wilbur M. Smith, *The Glorious Revival* (Grand Rapids, MI: Zondervan, 1954), 5.

3. Kaiser, *Revive Us Again*, 118.

4. *America's Great Revivals* (Grand Rapids, MI: Bethany House, 2004), 9–10.

CHAPTER 10

1. Henrietta C. Mears, *What the Bible Is All About* (Ventura, CA: Gospel Light Publications, 1966), 33.

2. F. B. Meyer, *Old Testament Men of Faith* (Westchester, IL: Good News Publishers, 1979), 191.

3. Del Fehsenfeld III, *Heartcry!*, 25 (Fall 2003), 53–54.

4. Vance Havner, *Seasonings* (Grand Rapids, MI: Fleming H. Revell, 1970), 64.

5. Jack Taylor, *After the Spirit Comes* (Nashville: Broadman Press, 1974), 45.

6. Mike Minter, *A Western Jesus* (Nashville: Broadman & Holman, 2007), 5.

CHAPTER 11

1. Interview with Joni B. Hannigan, managing editor, *Florida Baptist Witness*, www.bpnews.net